Facebook®

FOR

DUMMIES®

2ND EDITION

by Carolyn Abram and Leah Pearlman
Facebook Product Managers

WILEY

Wiley Publishing, Inc.

Facebook® For Dummies,® 2nd Edition

Published by
Wiley Publishing, Inc.
111 River Street
Hoboken, NJ 07030-5774

www.wiley.com

Copyright © 2010 by Wiley Publishing, Inc., Indianapolis, Indiana

Published by Wiley Publishing, Inc., Indianapolis, Indiana

Published simultaneously in Canada

For general information on our other products and services, please contact our Customer Care Department within the U.S. at 877-762-2974, outside the U.S. at 317-572-3993, or fax 317-572-4002.

For technical support, please visit www.wiley.com/techsupport.

Wiley also publishes its books in a variety of electronic formats. Some content that appears in print may not be available in electronic books.

Library of Congress Control Number: 2009937277

ISBN: 978-0-470-52761-0

Manufactured in the United States of America

10 9 8 7 6 5 4 3 2

WILEY

About the Authors

Carolyn Abram: One of the first Facebook users on the west coast, Carolyn took her English degree from Stanford University (Class of 2006), and decided the best career move was to get paid to be on Facebook all day long. At Facebook since 2006, Carolyn currently works on the User Experience Team as a Language Designer. This is a very fancy way of saying she works on site copy, voice, tone, and messaging. Originally from Ardsley, New York, Carolyn currently resides in Palo Alto. She boasts the highest ratio of mess to desk at the office. Her hobbies include hiking, writing, enjoying sunshine, mocking her friends, and playing Ultimate Frisbee.

Leah Pearlman: Leah graduated with a degree in computer science from Brown University, where she first signed up for Facebook to find out the name of a boy in a class. Typical. She spent two years at Microsoft learning the product management ropes (seriously, there are ropes) before becoming a Product Manager for Facebook. Since joining, she has worked on a wide range of projects including messaging and the Inbox, News Feed, Pages, and Ads. At the office, Leah's desk is always clean, except sometimes when it's not, and instead of a chair, she sits on an inflatable ball — she has only fallen twice while people were watching. Her hobbies include snowboarding (though she feels pretentious every time she says it), writing (see previous parenthetical comment), and playing Ultimate Frisbee.

About the Contributor

Blake Ross: Blake is currently on leave from Stanford University to oversee development of the new user experience at Facebook. He is three times the dummy as his fellow authors, having written *Firefox For Dummies* in 2005. Or is that twice the dummy? We told you he was dumb.

Deemed *untannable* by scientists, Blake grew up in sunny Miami, Florida, before being shipped out to even sunnier Palo Alto, California. He enjoys writing, playing piano, and programming.

Authors' Acknowledgments

First and foremost, we'd like to thank Blake Ross, double agent and ghost writer extraordinaire. We also could never have started (or finished) this book without the help of everyone at Wiley: Steve Hayes, Linda Morris, and Emily Crespin, as well as everyone listed on the other side of this page. We don't have space to list by name everyone on the Facebook team we'd like to thank; everyone who makes Facebook such a great product to work on, write about, and use.

Leah gives her personal thanks to Mom and Dad (in reverse alphabetical order) for the endless supply of you-can-do-its and nose-to-the-grindstone-kiddos. Special shout-out to brother DJ, nephew Collin, and Uncle Marc for graduating from newbie to Facebook-JV, without the help of this handy how-to. Thanks Maggie and Emily for your sisterly and BFF-erly love, respectively. An obvious, yet totally genuine thanks to Carolyn; if you had an Awesome button, I'd press it. Finally, thank you, spell-check; without ewe nothing eye right wood make any cents.

Carolyn gives her personal thanks to Mom and Dad, Becca and Matt, Charlotte, Grandma and Grandma. Eric (Boyfriend) gets special thanks as usual, especially for the use of his ergonomic desk chair. Thank you friends for asking if they'd get a second party out of this. Lastly, to Leah: If you had any of the following buttons, I'd press them: Awesome, Awkward, and Spell Check.

In closing, we'd like to thank the millions of Facebook users around the world who are busy connecting, organizing, and generally having fun on Facebook. Keep on signin' on.

Publisher's Acknowledgments

We're proud of this book; please send us your comments through our online registration form located at http://dummies.custhelp.com. For other comments, please contact our Customer Care Department within the U.S. at 877-762-2974, outside the U.S. at 317-572-3993, or fax 317-572-4002.

Some of the people who helped bring this book to market include the following:

Acquisitions and Editorial

Project Editor: Linda Morris

Executive Editor: Steve Hayes

Copy Editor: Linda Morris

Technical Editor: Emily Crespin

Editorial Manager: Jodi Jensen

Editorial Assistant: Amanda Graham

Sr. Editorial Assistant: Cherie Case

Cartoons: Rich Tennant
(www.the5thwave.com)

Composition Services

Project Coordinator: Sheree Montgomery

Layout and Graphics: Ashley Chamberlain, Joyce Haughey, Christine Williams

Proofreaders: Jessica Kramer, Toni Settle

Indexer: Becky Hornyak

Publishing and Editorial for Technology Dummies

    Richard Swadley, Vice President and Executive Group Publisher

    Andy Cummings, Vice President and Publisher

    Mary Bednarek, Executive Acquisitions Director

    Mary C. Corder, Editorial Director

Publishing for Consumer Dummies

    Diane Graves Steele, Vice President and Publisher

Composition Services

    Debbie Stailey, Director of Composition Services

Contents at a Glance

Table of Contents

Introduction

- -

*F*acebook connects you with the people you know and care about. It enables you to communicate, stay up-to-date, and keep in touch with friends and family anywhere. It facilitates your relationships online to help enhance them in person. Specifically, Facebook connects you with the *people* you know around *content* that is important to you. Whether you're the type to take photos or look at them, or write about your life, or read about your friends' lives, Facebook is designed to enable you to succeed. Maybe you like to share Web sites and news, play games, plan events, organize groups of people, or promote your business. Whatever you prefer, Facebook has you covered.

Facebook offers you control. Communication and information sharing are powerful only when you can do what you want within your comfort zone. Nearly every piece of information and means of connecting on Facebook comes with full privacy controls, allowing you to share and communicate exactly how — and with whom — you desire.

Facebook welcomes everyone: students and professionals; grandchildren (as long as they're at least age 13), parents, and grandparents; busy people; socialites; celebrities; distant friends; and roommates. No matter who you are, using Facebook can add value to your life. Results are typical.

About Facebook For Dummies

Part I of this book teaches you all the basics to get you up and running on Facebook. This is more than enough for you to discover its value. Part II and Part III explore all the powerful ways of sharing all kinds of information with the people you care about. Part IV does a deep dive into some of the more advanced ways of using the site that can be of great additional value, depending on your needs. Finally, Part V explores the creative, diverse, touching, and even frustrating ways people have welcomed Facebook into their lives.

Here are some of the things you can do with this book:

- ✔ **Find out how to represent yourself online in a way that's specific to each member of your online audience.** Friends may see you one way, family another way, co-workers another, and friends of friends yet another (or not at all).

✔ **Connect and communicate with people you know.** Whether you're seeking close friends or long-lost ones, family members, business contacts, teammates, businesses, and celebrities, Facebook keeps you connected. Never say, "Goodbye" again . . . unless you want to.

✔ **Discover how a rich toolset online can help enhance your relationships offline.** Event and group organizational tools, photo-sharing, and direct and passive communication capabilities all enable you to maintain an active social life in the real world.

✔ **Bring your connections off of Facebook and on to the rest of the Web.** Through Facebook Platform and Connect, you see how many services you already use can be made more powerful by using them in conjunction with your Facebook friends.

✔ **Bring your business to the consumers who can bring you success.** Productive audience engagement coupled with deeply targeted advertising can help you ensure your message is heard.

Foolish Assumptions

In this book, we make the following assumptions:

✔ You're at least 13 years of age.

✔ You have some access to the Internet and an e-mail address.

✔ There are people in your life with whom you communicate.

✔ You can read the language in which this sentence is printed.

Conventions Used in This Book

In this book, we stick to a few conventions to help with readability. Whenever you have to type text, we show it in **bold**, so it's easy to see. Monofont text denotes an e-mail address or Web site URL. When you see an *italicized* word, look for its nearby definition. Facebook pages and features — such as the Friends box or the Privacy Overview page — are called out with capital letters. Numbered lists guide you through tasks that must be completed in order from top to bottom; bulleted lists can be read in any order you like (from top to bottom or bottom to top).

Finally, we, the authors, often state our opinions throughout this book. Though we are employees of Facebook, the opinions expressed here represent only our perspective, and not that of Facebook. We are avid Facebook users and have been since before we joined the company. While writing this book, we took off our "employee hats" and put on our "user hats" to allow us to serve as reliable tour guides, and to share objectively our passion for the site.

What You Don't Have to Read

This book is written with the new Facebook user in mind. Some information pertains to readers looking to use Facebook to launch or expand a business. If you want to get on Facebook primarily to keep in touch with family and friends, feel free to skip these sections. Sprinkled throughout the book, sidebars cover many bits of extra information; these are simply added points of interest that can be skipped without detriment to your Facebook experience.

How This Book Is Organized

Facebook For Dummies, 2nd Edition, is split into five parts. You don't have to read it sequentially, and you don't even have to read all the sections in any particular chapter. We explain the most generalized functionality — that which applies to just about everyone — up front. The first chapter of each part gives you an overview of the application and functionality covered in that particular part, along with a description of the likely audience for that part. If you're unsure whether a part of this book pertains to you, try reading its first chapter; if you're unsure about a particular chapter, try reading its introduction to decide.

Topics in this book are covered mostly in the order in which most people use each particular feature. We recommend that you feel comfortable with the material in Part I before you move to Part II, and so on. As the book progresses, we dive deeper into specialized functionality that may be relevant only to certain audiences.

Don't forget about the Table of Contents and the Index; you can use these sections to quickly find the information you need. Here's what you find in each part.

Part I: Getting Started with Facebook

Chapter 1 introduces you to Facebook and gives you an overview of the most popular and useful ways different types of people incorporate Facebook into their lives. In the few chapters that follow, we help you get your profile set up and orient you to the site so you can always find your way around. Finally, you discover all the privacy tools and safety tips you need to take full control of your own Facebook experience; when each individual feels safe, the entire Facebook community benefits.

Part II: Sharing Your Life on Facebook

When you're familiar with the basics, Part II helps you create an honest, interactive online presence, linking you with all the people you know in the Facebook community, a community that is getting larger every day. We introduce some of the most popular uses of Facebook, including Photos, and explain how you can tailor the system to meet your specific needs.

Part III: Getting Organized

Part III covers how Facebook can help you stay connected and close with the people you know. We explain the differences between private and public communication, and active and passive interactions, all of which fulfill different needs in different social situations. In this part, you discover how people also keep connected and in touch using Facebook Groups and Events.

Part IV: Delving Further into Facebook

Along with providing value for people in their personal lives, Facebook can also help businesses connect with their customers in specialized ways. Whether in the Facebook Platform or in Facebook's spam-free ad system, your business's message can reach consumers in an engaging and uniquely targeted way.

Part V: The Part of Tens

The final section of this book gives fun-to-read and easy-to-digest views on the creative ways people use Facebook. We highlight ten very different applications other companies have integrated into the Facebook environment, including one that helps people raise money for nonprofit causes. Next you get the answers to ten of the questions these authors hear most often about how to use Facebook. Ten real-world scenarios provide you a perspective on the value of integrating Facebook with your lifestyle. Finally, we share ten truly amazing tales of Facebook.

Icons Used in This Book

What's a *For Dummies* book without icons pointing you in the direction of great information that's sure to help you along your way? In this section, we briefly describe each icon we use in this book.

The Tip icon points out helpful information that is likely to improve your experience.

The Remember icon marks an interesting and useful fact — something that you may want to use later.

The Warning icon highlights lurking danger. With this icon, we're telling you to pay attention and proceed with caution.

Where to Go from Here

Whether you've been using Facebook for years, or this is your first time, we recommend you start by reading Chapter 1, which sets the stage for most of what we describe in detail in the rest of this book. After reading the first chapter, you may have a better sense of which topics in this book will be more relevant to you, and you can, therefore, flip right to them. However, we recommend that *everyone* spend some quality time in Chapter 5, which covers privacy on Facebook. Facebook is an online representation of a community, so it's important that each person understand how to operate in that community to ensure a safe, fun, and functional environment for everyone.

If you're new to Facebook and looking to use it to enhance your own personal connections, we recommend reading this book from Part I straight through Part III. If you're *so* new to Facebook that you're not even sure that it's for you, you'll find your answer in Chapter 1. (We'll go ahead and ruin the surprise by telling you now that Facebook *is* for you, whoever you are.)

You may already be quite familiar with Facebook when you pick up this book. But because the site is constantly growing and changing, there is always more to know. Part IV is the section of the book that will keep you ahead of the curve.

No matter which category you fall into, it's time to get started: Let one hand flip the pages of this book, the other drive your computer mouse, and let your mind open up to a revolutionary way to enhance and experience your real-world relationships.

Part I
Getting Started with Facebook

The 5th Wave   By Rich Tennant

"I know Facebook is great and you want to be a part of it. But you're my mom - you <u>can't</u> be my 'friend.'"

In this part . . .

So, we've persuaded you to read beyond the Introduction. Go team! (You can't see it, but we're high-fiving right now.) Because you started at the beginning, we assume that you have some pretty basic questions, such as

What is Facebook?

Am I too old for Facebook?

How do I use Facebook effectively?

I know I want to use Facebook, but how do I get started?

These are all great questions for starting a journey into the 'book. In this part, we answer all these and more. We start with the bigger picture of who's using Facebook and how, and then we move into the nitty-gritty of signing up, creating your Profile, and finding a few friends. Additionally, we show you how to navigate around the site and protect your information.

Chapter 1

The Many Faces of Facebook

*I*magine trying to get from New York to California via some way other than riding an airplane. Try baking a pie (pecan, please) without an oven? Or getting to the seventieth floor without riding an elevator. Certainly there are ways to achieve those tasks, but without the right tools, they may take longer, come out less-than-perfect, and *really* make you sweat.

Like an airplane, an oven, or an elevator, Facebook is a tool that can make life's *To-Do*s fun and easy. Facebook enables you to manage, maintain, and enhance your social connections. Think about how you accomplish these tasks:

✔ Getting the phone number of an old friend.

✔ Finding out what your friends are up to today.

✔ Making a contact in a city you're moving to or at an office where you're applying for a job.

✔ Planning an event, tracking the guest list, and updating everyone when the time changes.

✔ Garnering support for a cause.

✔ Getting recommendations for movies, books, and restaurants.

✔ Showing off the pictures from your latest vacation.

✔ Telling your friends and family about your recent successes, showing them your photos, or letting them know you're thinking of them.

✔ Remembering everyone's birthday.

The preceding list is merely a sampling of life's tricky tasks that Facebook can help you accomplish more easily and enjoyably. The list could go on, but we need to leave *some* space in the book to tell you how to solve these problems.

Facebook facilitates and improves all your social relationships — we realize that's a big claim. Almost as big as the claims about the blender that can prepare a seven course meal in six minutes, the pill that can give you the abs of Chuck Norris and the legs of Tina Turner, or the six easy steps that can make you a millionaire. However, Facebook is a little different than these in at least three ways. First, we won't claim it's so easy your Chihuahua can do it. Getting set up and familiar with Facebook does take a little work (which you know or you wouldn't be starting out on this 360-page journey). Second, Facebook costs only three low payments of $0, but if you aren't totally satisfied, you can be fully refunded. Finally, unlike the blender or the pill, Facebook *will* actually change your life, make it better, more fun, easier, and, did we mention . . . more fun?

Figuring Out What Facebook Is Exactly

Think about the people you interacted with in the past day. In the morning, you may have gone to get the paper and chatted with the neighbor. You may have asked your kids what time they'd be home and negotiated with your partner about whose turn it is to cook dinner. Perhaps you spent the day interacting with co-workers, taking time out for lunch with a friend who's in town for business. In the evening, you may have shot off an e-mail to an old college roommate, called your mom (it's her birthday after all), and made plans with the gang to get together this weekend. At the end of the day, you unwound in front of your favorite newscaster telling you about the various politicians, athletes, businessmen, and celebrities whose lives may (or may not) interest you. Every day, you interact with so many different people in unique ways. You exchange information: "Did you catch the news this morning?" You enjoy another's company: "Who's up for a good joke?" You enrich lives: "I made you something at school today." Throughout your day, most of the decisions you make and actions you take are thanks to, or on behalf of, someone that you know.

That's a one-foot view of the world in which you're the center. Pan the camera back a ways (farther . . . farther . . . even farther), and you see that each person you interact with — family, friends, the newspaper delivery guy, the lunch lady, your favorite musician, and even the people who are writing this book — are at the center of their own realities. So is each person *they* know. The connections between every single person in the world intertwine, interplay, and interlock to form *the social graph*. Bold claim: This living, throbbing, shifting, growing web of human relationships is one of life's most awesome and powerful concepts.

The power of the social graph refers to how information travels quickly and (somewhat) reliably among folks who are connected with one another. Facebook's function is to make the social graph accessible — that is, to help people keep track of and reach the people they know and help individuals leverage the power of the graph by enabling them to communicate and exchange information with anyone or everyone they trust.

Another powerful aspect of the social graph on Facebook is that it builds and maintains itself. Each member helps define his or her place in the graph. When you sign up for Facebook, you start by finding the Profiles of the people you know and establishing your virtual connection to them. As a Facebook user, it's in your best interest to keep your portion of the graph mapped as accurately as possible — form a complete set of connections to the people you know. Facebook can become your single access point for the people you know, so it becomes more useful when you can confidently find exactly who you're looking for. Because of how Facebook is built, you are not the only one responsible for connecting with everyone you know (imagine the longest game of Hide and Seek *ever*). After you make a few connections, mutual friends are automatically made aware of your presence on the site, and they seek *you* out to establish a connection. ***Remember:*** It's also in their best interest to keep their contact list up to date.

Discovering What You Can Do on Facebook

Now that you know that Facebook is a means by which you can connect with people who matter to you, your next question may be, "How?" It's a good question — such a good question that we spend almost the rest of this book answering it. But first, an overview.

Establish a Profile

When you sign up for Facebook, one of the first things you do is establish your *Profile*. A Profile on Facebook is a social résumé — a page about you that you keep up-to-date with all the information you want people to know.

Facebook understands that if you were handing out résumés in the real world, you'd probably give different documents to different people. Your social résumé may have your phone number, your favorite quotes, and pictures from that crazy night in you-know-where with you-know-who. Your résumé for a potential employer would probably share your education and employment history. Your résumé for your family may include your personal address as well as show off your recent vacation photos and news about your life's changes.

You show different slices of your life and personality to different people, and a Facebook Profile, shown in Figure 1-1, allows you (no, *encourages* you) to do the same. To this end, your Profile is set up with all kinds of privacy controls to specify *who* you want to see *which* information. Many people find great value in adding to their Profile just about every piece of information they can and then unveiling each particular piece cautiously. The safest rule here is to share on your Profile any piece of information you'd share with someone in real life. The corollary applies, too: Don't share on your Profile any information that you wouldn't share with someone in real life. We provide more detail about the Profile in Chapter 2. For now, think of it like a personal Web page with privacy controls for particular pieces of information. This page accurately reflects you so that you hand the right social résumé to the right person.

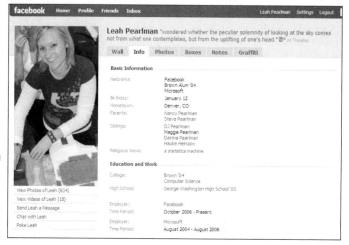

Figure 1-1:
Leah's
Facebook
Profile.

The motivations for establishing a Profile on Facebook are twofold. First, a Profile helps the people who know you in real life find and connect with you on Facebook. Each individual is actively (or actively trying) to keep track of the people she knows. If your name is something relatively common, such as James Brown or Maria Gonzales, it's difficult for people to find you without additional identifiers. Information about you, such as your home town, your education history, or your photos, help people find the right James or Maria.

The second (and way cooler) reason to establish an accurate Profile is the work it saves you. Keeping your Profile detailed and relevant means that your friends and family can always get the latest information about where you live, who you know, and what you're up to. You no longer have to read your phone number to someone while he fumbles to find a pen. Just tell him, "It's on

Facebook." If a cousin wants to send you a birthday present, he doesn't have to ruin the surprise by asking you for your address. When your Profile is up to date, conversations that used to start with the open-ended, "How have you been?" can skip straight to the good stuff: "I saw your pictures from Hawaii last week. *Please* tell me how you ended up wearing those coconuts."

Connect with friends

After you join Facebook, start seeing its value by tracking down some people you know. Facebook offers the following tools to help you:

- ✔ **Facebook Friend Finder:** Allows you to scan the e-mail addresses in your e-mail address book to find whether those people are already on Facebook. Selectively choose among those with whom you'd like to connect.

- ✔ **Suggestions:** Will show you the names and pictures of people you likely know or celebrities whose news you'd like to follow. These people are selected for you based on various signals like where you live or work, or how many friends you have in common.

- ✔ **Search:** Helps you to find people whom you expect are already using Facebook.

After you establish a few connections, use those connections to find other people you know by searching through their connections for familiar names. We explain how to find people you know on Facebook in Chapter 3.

Communicate with Facebook friends

As Facebook grows, it becomes more likely that anyone with whom you're trying to communicate can be reached. These days it's a fairly safe assumption that you'll be able to find that person you just met at a dinner party, an old professor from college, or the childhood friend you've been meaning to catch up with. Digging up a person's contact information could require calls to mutual friends, a trip to the white pages (provided you know enough about that person to identify the right contact information), or an e-mail sent to a potentially outdated e-mail address. You may have different methods of reaching people depending on how you met the person, or what limited information you have about him or her.

Facebook streamlines finding and contacting people in a reliable forum. If the person you're reaching out to is active on Facebook, no matter where she lives or how many times she's changed her e-mail address, you can reach one another.

Share your words

You have something to say. We can just tell by the look on your face. Maybe you're proud of the home team, maybe you're excited for Friday, or maybe you can't believe what you saw on the way to work this morning. All day long, things are happening to all of us that make us just want to turn to our friends and say "You know what? . . .That's what." Facebook gives you the stage and an eager audience. In Chapter 6, we explain how you can make short or long posts about the things happening around you, and how they're distributed to your friends in an easy, non-intrusive way.

Share your pictures

Since the invention of the modern day camera, people have been all too eager to yell, "Cheese!" Photographs can make great tour guides on trips down memory lane, but only if we actually remember to develop, upload, or scrapbook them. Many memories fade away when the smiling faces are stuffed into an old shoe box, remain on undeveloped rolls of film, or are forgotten in some folder on a hard drive.

Facebook offers two great incentives for uploading, organizing, and editing your photos:

- ✔ **Facebook provides one easy-to-access location for all your photos.** Directing any interested person to your Facebook Profile is easier than e-mailing pictures individually, sending a complicated link to a photo site, or waiting until the family reunion to show off the my-how-the-kids-have-grown pics.

- ✔ **Every photo you upload can be linked to the Profiles of the people in the photo.** For example, you upload pictures of you and your sister and link them to her Profile. Whenever someone visits her Profile, he sees those pictures; he doesn't even have to know you. This is great because it introduces a longevity to photos they've never had before. As long as people are visiting your sister's Profile, they can see those pictures. Photo albums no longer have to be something people look at right after the event, and maybe then again years later.

Plan events, join groups

Just about anything you do with other people is easier on Facebook . . . except cuddling. Facebook isn't meant to be a replacement for face time; it's meant to facilitate interactions when face time isn't possible or to facilitate the planning of face time. Two of the greatest tools for this are Facebook Events and Facebook Groups.

Groups are basically Web pages people can subscribe to, or *join.* One group may be intimate, such as five best friends who plan several activities together. Another group could be practical, for example, PTA Members of Denver Schools. Some groups garner support, such as AIDS Awareness. Others exist for solidarity; for example, When I Was Your Age, Pluto Was a Planet Groups allow people to come together in the name of some common interest or goal. Depending on the particular group's settings, members may upload photos or videos, invite other people to the group, receive messages, and check on news and updates.

Events are similar to groups, with the addition of being time-based. Rather than joining, users RSVP to events, which allows the event organizers to plan accordingly and allows attendees to receive event reminders. Facebook Events are often used for something as small as a lunch date or something as big as a march on Washington, D.C. Sometimes events are notional rather than physical. For example, someone could create an event for Ride Your Bike to Work Day and hope the invitation spreads far and wide (through friends and friends of friends) to promote awareness. At Facebook headquarters, Events are used to plan company meetings, happy hours, ski trips, and more. Read more about Facebook Groups and Facebook Events in Chapter 10.

Facebook and the Web

Facebook Photos, Groups, and Events are only a small sampling of how you can use Facebook to connect with the people you know. In Chapter 13, we explain in detail the *Facebook Platform.* In short, Facebook is a service that helps you maintain connections with your friends, but any company can build the tools, Web sites, or *applications,* that allow sharing. Photos, Groups, and Events are tools that are built on top of the Facebook Platform; they are the means by which people can use share information through their social connections.

Examples of Web sites and applications that have been built by other companies include tools to help you edit your photos, create slideshows, play games with friends across the globe, divvy bills among people who live or hang out together, and exchange information about good movies, music, and books. After you get a little more comfortable with the Facebook basics, you can try some of the thousands of applications and Web sites that allow you to interact with your Facebook friends through their services. One example is shown in Figure 1-2. We simply mention it here to pique your curiosity about the potential; Chapter 13 gives all the juicy details about third-party applications.

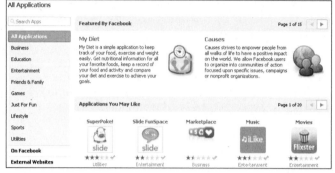

Promote your business

Say, you have something to sell — that fancy blender, maybe. How do you get people's attention? You don't go to a deserted parking lot and yell, "Hey! Buy my blender!" do you? Of course not. You go to where the people are, and the people are on Facebook. Although anybody can (and should) use Facebook to connect with their friends and family, more and more people are using it to connect with their patrons, fans, or supporters. In addition to their personal Profiles, people create additional Profiles to promote their bands, businesses, brands, products, services, or themselves, in the case of celebrities or politicians. These Profiles are similar to user Profiles in that they're a page on Facebook meant to

 ✔ Represent a specific real-world entity.

 ✔ Consist of truthful, necessary information required to engage with that entity.

These Profiles differ from user Profiles in that the relationships are essentially one way. We may have a relationship to Starbucks, but Starbucks doesn't really have a specific relationship with us, which leads to a number of differences in the functionality of business Profiles. We discuss the details of those differences and explain the benefits of promoting your business on Facebook in Chapter 12.

Chapter 15 discusses how you advertise your business without, or in addition to, establishing a business Profile on Facebook. Because Facebook users enter detailed information about themselves (and their actions on Facebook reveal even more about the kinds of people they are), Facebook can offer a compelling advertising platform by allowing advertisers to reach a targeted audience based on who people are and what they like.

Facebook also offers another kind of targeting, which is *social targeting.* For many kinds of commercial goods, we're often more likely to buy something if we know people who've already had a positive experience with the particular good or the company selling it. When Facebook shows someone an ad, it lets that person know whether any of their friends had an experience with that product, service, or business. In fact, if that person has a friend who interacted an ad, that person is more likely to see that same ad than someone with friends who haven't interacted with that ad. This type of targeted advertising is a win-win for business owners and consumers because business owners don't have to waste money or dilute their message on people who don't care about their product, and users are more likely to see ads for products that actually interest them — or, at the very least, tell them something about their friends' consumer habits.

Keeping in Mind What You Can't Do on Facebook

Facebook is meant to represent real people and real associations; it's also meant to be safe. Many of the rules of participation on Facebook exist to uphold those two goals.

Note: There are things you can't do on Facebook other than what we list here. For example, you can't message multiple people unless you're friends with all of them; you can't join the school network of a school you didn't attend (or a workplace network of a company you don't work for); and you can't spin hay into gold. These rules may change how you use Facebook, but probably won't change *whether* you use it. We separate the five rules in this section because, if any are a problem for you, you probably won't get to the rest of the book.

You can't lie

Okay, you can, but you shouldn't, especially not about your basic information. Lying about your identity is a violation of the Facebook Terms of Use and grounds for Profile deactivation. In other words, thank you, bye-bye. Although many people try, Facebook doesn't let anyone sign up with an obviously fake name like Marilyn Manson or Fakey McFakerson. Those who do make it past the name checks will likely find their account tracked down and deactivated.

Some fake accounts survive on Facebook undetected for a very long time because the Facebook user operations team goes after people who are breaking serious and safety-compromising offenses first. So, if you're considering setting up a fake Profile to test our claim, you're probably better off just going outside to play. Take a Frisbee.

You can't be twelve

Or younger. Seriously. Facebook takes very seriously the law that prohibits minors under the age of 13 from creating an online Profile for themselves. This rule is in place for the safety of minors, and it's a particular safety rule that Facebook takes extremely seriously. If you or someone you know on Facebook is under 13, deactivate (or make them deactivate) the account now. If you're reported to the Facebook user operations team, your account is deleted instantly, and Facebook (and Carolyn and Leah as well) will be very unhappy. Facebook is vigilant about keeping minors off the site, so if you're under 13, be aware that the people you hang out with won't be on Facebook either. If you happen to be older than 13 and looking for people under 13, check out the next section for what else you can't do.

You can't troll

We can't stress this enough, and putting it in bold definitely isn't enough stress. Maybe we should add underline, italics, or all caps. Let's try.

YOU CAN'T TROLL.

Facebook is about real people and real connections. It's one thing to message a mutual friend or the occasional stranger whose Profile implies being open to meeting new people if the two of you have matching interests. However, the moment the people you contact have a problem with you sending unsolicited messages, your account is flagged; if the behavior continues, your account is deactivated.

Imagine going to a coffee shop and introducing yourself to each and every person while they try to mind their cup of Joe. That is how we view the sending of unsolicited messages on Facebook, and the user operations team will make like an angry barista and kick you to the coffee shop curb.

You can't upload illegal content

Respecting United States law is something Facebook has to do regardless of its own position on pornography (where minors can see it), copyrighted material, hate speech, depictions of crimes, and other offensive content. However, doing so is also in line with Facebook's value of being a safe, happy place for all people (older than the age of 12). Don't confuse this with censorship; Facebook is all about freedom of speech and self-expression, but the moment that compromises anyone's safety or breaks any law, disciplinary action is taken.

Realizing How Facebook Is Different from Other Social Sites

Several social sites besides Facebook try to help people connect. Some of the most popular sites are MySpace, Friendster, Orkut, LinkedIn, Windows Live Spaces, Bebo, Meebo, Match.com, Twitter, and QQ.

In some cases, these sites have slightly different goals than Facebook. LinkedIn, for example, is a tool for connecting with people specifically for career networking. MySpace initially started out as a way for small, local bands to gain popularity outside of the politically-complicated music industry by creating a space for people to connect with others who had similar tastes in music. Match.com is a social networking site specifically geared toward people looking to date. Alternatively, other sites have the same goals as Facebook; they just have different strategies. MySpace gives users complete customization over the look and feel of their Profile, whereas Facebook maintains a pretty consistent design and expects users to differentiate their Profiles by uploading unique content. On the other extreme, Twitter allows its members to share only very short bits of text to achieve super-simple and consistent information sharing, whereas Facebook allows more flexibility with respect to sharing photos, videos, and more. That's not to say one model is better than another; different models may appeal to different people.

Who Is on Facebook

Originally, Facebook was created as a way for students at a particular college or university to find and connect with each another. In fact, when Facebook launched, only those people with a verified college e-mail address were permitted to sign up.

After the success of the university-only model, Facebook opened its doors to high school students in the United States as well. High school students don't have e-mail addresses to verify which high school they attend; therefore, Facebook has a fairly complicated system that relies on students verifying one another before gaining access to a particular high school network.

Facebook took off in high schools with such momentum that Facebook next opened its doors to workplace networks. Workplace networks followed the same model as the college networks — in order to join, you had to sign up with a verified e-mail address, this time, from a particular corporation. Therefore, workplace networks existed only for the companies big enough to offer its employees e-mail addresses, such as Microsoft, Apple, Amazon, and others.

Finally, in the fall of 2004, rather than opening any more doors, Facebook just knocked down its walls. Today, anyone with any e-mail address is welcome to join the Facebook party.

People can still limit the visibility of any part of their Profiles to people in their verified networks, or they can open up parts of their Profiles to anyone. Now that Facebook is used by more than 200 million people, the name of the game is control and choice. You can share as much or as little with as many or as few people as you so desire. Put under lock and key the parts of your Profile you *don't* want to share with everyone. Chapter 5 goes into much greater detail on how to protect yourself and your information.

Here are two reasons Facebook made the leap from *verified networks* (those in which you must offer some kind of proof of identity, such as an e-mail address, in order to join) to enabling people to share with everyone:

- ✔ **Facebook was offering a tremendous amount of utility to the people who had access to it.** Before opening to the general public, about 85 percent of registered users were logging in at least once per month, and 75 percent of those people were logging in daily. Numbers like that proved Facebook creators were onto something special and that other people — in addition to students and employees of large corporations — could gain value from access to Facebook.

- ✔ **Facebook is better when lots of different people are active on Facebook.** This reason for allowing any and everyone on Facebook is a little less obvious, so we offer this example as an explanation:

  A University of Colorado alumnus wants to throw himself a birthday party. At college, he used Facebook to plan his events and manage his guest lists, but now some of his friends are older and were out of college before Facebook became popular. Creating the event on Facebook could lead to an incomplete guest list. If he chooses not to use Facebook, he may end up using a less efficient means of communicating, such as e-mail, which requires that he dig up the e-mail address of everyone he wants to invite and then manage all the RSVPs as they flood his inbox. He may also decide that it's not worth the hassle and invite only people who are on Facebook. Facebook actually allows him to create an event and generate special invites to those not on the site, but he still has to locate those friend's e-mail addresses and enter them on Facebook.

Facebook has great tools for organizing people, information, and communication. Their utility, however, depends on you being able to reach your friends with them. The more contacts you have on Facebook, the more useful each of these tools become.

Significant to the utility of the social graph is its reliability. Having a single source to find and interact with friends, mutual acquaintances, family, or others with shared interests and beliefs would be one of the greatest solutions to many of life's most complicated tasks. Managing our relationships with everyone we know or want to know is the service Facebook is trying to provide. To anyone for whom Facebook has become the primary source for information and interaction, the moment someone in particular isn't represented on Facebook, the whole service becomes less powerful because its reliability for finding whomever you're looking for is reduced. To that end, welcoming everyone onto Facebook was a way to make the service more valuable to those already using it.

A majority of Facebook users are not, nor have ever been, part of a school network, and most of Facebook's growth is in demographics other than high school or college. In the following sections, we talk about how people in different demographics use Facebook. Note that these cases aren't exclusive to the particular category they're listed under; people in workplace networks may use many of the same features and functionality as students, and international users clearly span all three of the demographics. These sections simply emphasize the general trends in particular demographics and highlight some of the differences between them.

Students of the 'Book

Students live in somewhat of a unique environment in that the shared affiliation to the same school implies a level of trust. This allows students to create Profiles for themselves, and if they choose, share their information only with other students at their school (and people they manually verify). Because of the close quarters and accountability of their peers, students are perhaps the most open about the information they exchange on Facebook. As long as students are safe about the information they choose to share (see Chapter 5), this abundance of information flow is actually a very good thing that can make their lives and relationships extremely rich.

Students use Facebook for all kinds of fun and practical things:

- **Getting information:** Students can easily connect with others who live in their dorm or take the same classes. This can be great for (approved) collaboration on class work, finding out when homework's due, or borrowing a book for research.

- **Planning events:** A big source of student engagement is event planning. Say, Tau Phi Beta wants to plan an event. The fraternity's officers can create the Event page on Facebook, and with a few clicks of a few buttons, invite everyone they want to. They can specify whether the invite should go only to those initially invited — say, a Tau Phi Beta brothers–only dinner — or whether anyone can be invited (a must for a giant frat party — er, *fundraiser*). This is just one example, but events are rampant across universities. Every club, dorm room, sports team, and group of friends organize their events on Facebook.

✔ **Tagging photos:** The Photos feature is one of the most popular on Facebook. Students regularly engage in a lot of memorable activities, such as dances, games, and rallies. Generally a large number of students and a nearly-as-large number of cameras attend these events. We hear many students confess that in the time it takes them to hop a shuttle or stumble to their dorm room, someone has already uploaded photos from the event to Facebook. No sooner does a student experience a magical moment than she gets to remember it.

One of the fancy aspects of Facebook Photos is that each photo can be tagged with links to the Profiles of the people in the photo. All the photos a particular person is tagged in are aggregated into one album, so when you look at a person's Profile, you see all the photos he's ever been tagged in. After a big night on campus, students can see all the pictures their friends took or go straight to all the photos of them. Narcissistic maybe, but also human.

✔ **Keeping up with friends from home:** Sometimes college can feel like its own little universe, especially for those who travel far from home to attend. By establishing friend connections with those friends they *don't* see every day, they can more easily stay in touch. When they upload photos from the University Gala, friends from home can send a message to say, "Nice dress!" or "Who's the boy?" An RSVP to an event, such as the National Championship Dinner, informs friends from back home of their friend's recent success. And, even though students often get caught up in the action of campus life, sometimes they'll hear a song or read a passage that reminds them of a friend back home. Rather than digging for the e-mail address or finding time to call, they can just use Facebook to drop their friend a *thinking of you* Wall post, Poke, or message. (Find out more about these options in Chapter 9.)

✔ **Flirting and gossip:** We should've stuck this bullet point first because it's probably the biggest piece of the time-spent-on-Facebook pie. Mmmm, Facebook pie. Throughout this book, you read about messaging, poking, chatting, and gifting, which are all ways that students virtually bat their eyelashes at one another — and avoid doing their homework.

Everyone has the ability on their Profile to inform people who they're looking to meet (women, men, or both) and for what purpose (relationship, dating, friendship, and so on). Those already in a relationship can link to their significant other for the world to see. Provocative *Wall posts* (one friend can write a public message on a friend's *Wall*), intriguing photo uploads, and changing relationship statuses are all sources of juicy gossip without which high school or college just wouldn't be the same.

The School of Life

Chronologically speaking, there's only a small difference between someone nearing the end of their school career (whether that be high school, college, or graduate school) and someone starting life after school. But these two phases share a few other similarities. During school, most people have a set crowd of folks they interact with. They're very familiar with the city or town they live in and the daily routine (class, sports, studying) they've been doing for years. After school, things can change. Many folks move to new cities, start new jobs, and meet new people. Their groups of friends start to disperse (geographically and emotionally), and creating environments for social interaction requires more effort when people cut out lunch time, study hall, or Friday nights at the student center. Because Facebook is all about nurturing relationships, when the nature of people's relationships change, their usage of Facebook changes as well. After school, people find different kinds of utility from their social graph:

- ✔ **Moving to a new city:** Landing in a new city with all your worldly belongings and an upside down map can be hugely intimidating. Having some open arms or at least numbers to call when you arrive can greatly ease the transition. Although you may already know some people who live in your new city, Facebook can help connect with all the old friends and acquaintances you either forgot live there or have moved there since you last heard from them.

  When Leah first moved to the Bay area, she filtered her Friend List to everyone in the San Francisco and Silicon Valley networks. The final list probably contained four times as many people as she remembered living in the area. She sent messages announcing her imminent arrival and then connected with her various contacts to get settled into an apartment, meet other people, and find doctors, bike routes, Frisbee leagues, and restaurants. Even if you don't have friends or acquaintances in your new city, someone you know probably does. Your friends can give you names of people to look up when you arrive — use Facebook to do that.

- ✔ **Getting a job:** Recently, more and more people began using Facebook as a tool for managing their careers as well as their social lives. If you're looking at a particular company, find people who already work there to get the inside scoop or to land an interview. If you're thinking about moving into a particular industry, browse your friends by past job and interests to find someone to connect with.

- ✔ **Finding activity partners:** Many folks would agree that it's harder to meet people after they leave school. Facebook is a great tool for meeting new friends with similar interests, activity partners, or even potential love interests. You can browse Profiles of people in your network based on various kinds of information, such as age, political views, and work history. Plenty of online sites offer these kinds of services, but Facebook works particularly well because the connection you make is often based on mutual acquaintances, making them less awkward, better informed, and safer.

Putting Facebook to work at work

Facebook is still finding its footing within the workplace networks. Therefore, it's tricky to generalize how people in workplace networks use Facebook because it really depends on the particular workplace. However, here are some uses we've heard about anecdotally:

- ✔ Getting to know co-workers and putting names to faces.

- ✔ Hosting events specific to the company. Facebook uses Events to plan company parties and host happy hours.

- ✔ Using Groups for people in the company with similar interests or needs. This may range from those with similar athletic endeavors, carpool requirements, or artistic interests.

- ✔ These days, many companies have a business presence on Facebook. Advertising on Facebook is one way to use Facebook at work. Additionally, when companies work together, sometimes their employees become fans of one another's businesses on Facebook to show support.

- ✔ Posting and sharing stories about the company relevant to the business.

Facebook maturing

Facebook isn't just for students. Anything you've heard to the contrary is dated information. Like we mention before, the fastest growing group of Facebook users is those for whom school is a distant memory. Many of these folks find the same value in Facebook as people in other demographics; however, they also use it for some different kinds of interactions.

Keeping in touch with family

These days, families are often spread far and wide across state or country lines. Children go to college, parents travel for work, grandparents move to Florida. These distances make it hard for families to interact in any more significant way than gathering together once per year to share some turkey and pie (pecan, preferably). Facebook offers a place where families can virtually meet and interact. Parents can upload photos of the kids for everyone to see, grandparents can write notes about what everyone is up to, and college students can gather support for a cause, plan a graduation party, or show off their class schedule — great information for family members who may have a hard time extracting the information in other ways.

We often hear parents and older family members say they feel being on Facebook may infringe on their kid's social life. If you fit this description, we have a few comments for you:

✔ **You may be right that your kids want you nowhere near their social lives.** If that's the case, and you respect that, don't connect with them on Facebook. Exist within your social graph on Facebook, and let them exist within theirs — you never have to interact with one another whatsoever. Not joining Facebook because your kids are using it is like not eating ice cream because your kids eat ice cream. Sure, you *can* go for ice cream together (or be connected on Facebook), but you certainly don't have to. Don't deprive yourself of the sweet creamy deliciousness just because your kid may be offended that you have similar taste in desserts.

✔ **You may be wrong that your kids don't want you on Facebook.** Depending on your kids' age and personality, they may actually prefer that you join Facebook. Some kids, especially the college-aged or twenty-somethings, are very busy and active. It can be hard for them to remember to call home, let alone call the grandparents, aunts, and uncles. Even when they do, they may leave out interesting information about their lives simply because they forget (this hypothetical is coming from personal experience). These relationships can be much stronger when everyone is on Facebook. Relatives can always see the latest news or photos even when they've been out of touch for some time; they can also connect in a lightweight way in between longer phone conversations. (See Chapter 10 on communicating through Facebook.)

✔ **Kids are *really* good at using Facebook.** If you are connected to your children on Facebook and they want to upload something they don't want you to see, they know exactly which privacy controls to put in place so that you don't see it. It may be easy for them to connect with you and share only the information they want to and hide the information they (and you) may be better off not sharing. Whether this is a relevant concern to you, we recommend sitting down with your kids (sometime after the birds-and-bees conversation but before the how-to-pay taxes conversation) and figuring out how to happily cohabitate on Facebook.

Facebook reunion

Thanks to life's curve balls, whoever your friends are at any given time may not be the people in your life at another. People you consider to be most important in your life fade over the years so that even trying to recall a last name causes you pause. The primary reason for this is a legitimate one: There are only so many hours in a day. While we make new, close friends, others drift away because it's impossible to maintain many intense relationships. Facebook is an extremely powerful tool; however, it hasn't yet found a way to extend the number of hours in a day, so it can't exactly fix the problem of growing apart. Facebook can, however, lessen the finality and inevitability of the distance.

Assuming Facebook achieves the longevity and reach it's striving for, those who have started using Facebook at a young age (13 is the minimum) will, at an old age, actually have a lead on every single person they've ever been friends with. This extremely powerful concept actually alters how people keep and maintain human relationships. Thirty years after you last speak to someone, you may have a funny memory, something important to share, or just genuine curiosity about that person's whereabouts. If you keep her on your Facebook Friend List, it doesn't matter how many times you both move, change your phone numbers, or get married and change your name, you can still get in touch with each another. If that concept scares you, Facebook also has the tools to explicitly sever connections with people you'd rather didn't find you.

Because Facebook is fairly new (and because you're reading this book), you probably don't have your entire social history mapped out. Some may find it a daunting task to create connections with everyone they've ever known, which we don't recommend. Instead, build your graph as you need to or as opportunity presents. Perhaps you want to upload a photo taken from your high school graduation to tag various classmates. Search for them on Facebook, form the friend connection, and then tag them. Maybe you're thinking about opening a restaurant, and you'd like to contact a friend from college who was headed into the restaurant business after graduation. Perhaps you never told your true feelings to the one who got away — your unicorn. For all these reasons, you may find your cursor in the Facebook Search box.

Frequently, we receive reports from adopted children who connect with their biological parents, or estranged siblings who find each other on Facebook. Carolyn recently heard from her sixth-grade bully, who found her on Facebook to apologize for how he terrorized her back then.

Organizing groups

Unlike students, adults don't often have the luxury of participating in lots of events organized by other people. Instead, they organize their book clubs and cooking groups or gather to watch sporting events and have dinner parties. Facebook Groups can add value to all these events. Creating a group on Facebook for your book club makes it easy for someone to update everyone each week about times, dates, locations, who should bring what, and what everyone should read before attending. People can join and leave groups as they see fit, so you never have to worry about notifying those who've moved or are no longer interested in your group.

The birth of the 'Book

In the old days, say, four or five years ago, most college freshmen would receive a thinly bound book containing the names and faces of everyone in their matriculating class. These *face books* were useful for matching names to the students seen around campus, or for pointing out particular people to friends. There were several problems with these face books. If someone didn't send his picture in, they were incomplete. They were outdated by junior year because many people looked drastically different, and the book didn't reflect the students who had transferred in or who were from any other class. Finally, they had little information about each person.

In February 2004, Mark Zuckerberg, a sophomore at Harvard, launched an online "book" that people could upload their photos and personal information to, which solved many of these problems. Within a month, more than half the Harvard undergraduates had created their own Profiles. Zuckerberg was then joined by others, including Dustin Moskovitz and Chris Hughes, to help expand the site into other schools. Your very own author, Carolyn Abram, was the first non-Harvard student to receive an account. During the summer of the same year, Zuckerberg, Moskovitz, and another partner, Andrew McCollum, moved the company to Palo Alto, California, where the site and the company kept growing. By December 2004, the site had grown to 1 million college students. Every time Facebook opened to a new demographic — high school, then work users, then everyone — the rate at which people joined the site continued to increase. In November 2006, the site had more than 11 million users; by November 2007, it had grown to 50 million active users (*active users* are defined as unique accounts that accessed the site in the last 30 days). By August 2009, only two years later, Facebook reached more than a quarter of a billion users and 1,000 employees. At this point, Facebook's growth shows no sign of slowing.

For one-time gatherings, such as a Super Bowl party, Facebook Events offers a great solution. All you have to do is fill out the guest list and event description — the rest takes care of itself. For the three days prior to the event, everyone receives a reminder on their Facebook Home pages, so they have no excuse for not showing (unless someone invited them to a better party). If you want to ensure your guest list is accurate or that people don't forget, message everyone who RSVP'd (attending or tentative, that is) or who hasn't replied. After the event is over, upload photos or leave funny comments and quotes on the event's Wall. Your Super Bowl party is forever immortalized online — and everyone who RSVP'd has total access.

Le Facebook International

Facebook launched in universities in the United States and then spread to U.S. high schools. As a result, it wasn't until the fall of 2006 (when Facebook opened to everyone) that Facebook started making a showing in any other country. When Facebook finally ventured into Canada and the United Kingdom, it took off fast, like Vin Diesel fast. Many people speculate that the reason for Facebook's insta-popularity in these countries, more so than in the United States, came from the fact that citizens in Canada and the U.K. (and, randomly, Norway) didn't have the same preconception that U.S. citizens had: that Facebook was only meant for students. People in the United States had heard the buzz about Facebook for two years when it was only for students. This stigma used to be a significant hurdle for Facebook's growth in older U.S. demographics. However, for the last year, the fastest growing demographic of U.S. Facebook users has been in the over thirty-five age group, and the notion that Facebook is only for the kiddies is becoming a distant part of Facebook history.

The next major leap for Facebook's growth came at the start of 2008, when it was clear that many people on Facebook wanted to be connecting with people who spoke other languages. Facebook is more valuable for each person when more of their friends use the site. Facebook's strictly English interface was keeping many people from connecting with people they knew. So Facebook launched the Facebook Translation Application. This allows any bilingual (English + Other) user of Facebook to volunteer to help translate Facebook into other languages. Volunteers are shown various English text on the site, and they can either offer a translation, or vote on translations that other people have suggested. When a suggested translation receives enough votes, that translation becomes the text that other people using the site in that second language see. People can sign up for the site and change their language setting to Spanish. Rather than seeing all the English text, they see all the text that the Spanish speaking volunteers have suggested and approved. In this way, Facebook has been translated into 60 languages in just more than a year.

Chapter 2

Adding Your Own Face to Facebook

In This Chapter

▶ Signing up and getting started

▶ Joining a network

▶ Creating your Profile

*I*n Chapter 1, we cover why you want to join Facebook. In this chapter, we actually get you signed up and ready to go on Facebook. Keep in mind a couple of things when you sign up. First, Facebook gets exponentially more useful and more fun when you start adding friends. Without friends, it can feel kind of dull. Second, your friends may take a few days to respond to your friend requests, so be patient. Even if your first time on Facebook isn't as exciting as you hope, be sure to come back and try again over the following weeks. Third, you can have only one account on Facebook. Facebook links accounts to e-mail addresses, and your e-mail address can be linked to only one account. This system enforces a world where people are who they say they are on Facebook.

Signing Up for Facebook

Officially, all you need to join Facebook is a valid e-mail address. When we say *valid,* we just mean that you need to be able to easily access the messages in that account because you're e-mailed a registration confirmation. Figure 2-1 shows the sign-up page. As you can see, you need to fill out a few things:

✔ **Full Name:** Facebook is a place based on real identity. It's not a place for fake names or aliases. Numerous privacy settings are in place to protect your information (see Chapter 4), so use your full real name to sign up.

✔ **E-mail:** You need to enter your valid e-mail address here. If you want to join a school or work network automatically, use your school or work e-mail.

✔ **Password:** Like with all passwords, using a combination of letters and numbers is a good idea for your Facebook password. It's probably not a good idea to use the same password for every site you join, so we recommend using something unique for Facebook.

✔ **Date of Birth:** Enter your date of birth. You can hide this information on your Profile.

✔ **Gender (I am):** Facebook uses your gender information to construct sentences about you on the site. Especially in other languages, it's weird to see sentences like "Jennifer added a photo of themself." If you want to hide your gender, or don't want to associate with either gender, you'll be able to do so after you sign up.

✔ **Security Check (not shown):** The security check on Facebook is in the form of a CAPTCHA. A CAPTCHA is that funky-looking word-in-a-box. Computers can't read CAPTCHAs, but humans can. Asking you to solve a CAPTCHA is Facebook's way of keeping out robots who want to spam you, while still letting you sign up. You see the CAPTCHA after filling out your information and clicking Sign Up.

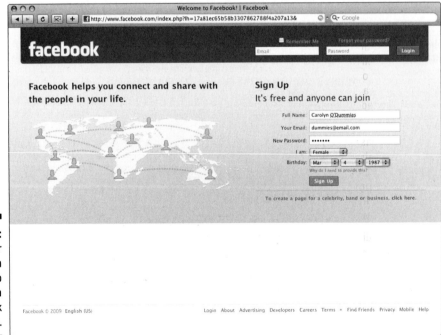

Figure 2-1:
Enter information here to create a Facebook account.

After you've filled out this information and agreed to the Terms of Service and Privacy Policy, click Sign Up. You'll be able to start using Facebook, but you won't yet be confirmed. *Confirmation* is Facebook's way of trying to make sure you are really you, and that the e-mail address you used to sign up is really yours. You receive a confirmation e-mail; click the link in that e-mail to make sure you are confirmed. When you log in to Facebook for the first time, Facebook takes you through a series of steps to help you get started and find your friends. These steps focus on entering information that helps you find friends, either immediately or later on. For example, these steps ask you to use the Friend Finder, which we cover in Chapter 6. The Friend Finder checks your e-mail address book and matches e-mails to Facebook accounts, so you can immediately send friend requests to people you know.

The set-up wizard has a tendency to change depending on what kind of e-mail address you join with and whether a friend invited you to use Facebook. Therefore, instead of going through every possibility for what Facebook may look like when you first log in, we suggest you read the "Making Facebook Revolve Around You" section, as well as the "Education and work history" section, later in this chapter. These concepts definitely come into play as you are prompted for information in the set-up process.

Am I too old for Facebook?

No. Most emphatically, no. This is a common misconception, mainly because Facebook was originally exclusive to college students. Facebook's origins, even its name, are rooted in college campuses, but its utility and nature aren't limited to being useful to only college students.

Everyone has networks of friends and people with whom they interact on a day-to-day basis. Young or old, in college or working, this is true. Facebook tries to map these real-world connections to make it easier for people to share information with their friends.

If you're reading this section and thinking maybe you're just too old for Facebook, you're wrong. More and more people in older age demograph-ics are signing up for Facebook every day to keep in touch with old friends, share photos, create events, and connect with local organizations. Almost everything we discuss in the book is non-age-specific.

Obviously, how people use the site can be very different at different ages, but you will discover these nuances when you use Facebook more and more. Generally, you should feel confident that you and your friends can connect and use Facebook in a meaningful way.

There are more than 200 million people using Facebook, and that number isn't made up of "a bunch of kids." Rather, it's a bunch of people from every age group, every country, and every walk of life.

Making Facebook Revolve Around You

For this section, try imagining Facebook as a map in a car navigation system. Except instead of only mapping out the streets of your neighborhood, Facebook layers on top of that the Profiles of your friends, the photos they've uploaded, and the coffee shops that are their favorites. Facebook is your own digital map of your life. Back in that navigation system, it's hard to figure out where to turn unless your car is right at the center, and the map shifts and reformats as you move through it. Adding your location — whether through your current city or networks — makes sure that Facebook is keeping you in the center of the picture.

Current city

At some point in the first few days, you will be asked — and we certainly encourage you to — identify your current city. Adding a current city helps centralize search results around you, so that if you search for pizza, you'll get local results before you get some pizza place in Italy. That's just a tease — for more details on searching, see Chapter 11.

Adding your current city also helps people around you find and connect with you through search. If you want to add it right now, you can do so from your Profile page. Look for the little pencil icon in the Basic Info section of your Info tab. Clicking it allows you to enter a current city.

Networks

The word *network* can be a bit overused around Facebook from time to time. After all, isn't Facebook a giant network? Aren't your friends, with whom you have direct connections, a network? What about if you're using Facebook for business networking? When getting started on Facebook, you're prompted to join a network. In this context, *network* refers to a group of people with a real-world connection but who may not actually know each other.

Each of the three types of networks has a real-world counterpart. High school networks and college networks mirror high school and college campuses; workplace networks mirror companies and businesses. Similar to your current location, joining a network re-centers the site around you and your location.

Unlike your current location, however, networks aren't for everyone. When you're deciding to join a network, keep in mind these limitations:

- ✔ **You cannot join a high school network unless you're actually in high school.** High school networks cannot, for security reasons, accommodate high school alums or even teachers.

- ✔ **You can join college and workplace networks only with authenticated e-mail addresses.** If you've already graduated from college but want the capability to see classmates, request an alumni e-mail address from your alma mater. Without it, you won't be able to join that school's network.

If you aren't in high school, and if you don't have an "authenticated" e-mail address, you can skip on over to "Setting Up Your Profile." Otherwise, read on to learn more about how you can and why you should join a network.

To join your most relevant networks, look for the link to the Settings page on the big blue bar at the top. Click the Networks tab, and enter the network you would like to join. Figure 2-2 shows the options you see if you haven't yet joined any networks.

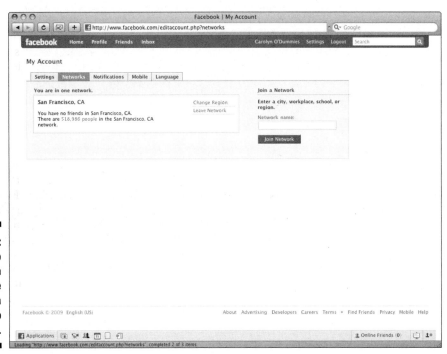

Figure 2-2: Look no farther than this page to find a network to join.

Networks are very useful as a privacy control; therefore, joining your network gives you more access to relevant information. There's more detailed information about privacy in Chapter 5, but we lay out some basics here. For example, let's say Carolyn and Leah both work at Company Q, but (and this is really sad) they haven't yet added each other as friends. Carolyn may take photos at the company picnic, and publish them to her "Friends and Networks." If Leah forgot to join the Company Q work network, she won't be able to see the photos (again, really sad).

This privacy setting doesn't just apply to photos, but to all sorts of information. Because you can give the people around you a little more access, and you can get a little more access, joining a network makes connecting and sharing even easier.

To join your workplace or school network(s), you need an e-mail address from your company or school.

Setting Up Your Profile

You're probably thinking, "Didn't I set up my Profile when I joined?" The answer to that is, not quite. Your account is what you already created; however, your *Profile* — what people can see about you — is probably still blank. We talk more about the bigger picture of Profiles and what they mean for you in Chapter 6. For now, just say that setting up your Profile is important so that when you start to find friends and friends start to find you, they can identify who you are, and that you really are you. The main pieces we cover here help people figure out who you are.

But what does your Profile actually consist of? You can check out your current Profile by clicking the Profile link, or your name, in the big blue bar on top of any page. Your Profile is made up of *boxes* and *tabs*. You see *boxes* — literally small rectangles each containing a type of information — running down the left side of your Profile. You see *tabs* — similar to the tabs that emerge from file folders — running across the top of the page. Together, the information contained in these boxes and tabs tells the story of you.

To get you set up on your Profile, we're going to focus on the Info tab. The Info tab contains mostly text fields that may not change that often. Go to the Info tab of your Profile. To fill out your Info tab, look for the Edit Information link at the top of that tab. Figure 2-3 shows the page for editing Basic Information; you can select any of the other sections (Personal Info, Work and Education Info, Contact Info) to edit that information as well. As you edit this information, you may wonder who can see it. By default, Everyone can see the sections we're diving in to right now. Sensitive stuff like your contact information is available only to your confirmed friends by default. You can restrict both of these settings further using your privacy settings, if you choose (see Chapter 4).

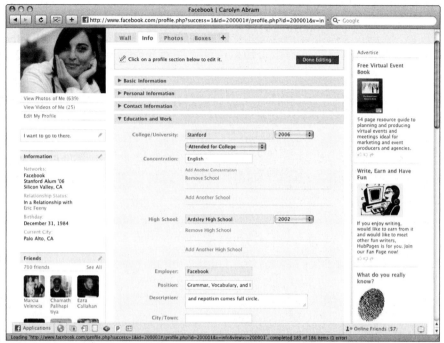

Figure 2-3:
Updating your Info tab.

Look for the little pencil icon you see next to Edit Information all over Facebook. It often appears when your mouse is hovering over something as well. Wherever you see it, you'll be able to change or edit the content it marks.

In the rest of the chapter, we detail a few fields you should fill out early on. Here, we briefly describe the types of fields contained within each section (and we get into more depth with a lot of these in Chapter 5):

✔ **Basic Information:** Basic Information contains a variety of fields that you may want to share with people. This includes things ranging from your political and religious views to your relationship status. None of these fields are required, but they are meant to encourage you to share some biographical details that help people understand who you are.

✔ **Personal Information:** Personal information includes a lot of free-form fields. For example, you can enter your favorite books, movies, activities, TV shows, and music. You can also enter representative quotes, as well as tell people "about me."

✔ **Contact Information:** Facebook has an amazing ability to be a one-stop address book. Because of the ability to restrict visibility, you can share your phone number, address, e-mail addresses, and screen names easily. The Contact tab has built-in privacy drop-down menus that enable you to control who sees what.

✔ **Education and Work:** We spend a lot more time on this in the following section. It's pretty self-explanatory; this section allows you to share where you went (or go) to school and the various places you've worked.

Basic Information

Basic Information — the information that appears at the top of your Profile next to your Profile picture and below your name — is a sort of "at-a-glance" window into you. As we said previously, it includes a range of fields, all of which are optional. We recommend filling in *at least* your hometown because that's a really common way old friends may want to make sure that it's really Susan from gym class. If you want to fill out these other fields, that's great too. All of the fields help you tell your friends about you and what matters to you.

Education and work history

Entering your education and work history usually helps people identify how they know you when you request a friend or send someone a message. For example, if you meet someone at a conference or social function, the ability to remind them, "Remember me, the one with the cool job writing books for dummies?" is built right into your Profile. Additionally, if someone performs a search for a certain class year from your school, you appear in the search results, and old friends can get in touch with you.

Profile picture

Your Profile picture is another way that people can identify you, especially if you have a common name. If your Profile picture features a light blue silhouette, you can change it by rolling your mouse over it and clicking the Change Picture link that appears. A few considerations about Profile pictures that fit into the larger idea of a Profile are covered in Chapter 6. For now, keep these points in mind when choosing a Profile picture:

✔ **Make a good first impression.** Your Profile picture is one of the first ways people interact with your Profile and how you choose to represent yourself. Most people pick pictures that are more or less flattering, or that represent what's important to them. Sometimes, Profile pictures include other people — friends or significant others. Other times, the location matters. If the first photo you see of someone is at the beach versus at a party or sitting at his desk, you may draw different conclusions about that person. What picture represents you?

✔ **Consider who will see your Profile picture.** By default, your Profile picture appears in search results that are visible to all of Facebook, and can even be made available to the larger Internet population. So, generally, people who search for your name can see that picture. You can control this with privacy settings. For more about privacy settings, see Chapter 5.

✔ **Remember that you're not stuck with it.** After we put all this pressure on you to represent yourself and let people identify you, keep in mind that you can easily change your Profile picture at any time. Is it the dead of winter, and that photo of you on the beach last summer just too depressing to look at? No problem; simply edit your Profile picture.

Trust Me: Getting Verified

As we say over and over, Facebook is a Web site for real identity and real people. To protect this fact, Facebook has systems in place to detect any fake Profiles. Fake Profiles may be jokes (for example, someone creating a Profile for her dog), or they may be *spammers* (robots creating accounts to send thousands of fake friend requests). Regardless, they're not allowed on the site.

You, however, aren't fake or a spammer; how does Facebook know that? Facebook figures that out by verifying you. Now, you may start out verified, or it may take a little while. To figure out whether you still need to get verified, look at these questions:

✔ **Did you join with an *authenticated* e-mail address?** *Authenticated* e-mail addresses are ones that not just anyone can get. For example, Google provides e-mail addresses to its employees that end with a specific domain (in their case, @google.com). You can't have that address unless you work for Google. Most colleges and workplaces have authenticated e-mail addresses. If you joined with one of these, you were automatically verified.

✔ **Do you have an authenticated e-mail address that you didn't join with?** Joining a network with your authenticated e-mail address also serves to verify you. (Refer to Figure 2-2 to see how you join an authenticated workplace or school network.)

✔ **Do you not have an authenticated e-mail address?** You will need to get verified as you use the site. To do that, keep reading this section.

Without an authenticated e-mail address, Facebook unfortunately has to assume the worst about you. You may send spam or inappropriate content to people on Facebook. It's suspicious and paranoid. But it wants to trust you, so it's going to start testing you.

Remember the CAPTCHA you filled out when you joined? Until Facebook trusts you, you will continue to see these when you interact with other people on Facebook. Through normal use of the site, eventually Facebook will believe you are not, in fact, malicious, and it will stop showing you CAPTCHAs wherever you turn. You can forgo having to solve many of these by instead being verified through your mobile phone. In order to do this, your mobile phone needs to be able to receive text messages (also known as SMS messages). If you don't have a mobile phone, or it doesn't have this capability, don't worry — you'll still get verified as you start using Facebook.

To get verified via mobile, follow these steps:

1. **Search for someone and click Add to Friends.**

2. **On the Add to Friends pop-up that appears (shown in Figure 2-4), click the Verify Your Account link (located beneath the CAPTCHA).**

   A new Confirm Your Phone pop-up appears, as shown in Figure 2-5.

Figure 2-4:
Still seeing a CAPTCHA like this? End the madness with mobile verification.

Figure 2-5:
Confirm your phone to prove you're real.

3. **Select your country and enter your mobile phone number.**

4. **Check your mobile phone for a text message that contains a code.**

5. **Enter the code into the Code field in the Confirm Your Phone pop-up.**

6. **Click Confirm.**

Facebook won't send you any other mobile messages unless you choose to opt into Facebook Mobile. (For more information about Facebook Mobile, see Chapter 14.)

If you're already verified, you won't see a CAPTCHA. You may not be able to use mobile verification if your phone can't receive text messages, but don't worry, you'll still get verified eventually just by being a normal user of the site.

Chapter 3

Finding Your Way Around Facebook

*I*magine a universe at which you are the center. The one thing that every person and piece of information have in common is you. Cool, huh? This is how you can think of the page you see each time you log in to Facebook. The Facebook Home page is entirely oriented toward you and *your* friends. The main column tells you everything all your friends have been up to recently. In the right column, you'll find key pieces of information, like what events you have coming up, and people you may know with whom you have not yet connected. Even the ads in the right column are targeted specifically to you and your interests. Navigation bars line the top and bottom of this page and every other page on the site. These ensure that you can always find your way back to a page you recognize, no matter where you end up. In this chapter, we explain everything you see when you log in, and how to use this page to get around the rest of the site.

Checking Out the Blue Bar on Top

Leah and Carolyn both happen to spend a lot of time in coffee shops working alongside writers, students, business people, and hobbyists — all drinking steamy beverages and manning laptops. We can always tell at a glance when someone is browsing Facebook by the big blue bar across the top of the page.

The blue bar is home to the most important navigational links on Facebook. When you can sufficiently navigate the blue bar, kick off your shoes and put up your feet (unless you're in a coffee shop), because you'll undoubtedly feel right at home on Facebook. Figure 3-1 shows the blue bar links from left to right. Here's what you need to know about each one:

- **Facebook home:** The Facebook logo followed by the Home link on the top left of the page serves two purposes. The first purpose is to remind you what Web site you're using, lest you should forget. When you hover your mouse over the Facebook logo, a little house icon appears — the second purpose. No matter where you are on Facebook, all you have to do is click this icon (saying, "There's no place like home!" is optional), and you're back at the Facebook Home page.

- **Profile:** Next to the home link, you find a link to your own Facebook Profile. *Note:* You can also get to your Profile by clicking your own name or photo, wherever you see them on the site. (See Chapter 2 for more on Profiles.)

- **Friends:** The Friends link takes you to a page where you can manage your existing Facebook connections, or find more people with whom you may want to connect. When you first land on the Friends page, you see all the same friend-finding tools you saw during sign-up (Chapter 2). Clicking the tabs down the left side of the Friends page shows you all of your friends, or, if you've organized your friends into different lists, you see those lists here along with all the tools to edit them. We explain the Friends page in much more detail in Chapter 4.

- **Inbox:** Anyone on Facebook can send you a message unless you change the messaging privacy settings. The Inbox is where you retrieve those messages. The number of new or unread messages you have in your Inbox is shown in a light blue dot next to the Inbox link. Hovering your mouse over the Inbox link lets you quickly navigate to the compose window for sending a new message described in Chapter 9.

- **<Your Name>:** Clicking on your own name always takes you to your own Profile. Some people find the Profile link more intuitive, but for people who often use a shared computer, it's reassuring to see your name up there in the blue bar to quickly verify you're logged in to the right account.

Figure 3-1:
The blue bar
at the top:
link by link.

facebook   Home Profile Friends Inbox   Leah Pearlman Settings Logout Search

✔ **Settings:** Clicking this link brings you to a single page in which you can configure nearly everything to do with your Facebook account. The page is divided into several tabs, each one home to different types of settings. Here is a high-level run-down:

  - *Account* settings include things like changing your name, your e-mail address or password, your mobile information, which allows you to access the site from a mobile phone, the language in which you want to use the site, and also where you go to deactivate your account.

  - *Privacy Settings* is where you set the visibility of all of the information in your Profile. We talk about this in great detail in Chapter 4.

  - *Application Settings* has a few different kinds of settings. On a per-application basis, you can make various privacy and setting configurations from this page. You can also make choices about which pieces of information from your Profile you want to share with applications. Applications use this information to personalize your experience on their sites. More on this in Chapter 13.

  - *Help* takes you to the Help page, which gives you tools for using the site, staying safe on Facebook, and sending your suggestions about how the site may be improved.

✔ **Logout:** Use this link to explicitly log out of Facebook. This is particularly important on computers to which others may have access: Someone can do a lot of damage to your social life with free reign over your Facebook account. *Note:* One other way to log out of Facebook is to end your browser session. However, if you have the Remember Me option selected, you won't ever be logged out until you explicitly hit Logout. That option keeps you logged in despite closing the browser; therefore, we recommend only using that check box on a personal computer.

✔ **Search:** In Chapter 7, we go into all kinds of detail about Search on Facebook. The short version is that Facebook search can be used to find any people, groups, Events, or applications on Facebook. It can also be used to see what your friends or anyone in the world is publishing about a particular topic. You can find your long-lost elementary school friend, a gaming application, what people are saying about the recent election, what they think of a product you're thinking of buying, or even the up-to-the-minute score of a sports event. However, searching for elements of Facebook itself, such as Account or Privacy, doesn't give you what you're looking for. A better way to discover, or navigate to, a particular feature of the site is to scroll to the bottom of the page and click Help. The Help page features a different search box specifically designed for these types of queries. Another common misuse of the Search box is entering attributes of people or things, such as Events happening this Saturday in Denver or Liberal men in Seattle. Search focuses solely on names plus a few facts about people such as where they work, and specific things people are saying.

Exploring the Blue Bar on the Bottom

Fixed to the bottom of any Facebook Page is another set of tools that follow you around the site. It's even more fixed than the blue bar on top, because even as you scroll, it stays right where it is. The blue bar on the bottom houses four different key Facebook elements: your Application bookmarks, Chat, your instant messenger service on Facebook, and your notifications flag.

Application bookmarks

In Chapter 1, we introduce the term *application* as it's defined on Facebook. *Applications* are the services that leverage the core Facebook elements, including Profile information, Friends, and the Inbox. These enable you to engage in more specific and sometimes niche activities.

When you join Facebook, bookmarks to seven default applications already added to your account are listed next to Applications in the light blue bar at the bottom:

 ✔ The Photos application enables you to browse your friends' recent photos, view photos in which you're tagged, and upload your own photos. For more details on the Photos application, see Chapter 7.

 ✔ The Video action is exactly the same as the Photos application, except that all the pictures move! 'Cause they're videos. Not pictures. Click on the Videos Application to see recent and popular videos that your friends have posted or in which they are tagged. You can upload videos here, too. More on the Videos application in Chapter 8.

 ✔ Groups on Facebook can be created by any user for any reason and are usually meant to bring people together (virtually) around common causes or interests. The Groups bookmark takes you to a page for viewing groups recently joined by your friends, groups to which you belong that have recently been updated, or generally popular groups that you can browse. See Chapter 10 for more details on Groups.

 ✔ The Events application is most often used to enable people to organize real-life events with guest lists, reminders, and a space to add relevant comments and photos. The Events bookmark takes you to a page for viewing your upcoming and past Events, friends' Events, and other popular Events that you can browse. For more on Events, see Chapter 11.

 ✔ The Links application allows people to highlight interesting content from the Web or Facebook and provides them a forum for discussion. Clicking Links takes you to a list of items recently posted by your friends as well as your Links and other popular Links. We talk about links in greater detail in Chapter 6.

✔ Known to techy-types as a blogging tool, Notes offers users a blank page for sharing thoughts, anecdotes, tirades, diatribes, and more. The Notes link, located beneath More on the Applications menu, gives you quick access to Notes recently written by and about your friends. You also get quick access to Notes you've written and to other popular Notes. For more about Notes, see Chapter 8.

✔ The Gifts application is the seventh application. Because the blue bar only holds six bookmarks, you can access Gifts by clicking Applications, which brings up the full application menu. Chapter 6 goes into detail about how giving gifts to a friend is a sign of true affection. Why? Because they'll cost you hard earned cash . . . er, credit card.

If you've been using Facebook for a while, you may see a different set of applications than the ones we list here. This may have something to do with what you've used recently, or what you've added to or removed from your Profile. The applications described here are simply the defaults you have upon signing up, but ultimately you have complete control over which applications you add to your Facebook experience. You're free to remove or add as many applications as you like from the hundreds developed by Facebook or other companies (which we cover in Chapter 13).

Each time you start using a new application on Facebook, an icon for that application shows up in the Application Menu. You can add a bookmark to any application you've used by clicking the Application menu and dragging the desired icon underneath the line marked Bookmarks.

Chat

Chat allows you to see which of your friends are online at the same time you are, and then enables you to send quick messages back and forth with any of those people. Similar products are AOL Instant Messenger (AIM), Windows Live, or Yahoo! Messenger. In the bottom-right corner of the blue bar, you'll find the chat bar. The first thing you see is a little icon of a person next to a green dot, which means you are currently available for your friends to send you messages. Next you see the word Chat next to a number, which refers to how many of your friends are online and available to talk to you right at this minute. Clicking anywhere in the chat bar — which is that particular section of the bar on the bottom — is how you see who is online and begin chatting. Actually, reading Chapter 9 of this book, which covers Chat in great detail, may be an even better starting point.

Notifications

Say for a moment that someone on Facebook has done something to you. Maybe he's tagged you in a photo, written on your Wall, or given you a virtual gift. Don't you want to know about it? Facebook tries to let you know in a couple ways. For one thing, you'll likely get an e-mail about it. *Note:* You can turn on or off whichever types of e-mail notifications you choose by clicking Settings at the top and hitting the Notifications tab. If you do turn off your e-mail notifications, or if you sign in to Facebook before you check your e-mail after one of your friends has taken an action like this, you'll be notified about in the blue bar at the bottom.

When a friend takes an action on the site that affects you or your Profile, such as accepting your friend request, inviting you to try an application, tagging you in a Note, and so on, a little red speech bubble appears at the bottom of the page alerting you to notifications of it. Clicking the bubble brings up a list of the last five notifications you received, and a See All link to see the rest. Each notification contains a link to the content that was added, whether that's the photo you were tagged in, or the Wall post someone left for you. We go into notifications in a little more detail in Chapter 9. But when you see the red bubble down there, click it; when you don't, don't worry about it.

Discovering the Home Page

The Home page refers to what you see when you first log in to Facebook. It's comprised of two major sections: The Stream and, um, the right column, which doesn't have a name but rather a theme, which we cover in just a minute.

Note: Before you have even a single friend, the Home page looks very different than it does after you start making connections. Because the sign-up flow described in Chapter 2 guides you through finding your first friends, everything that follows in this section assumes that you've connected to at least one person on Facebook. If you haven't, flip ahead to Chapter 4, which goes into great detail about finding and connecting with people you know. Then flip back: This is a juicy chapter.

Get published

Hey, reader: What's on your mind? Don't answer us here; we can't hear you. Answer us at the top of your Home page, in the box that asks this very question. This box, called the Publisher, is introduced in Chapter 2 as a key part of the Profile. The Publisher box on the Home page works just like the one on your Profile: Any time you have something you want to share, whether it's just a quick update about what you're doing, where you are, or where you like to go for dinner, a photo from your recent trip to Vegas, or a link to a hilarious comic strip about sarcastic dinosaurs — anything you care to share — you can do it through the Publisher. Anything you post in the Publisher shows up on your Profile for those people who you allow to see it. In Chapter 2 and 5, we go into great detail about how you can set the privacy on each piece of content you post to Facebook.

The Stream, News Feed, and Live Feed

Imagine if your morning paper, news show, or radio program included an additional section that featured articles solely about the *specific* people you know. This is the Stream. As long as the people you know are active on Facebook, you can stay up-to-date with their lives via the Stream. Through *his* Publisher, a friend may post photos from his recent birthday party, another may write a Note about her new job, and several others may RSVP to a wine-tasting party you may be interested in attending as well. All these may show as stories in your Facebook Home Stream. Recently, in her Stream, Leah read that 86 of her friends are attending Facebook Game Day, another friend is headed to the new *Star Trek* movie at 9:55pm tonight, another friend quit her job, two more friends got engaged — plus 20 other stories of this kind.

A Stream bonus: You can often use it to stay up-to-date on current events just by seeing what your friends are talking about. In one morning's Stream, Leah found out that the latest news on swine flu, which movies were opening this weekend, and that the job losses in April weren't quite as bad as those in March. We're not recommending you rely on the stream for all your current event news, but sometimes it can be a decent proxy.

For the most part, the Facebook home stream shows the actions that your friends are taking on Facebook, such as photo uploads, comments, Wall posts, Profile changes, and others. Sometimes, however, you may read about what your friends are up to in life through their interactions on the rest of the Web. A feature called *Facebook Connect* allows other sites (such as Digg, CitySearch, CBS, CNET, Evite, Hulu, Twitter, Red Bull, and more) to publish stories to Facebook — with the user's permission. For example, Carolyn may write a review comment on Hulu, or Leah may RSVP to an Event on Evite. They can both have those stories printed in their friends' home Stream.

We dig into News Feed in greater detail in Chapter 7, but as an overview, News Feed is the default view of your stream. When you sign into Facebook, you'll see what Facebook deems to be the most interesting information your friends have recently posted. News Feed pulls out the stories Facebook thinks are the most interesting to you, and lets them linger on your home page so you have a chance to see them later if you missed them the first time around. Interesting stories are those that may have taken your friend a long time to create, such as a photo album, or stories that a number of people commented on, or said they like, or stories from those people you said you were particularly interested in hearing from.

The other view of News Feed is called Live Feed, which is simply a chronological list of every story all of your friends have posted on Facebook. **Note:** If you have more than 250, Facebook chooses the 250 it thinks you want to hear from based on who you interact with. You can also customize this set of 250 by clicking Live Feed, then scrolling to the bottom and selecting Edit Options. If you have fewer than 250 friends, you can also eliminate some of them from Live feed.

Fun with filters

Down the left side of your stream are three filters: Status Updates, Photos, and Links. *Note:* You may see more if you've joined a Network, as described in Chapter 2. These links allow you to filter the stream down to just the types of content you're interested in. Some people like to filter to status updates to get a quick snapshot about what their friends are up to right at the moment. Others like to filter to photos when they're in a browsing mood and feel like looking at pictures. Clicking more gives you even more filtering options.

These application filters allow you to filter down to the *types* of content in which you're interested; sometimes, however you may want to filter down your stream to content posted by certain *people*. You can create people filters by joining a network or creating lists of friends — all the friends who live in your city, for example, or work at your company — and turn that list into a filter. We'll go into a lot more detail about the Stream and filtering in Chapter 7.

Right column, what's up?

On the right side of the Home page, next to the Stream, you find a somewhat random smorgasbord of what's new, what's now, and what's coming up next on Facebook:

✔ **Requests:** An example of a request is someone on Facebook wanting you to confirm that you two are friends. The request contains links to accept or ignore the friend's request. Another example is an invitation to an Event to which you should RSVP. The request contains links to RSVP Attending, Not Attending, and Tentatively Attending. When any request is pending, a link to it appears at the top of the right column on your Home Page. If nothing shows there, you have no unanswered requests.

✔ **Suggestions:** Going out and finding all the people you know on Facebook would be a lot of work, which is why Facebook tries to bring the people you know *to you*. In the suggestions box, you'll see people, celebrities, and bands that Facebook believes you may know or like. These suggestions are calculated using a number of factors, the most important of which being how many mutual friends you have with the suggested person, or how many of your friends are fans of the suggested brand or celebrity. If you see someone you recognize, click on her photo to add that person as a friend. Also listed in the suggestion box are those friends with whom you haven't communicated with in while (communicated with on Facebook anyway). Facebook gives you a suggestion to write on that person's Wall or send a message, just in case maybe you've forgotten about someone you might want to get back in touch with.

✔ **Sponsored:** Facebook doesn't grow on trees, you know. Nor was it brought into this world hanging from the beak of a magical stork. Facebook is built from pure manual labor (where manual labor equals a lot of typing) and a whole lot of computers storing all the information you and you friends add to the site each day. Labor and technology, these things cost — and it's the ads that appear in the sponsored section that fund the entire system.

✔ **Events:** Reminders about all Events to which you're invited show in this column for three days prior to the start of the Event unless you RSVP Not Attending. Clicking See All shows you all the Events to which you've been invited. After Events, see all the friends who have birthdays coming up in the next three days. You won't see birthday reminders for those friends who have chosen to hide their birthday information from their Profiles.

✔ **Pokes:** Read about Poke in Chapter 9. Just know for now that if you receive a Poke, you find out about it on the Home page.

✔ **Connect With Friends:** This section doesn't particularly fall into the new, now, or next theme, but if getting someone you care about to join Facebook would improve your Facebook experience, you have easy access to invite them. Click the Invite Your Friends to Join Facebook link to start finding people you know. More on finding friends in the next chapter.

Looking at the Footer

At the bottom of every Facebook page, you see a set of links collectively called *the Footer*. The Footer is the catch-all for important information about Facebook the social network, Facebook for business, Facebook the company, and the Facebook policies. Descriptions of each link follow:

✔ **<Language>:** The first link on the footer shows the name of the language in which you're seeing the rest of Facebook written, English, for example. By clicking the name of the language, you can pull up all the languages in which Facebook is available.

✔ **About:** Takes you to the About Facebook page. Here, you can read about some key features of Facebook, see the latest headlines from the Facebook Blog, discover the newest Facebook features, and see links to recent articles written about Facebook. Also, follow this link to discover all the job opportunities at Facebook.

✔ **Advertising:** Explores two of Facebook's primary promotional offerings, Facebook Pages and Social Ads. In Chapters 12 and 15, we cover these advertising solutions in great depth.

✔ **Developers:** Most of the applications you can add to your Facebook Profile are written by developers who don't work at Facebook. Some of these outside developers write Facebook applications to help their businesses, some are students creating applications for programming classes, and some are simply developer hobbyists. If you're interested in creating a new Facebook application, this is your link.

✔ **Careers:** Wanna work for Facebook? Click this link to find out what jobs are available and all about the working environment.

✔ **Terms:** Although this link may see the least traffic of all the links on the site, it's one of the most important. Facebook is eerily adept at catching users who break the Terms of Use in any damaging way. For the sake of those who use the site in a respectful way, Facebook takes violations of the Terms of Use seriously. The use of fake birthdays, fake names, pornographic or copyrighted content, and spam-like behavior are all grounds for disabling an account.

✔ **Find Friends:** This link gives you the same tool you saw on the Friends page, and from the Find Friends link in the right column. Go here to invite friends to Facebook and see who's already on it that you may know.

✔ **Privacy:** Details the Facebook Privacy Policy, which states

Facebook's Privacy Policy is designed to help you understand how we collect and use the personal information you decide to share, and help you make informed decisions when using Facebook.

✔ **Mobile:** Facebook has rich offerings for integration with your mobile phone. You can download clients to your mobile phones, use a phone compatible version of the site, and interact with your friends through Facebook using text messaging. All of these features are explained both here, behind the mobile link, and in Chapter 14.

✔ **Help:** This link takes you to the same Help page as the link in the Settings menu described earlier.

Chapter 4

Finding Facebook Friends

In This Chapter

▶ Understanding what *friending* someone means

▶ Finding friends on Facebook in various ways

▶ Organizing and controlling your Friend List

*H*undreds of sayings abound about friendship and friends. We looked up a bunch of them online, and we boiled them down into one catch-all adage: Friends, good; no friends, bad. This is true in life, and it's also true on Facebook. Without your friends on Facebook, you find yourself at some point looking at a blank screen and asking, "Okay, now what?" With friends, you find yourself at some point looking at photos of a high school reunion and asking, "Oh, dear. How did that last hour go by so quickly?"

Most of Facebook's functionality is built around the premise that you have a certain amount of information that you want your friends to see (and maybe some information that you don't want *all* your friends to see, but we get to that later). So, if you don't have friends that are seeing your Profile, what's the point in creating one? Messages aren't that useful unless you send them to someone. Photos are made to be viewed, but if the access is limited to friends, well, you need to find some friends.

On Facebook, all friendships are *reciprocal,* which means if you add someone as a friend, they have to confirm the friendship before it appears on both Profiles. If someone adds you as a friend, you can choose between Confirm and Ignore. If you confirm the friend, congrats: You have a new friend! And if you ignore the friend, the other person won't really find out.

Now that we made you feel as though you're the last kid picked for the team in middle-school dodge ball, we're also here to tell you to have no fear because there are many ways to find your friends on Facebook. If your friends haven't joined Facebook, invite them to join and get them to be your friends on Facebook as well as in real life.

What Is a Facebook Friend?

Good question. In many ways, a *Facebook friend* is the same as a real-life friend (although, to quote many people we know, "You're not real friends unless you're Facebook friends"). However, subtle differences exist among your real life friends and your Facebook friends: There are a few Facebook-specific things about friendship that you should know.

A reflection of reality

The first and foremost definition of Facebook friends is that they're just friends. These are the people you hang out with, keep in touch with, care about, and want to publicly acknowledge as a friend. These aren't people you met on Facebook but rather the same people you would call on the phone, stop and catch up with if you crossed paths at the grocery, or invite over for parties, dinners, and general social gatherings.

In real life, there are lots of shades of friendships. Think of the differences between acquaintances, a friend from work, an activity buddy, an "ex-significant other but we're still friendly," and a BFF (best friend forever). In real life, these designations are always shifting — say, when you start calling up an activity buddy for advice, or it turns out that you and your significant other really can't be just friends. On Facebook, though, all these nuanced relationships are still your friends.

There are ways to account for these different relationships using Friend Lists, which we discuss later in this chapter. For the most part, though, all friendships are created equal on Facebook. When people see your Friend List, they see a big list that can be sorted only by networks, not your personal designations of *best friends* and *too awkward to say no.*

A contact

A Facebook friend is also a contact, meaning that you are giving all your Facebook friends a way to get in touch with you. In many cases (depending on privacy settings and what information you choose to share), you are also giving your friends access to other info, such as your phone number, address, and e-mail address.

In return, your friends become your contacts: You can always contact them through Facebook, in addition to having access to their phone numbers, addresses, and e-mail addresses.

A privacy implication

One important thing to remember when you send and confirm friend requests is that friends likely get access to your Profile. You can limit the visibility of most things on your Profile to a subset of friends, but most people have all of their Profile visible to all of their friends, if not more people. If your Profile is set up this way, accepting a friend request means you're granting that person access to anything to which you've giving all your friends access.

That may sound a bit scary, but it's similar to the access we give friends in real life. The only difference is that in real life, this process happens gradually, as opposed to at the click of a button. At some point, a person you know becomes someone you enjoy spending time with, care about, and are willing to listen to. This sort of friendship intimacy is akin to the intimacy of letting someone see your Profile. In addition to that, it's a way to acknowledge to the world, "Hey! This is someone I care about."

A News Feed implication

News Feed is a constantly updating list of stories about all the actions your friends take on Facebook, as well as a few stories about actions your friends take on other sites. Think of News Feed as a personalized cable news show. Instead of reporting on everything happening around the world, it reports on everything happening around *your* world. News Feed stories may be something like "Blake wrote on Will's Wall" or "Eric was tagged in a video." All these stories link to relevant content about your friends.

When you add people as friends the stories they post will automatically begin showing up in your News Feed. Right away you can start to see their statuses, what sorts of photos they upload, and so on. However, if you're less interested in that person (say it's someone you just met at work and you don't care much what she's up to on a day-to-day basis), or you find you're not interested in their posts, you can always hide them from News Feed later, which we cover in Chapter 7.

A real-time implication

Not only may you want to know what someone is up to in general, but you may want to know what certain people are up to *the moment* they are up to it. If you have a mobile phone, you can be notified in real-time about what your most favorite friends are doing as often as they choose to let you know.

When you add someone as a friend (or later, when you go to her Profile and look at the links beneath her picture) you can choose to subscribe to her updates via SMS. This means that after you set up your phone on Facebook Mobile, described in Chapter 13, each time she publishes something to her Profile, you get a text message containing the status update sent to your phone. This feature should be reserved for your absolute favorite, best, most wonderful people in the whole world, who generally update their Profiles with interesting relevant content (otherwise, you may start resenting the buzz of your phone).

You may want to know what your daughter, your spouse, your best friend, or maybe your close co-worker, is up to in real time. Subscribing to someone's status can be a neat way to discover that you're in the same physical location as someone, or be able to answer a time-sensitive question, such as "Who wants to go get dinner with me?"

If you ever change your mind about receiving real-time updates, head over to that person's Profile, and click Unsubscribe from SMS updates beneath the Profile picture.

Discovering the Facebook Friend Philosophy

You may hear different reports on the rules for Facebook. You may hear that it's rude to ignore a friend request. Pay no attention to these ugly rumors. The truth about Facebook Friend etiquette is here.

Choose your friends wisely

Generally, you send friend requests to and confirm friend requests only from people you actually know. If you don't know them — *random friend requests* — click Ignore. For all the reasons enumerated in the preceding section — your privacy, News Feed, and reflection of reality — don't declare friendship unless some kind of relationship actually exists. Remember the lecture you got about choosing good friends when you were in high school? It's every bit as true now. Accept a friend request that you shouldn't, and the next thing you know, you're fleeing for the border on the back of a motorcycle belonging to some guy who insists his name is Harley. Trust us: It will happen exactly like that.

It's quality, not quantity

Another common misperception about Facebook is that it's all about the race to get the most friends. This is very, very wrong. Between the News Feed and privacy implications of friendship, aim to keep your Friend List to the people you actually care about. Now, the number of people you care about — including the people you care about the most and those you care about least — may be large or small. The average number of friends that a person has on Facebook is around 120. Does a person with 120 friends care about them all equally? Probably not. Does this mean that person is shallow? No. It means that this person is keeping up with and keeping track of all the friends who have come and gone through a lifetime. Changing jobs, schools, and locations also comes with new friends, but that doesn't displace the fact that you care about the old.

Should you aim to have 120 friends? No. Carolyn's mom has a great Facebook experience with fewer than 20 friends. With that number, she still can share her photos with her friends, play Scrabulous with people she knows, and have a pretty active News Feed. Aim to have all the people you care about on your Friend List. Maybe that's a big number, or maybe it's a small number; the part that counts is that you want to see them in that list, smiling back at you.

Finding Your Friends on Facebook

Now that we impressed upon you how important friends are, you may be feeling a bit lonely. How do you get to the people you want to be your friends? Facebook is big, and if you're looking for your friend John, you may need to provide some more detail. Facebook has a couple of tools to show you people you may know and want to be your friend, as well as a normal search-by-name functionality for finding specific people.

If only real life had a Friend Finder

Friend Finder is a tool that matches e-mail addresses from your e-mail address book to people's Profiles on Facebook. Because each e-mail address can be associated with only one Facebook account, you can count on your matches finding the right people who you already know through e-mail.

With your permission, Friend Finder also invites those people who don't have a Facebook account that matches the e-mail in your address book to join Facebook. If they join from an invite that you send, they have a friend request waiting from you when they join.

To use Friend Finder, you need to give Facebook your e-mail address and e-mail password. Facebook doesn't store this information: It just uses it to retrieve your contacts list that one time.

Chances are that you came across Friend Finder when you first set up your account. The following steps make several assumptions: namely, that you use Web-based e-mail (Hotmail, Gmail, Yahoo! Mail, and so on), that you haven't used Friend Finder recently, and that the address book for that e-mail has a bunch of your friends in it. We cover other options, such as a client-based address book or using an Instant Messenger Buddy List later in this chapter. Here's how to use Friend Finder:

1. **Click Friends in the big blue bar on top; choose Find Friends from the tabs on the left.**

   Figure 4-1 shows the Friend Finder.

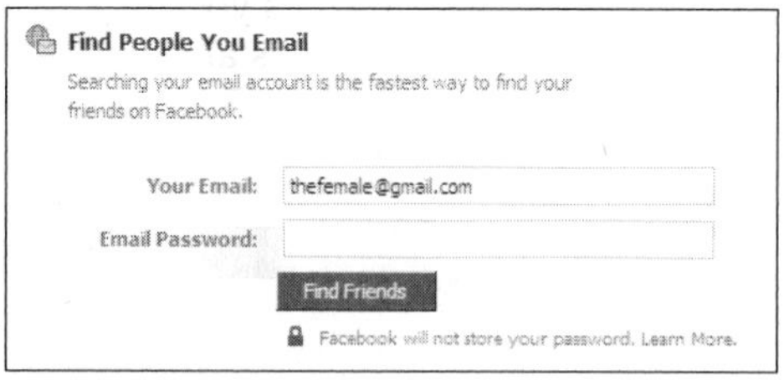

Figure 4-1:
An unfilled
Friend
Finder.

2. **Enter your e-mail address into the Your E-Mail field.**

3. **Enter your e-mail password (not your Facebook password) into the E-Mail Password box and then click Find Friends.**

   If Facebook finds any matches with the e-mails in your address book, you see a page that looks similar to Figure 4-2. (If it doesn't find any friends, go to Step 4.) These are the people who Facebook thinks you may know. Anyone you select is sent a friend request from you. You can the Select All link at the top if you'd rather not spend your afternoon checking off little boxes.

4. **Decide whether to**

   • *Add everyone as a friend.* Click Add as Friends.

   • *Not friend anyone.* Click Skip.

- *Add many people as a friend.* First click the Select All option at the top of the screen. Then deselect the check boxes to the left of the specific names that you don't want to be friends with. After you deselect all the people you don't want, click Add as Friends.

- *Add a few people as friend.* Check the box to the left of anyone's name who you want to add as a friend. When you've selected everyone you'd like to invite, click Add as Friends.

After you click either Add as Friends or Skip, you land on the Invite portion of Friend Finder. It should look something like Figure 4-3. These are e-mails that have no matches on Facebook.

5. **(Optional) Invite people to join Facebook and become your friend.**

Similar to adding friends, you can

- *Invite all these contacts.* Click Invite to Join.

- *Invite none of these contacts.* Click Skip.

- *Invite many of these contacts by deselecting the ones you don't want to invite.* Use the check boxes to the left of their e-mails and then click Invite to Join.

- *Invite some of these contacts to join.* Deselect the Select All/None check box on top. Then reselect the ones you want to add by using the check boxes to the left of their e-mails and clicking Invite to Join.

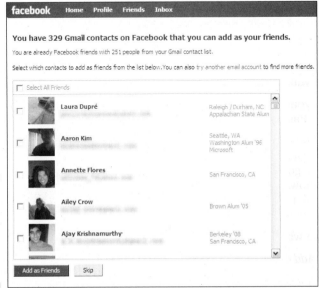

Figure 4-2:
The friend
selector
portion
of Friend
Finder.

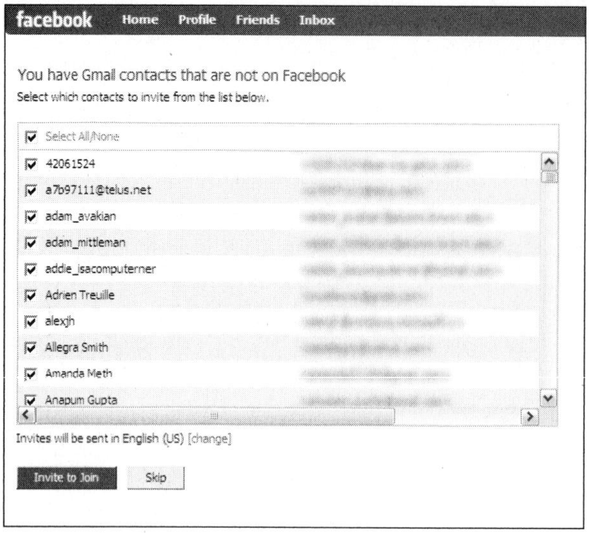

Figure 4-3:
The Invite
portion
of Friend
Finder.

After doing all this, we hope you manage to send a few friend requests. Your friends need to confirm your requests before you officially become friends on Facebook, so you may not be able to see your friends' Profiles until that confirmation happens.

If that whole experience yielded nothing — no friends you wanted to add, no contacts you wanted to invite — you have a few options. You can go through these steps again with a different e-mail address. You should probably use the one that you use for personal e-mail (from where you e-mail your friends and family). If that's not the problem, you have more ways to use Friend Finder.

Import an address book

If you're someone who uses a *desktop e-mail client* — a program on your local computer that manages your e-mail (like Microsoft Outlook, or Entourage) — create a file of your contacts and import it so that Facebook can check it for friend matches. The way to create your contact file depends on what e-mail client you use. Here's how to get the right instructions:

1. **Go to the Find Friends page (by clicking Friends in the big blue bar on top and clicking the Find Friends tab on the left).**

2. **Select Upload a Contact File, a blue link to the right of Find People You E-mail.**

    This first asks you to choose a contact file to upload. If you don't know where to find your contact file, click the How to Create a Contact File link just above the upload field. This expands a window that looks similar to Figure 4-4.

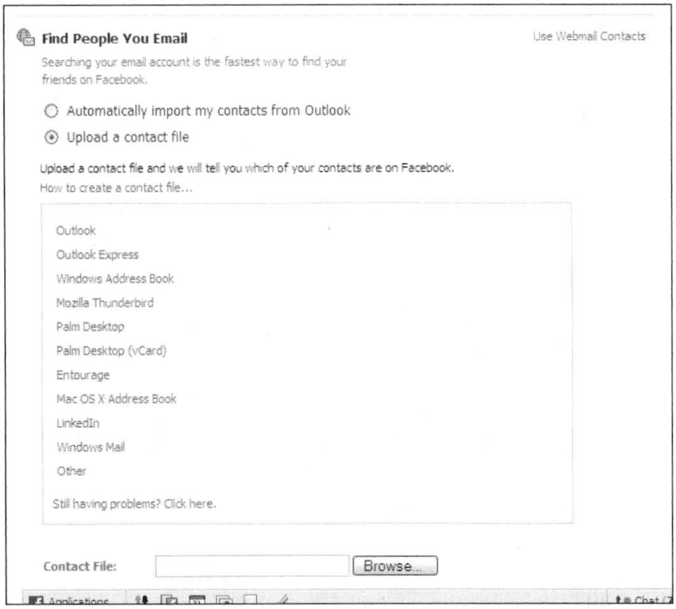

Figure 4-4:
Importing a
contact file.

3. **If you already have a contact file created, import it here.**

   After you do that, you're taken through Steps 4–5 from the preceding section.

   Also, if you're on a PC, you may have an option to Automatically Import your Microsoft Outlook Address Book, by choosing that option.

4. **If you haven't created a contact file already, click the How to Create a Contact File link and follow the instructions; then import the file, and follow Steps 4–5 in the preceding section.**

Windows Live Messenger and the AIM Friend Finder

This option works for you only if you use Windows Live Messenger or AIM (AOL Instant Messenger) as an instant messenger (IM) client for chatting with your friends. The biggest difference between these and the previous steps in the Friend Finder is that any invitations you send via here are delivered via instant message. Thus, instead of sending your friends an e-mail asking them to join, they get an instant message from Facebook Bot. Again:

1. **Go to the Find Friends page (by Friends in the big blue bar on top and clicking the Find Friends tab on the left).**

2. **Scroll to the bottom right. Under Find People You IM, click Import AIM Buddy List or Import Windows Live Contacts (whichever you use).**

The page expands to what's shown in Figure 4-5.

3. **Enter your screen name and password and then click Find Friends.**

4. **Follow Steps 4–5 above for the regular Friend Finder.**

If none of these methods yield any results for you, don't worry; you'll find friends in other ways, and you can still use the site.

Suggestions

After you have a friend or two, Facebook can start making pretty good guesses about who else may be your friend. It primarily does this by looking at people with whom you have friends or networks in common. In the Suggestions box shown in Figure 4-6, you see a list of people Facebook thinks you may know, and therefore may want to be friends with. If you see someone you know is a friend, simply add her as one by clicking the aptly named Add as Friend link beneath that person's name. If you're not sure, you can click on a name or Profile picture to gather more evidence from the Profile about if and how you know that person. Then you can decide whether to add that person as a friend. If you're sure you don't know someone, or you know someone, but are sure you don't want that person as your Facebook friend, click the X next to her name and picture, and she will stop appearing in your Suggestions list. As you add or remove people from suggestions, more will pop up to take their place: This fun can last for hours, so make sure you have time and a comfortable chair before you decide to start going suggestions-crazy.

Find what you're looking for: Search

Friend Finder is a great way to build your Friend List quickly without a lot of work. After you build it a bit, though, what if you find other people who may want to be your friends? Facebook Search has a few different methods that let you search for groups of people you may know; Facebook Search also offers you the capability to seek out certain friends by name.

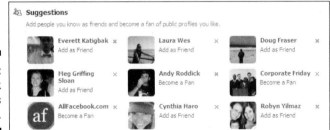

Figure 4-6:
Facebook
suggests
friends.

Classmate Search

Classmate Search takes the information from people's Profiles to create a big, searchable list. Classmate Search lets you easily find your friends from high school, college, graduate school, and so on. Ever wonder what that awkward kid from the dining hall wound up doing? Look no further.

To get to Classmate Search:

1. **Click Friends in the big blue bar and then select the Find Friends tab on the left.**

2. **Scroll to the bottom and select the links that read either Find Former High School Classmates or Find Current or Past University Classmates.**

   These take you to the Classmate/Coworker search page, as shown in Figure 4-7.

   If you've already entered your education information to your Profile, instead of a Find Current or past classmates links, you may see a link specific to searching people from the schools you've listed. Clicking these links takes you straight to searching within these schools/graduating years, but you can always search for people from other schools by clicking More Search Options in the upper right of the resulting page.

3. **Enter your high school or college, as well as the relevant graduating year.**

   The graduation year can be huge in filtering the results to the people you actually know. If you just search for *Brown,* you'd get thousands of results, which is too many to sift through looking for those few people you knew once upon a time. Limiting it to a certain graduation year makes it easier to find more people who you actually know.

4. **Click Search for Classmates.**

   See whether you know anyone in the search results.

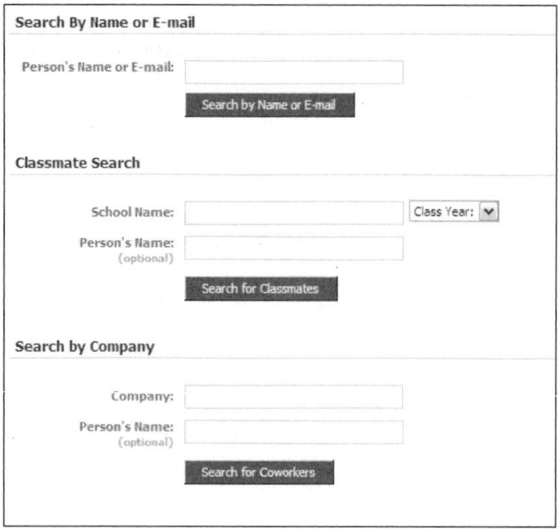

Figure 4-7:
Classmate
and
Coworker
Search.

Coworker Search

Coworker Search is based on information that people enter into their Profiles about their work history. Generally, people enter the company they worked for and the dates they worked there.

Coworker Search lets you search for people who work at the same places you do (or did). Depending on the size of the place where you worked, and how many of your co-workers have joined Facebook, this sort of search may yield entirely too many people or not enough. But keep your fingers crossed, Goldilocks: It may turn out to be just right. To account for the "too many" problem, search for specific names at specific companies, if you wish. It may be easier to search for "John" at Microsoft, rather than anyone at Microsoft. If you don't find people you expect, it doesn't necessarily mean they're not on Facebook. It may just mean they didn't list the relevant information on their Profiles, so you may have to try and track them down by name through normal search.

To get to Coworker Search:

1. **Click Friends in the big blue bar, and then select the Find Friends tab on the left. Scroll to the bottom and select the find Current or Past Coworkers link.**

   This brings you to the Search by Company page, as shown in Figure 4-7.

If you've already entered work information to your Profile, instead of a Find Current or past co-workers link, you may see a link specific to searching people from the places you've listed. Clicking these links takes you straight to searching within these companies, but you can always search for people from other companies by clicking More Search Options in the upper right of the resulting page.

2. **In the Company field, start typing the name of the company you want to search.**

   The Company field tries to autocomplete what you're typing.

3. **(Optional) If you want, enter a specific person you're looking for.**

4. **Click Search Coworkers.**

   Voilà! A list appears of people who listed that company in their Profiles.

Quick-Search

In directing you to Classmate Search and Coworker Search, we keep bypassing the convenient-sounding Quick-Search box. The Quick-Search box is (more or less) what it sounds like. You enter a name of someone you want to find on Facebook, press Enter, and very quickly get a list of search results.

If Friend Finder hasn't yielded any results and you're looking for more friends, try thinking of some people who you know are on Facebook. Enter their full name into the Quick-Search box and see whether that finds them. Read results, lather, rinse, repeat.

Keeping Track: Friend List Management

After you do all this work finding and adding your friends, at some point, you may get a little overwhelmed and yell, "Stop the madness!" at your computer. This may freak out your computer, so here are some ways to spare your computer's feelings and keep your Friend List under control.

Creating and applying Friend Lists

Friend Lists (capital L) are subsets of your giant list of friends (lower case l). Confused yet? Friend lists are a way of organizing your friends into lists to make your Facebook experience even easier and more personalized to you and your types of friends. Organizing your friends into Friend Lists can allow you to

✔ Share different types of information with different sets of friends. For example, your best friends may get to see your party photos, and you family may get to see your wedding photos. Using Friend Lists for privacy is discussed in Chapter 5.

✔ **See different information from different friends.** You can filter your News Feed down to specific Friend Lists. Some people make Friend Lists for the different places they've lived, so their friends in Seattle are in one list, San Francisco another list, and Denver another list. Then, when reading their News Feeds, they see first what's going on in Seattle, then SF, then Denver. Using Friend Lists for News Feed is covered in Chapter 9.

✔ **Communicate with the same groups of people.** Friend Lists can be used in the Inbox. Say that you always invite the same group of people biking. Add them all to a Friend List, and then you can simply message the list rather than typing their names each time. To send a message to a Friend List, simply type the name of the list in the To line, where you normally type a name.

✔ In Chapter 9, we discuss using Friend Lists in Chat so that you can show yourself as online or offline to different groups of people, or easily scan for certain types of friends currently online, such as social friends if you're looking for a dinner date, or carpool friends if you need a ride.

The options for how you create Friend Lists are virtually limitless. You can have 1,500 friends on each list, each friend can be on more than one list, and you can make up to 100 Friend Lists. Your lists can be for silly things (Girls' Night Out Girls), real-world needs (Family), or general bucketing (co-workers).

To create a Friend List:

1. **Go to the Friends page by clicking Friends on the big bar on top.**

2. **Click the All Connections tab on the left.**

3. **Click the Create New List button (on the top left of the screen).**

4. **In the window that opens, name your list.**

   Maybe something like *Dummies* for the Dummies Team (see Figure 4-8).

Figure 4-8:
Creating a
Friend List.

5. **Input the names of the people who belong on this list and then press Enter.**

   When you see the picture of the person you're looking for pop up, you click it with your mouse, or keep typing until there is only one person left, at which point that person is automatically selected.

6. **Click Create List.**

   Now, wherever Friend Lists appear on Facebook, including in privacy, News Feed, Chat, the Inbox, and the friends page, you have access to this new list you just created.

You can always edit the name or membership of a list later by selecting the list name from the tab on the left of the Friends page (beneath the Lists heading), and then clicking the edit list button at the top of the page. From there, you can change the name or delete or add members. Also, whenever viewing friends on the Friends page, you can add them to lists by selecting the Add to List drop-down to the right of their names, and checking of the list to which you'd like to add them.

Friend Lists are private, so even if the list you're messaging is known in your mind as *Annoying Co-Workers,* all that your annoying co-workers see is a list of names.

Spring friend–cleaning

Every now and then, no amount of Friend Lists can hide the fact that you just have too many friends you don't care about anymore. This isn't your fault: After all, you can't help being popular. If it's cluttering your Facebook Experience, though, it's time to do a little *friend pruning.*

No, friend pruning doesn't mean waiting for your friends to shrivel in the sun. Instead, go to your huge master Friend List and start working your way through all your friends. The rules that apply for friend pruning are similar to the rules for spring-cleaning: If you haven't used it in a year, you can probably throw it out. If you haven't even thought about a friend in a few years, or if you can't remember why you accepted a friend request in the first place, it's okay to remove that person as a friend. When you're looking at your friends on the Friends page, you see a small X to the right of that person's listing. Just click the X to remove your friend, and that friend is gone.

Don't worry — your friends are never told that they've lost a coveted place on your Friend List. Chances are that if you had no contact over several months, they won't notice, either. You merely disappear from his Friend List (and he from yours), and both move on happily with your lives.

Chapter 5

Privacy and Safety on Facebook

*U*nfortunately, a lot of horror stories are out there about the Internet, especially about social networking sites. A lot of them involve teenagers and predators, some of them involve identity theft, and others involve far less salacious (but no less real) problems, such as spamming and computer viruses. The bad news is that these things are out there. The good news is that Facebook has some of the most granular privacy controls on the Internet, enabling you to share real information comfortably on Facebook.

Facebook has created a trusted environment that provides three major assets to you:

✔ **In general, people create real accounts for themselves, and people are who they say they are on Facebook.** This means that the community enforces a standard of reality. When people ask you to view their Webcasts or click some mysterious link, those actions are reported by the community and are removed from Facebook. This also means that it's usually easy to tell a real person from a fake one and that you can make informed choices about with whom you interact online.

✔ **Facebook provides granular privacy controls that are built in to every piece of information you create on the site.** We discuss how these work in depth in this chapter. Before we get to that, however, we talk a bit about privacy in general and how Facebook approaches it.

✔ **Facebook makes it easy for you to see your own Profile as other specific people see it.** This means you can easily verify that you're sharing the information you want to share with the right set of people.

Seeing the Win-Win of Privacy

Would you display your phone number on a public billboard? Probably not. Would you write it down for your friends to hold on to? Probably yes. What Facebook has learned is that the more we control our information, the more likely we are to share it. If we feel confident that only those people whom we want will see our phone number, we post it on Facebook. The win-win of privacy is that the more we share, the better it is for information flow among us and our friends. So, when we each share more information, our friends share more information. As individuals, we win in that our information is shown to the specific people we want to see it, and not to the people we don't. Our friends win because they can have access to more information about us. If our friends see us sharing, and decide to do the same, we win again because we have access to more information about our friends. And then, well, the cycle keeps building.

Keeping this in mind, using your privacy options wisely is the best way to share the right information with the right people. Using your privacy options wisely is also the best way to keep your information away from the wrong people. With this control, Facebook becomes a place where you can share very personal things — not just in a "my phone number is private" way, but also in a "see photos of my new niece" way. Because of the privacy controls, Facebook is a place for you to truly share your life the same way you do in the real world.

Getting Familiar with Your Privacy Options

The Facebook privacy options are organized into three different sections on the site. The settings that control the information you share on you Profile is listed on the Privacy tab of the Settings page. The settings that allow you to control the visibility of information you share from the Web sites and applications you use in conjunction with Facebook (more on applications in Chapter 13) live on the Applications tab of the settings page. And finally, the control that allows you to set the privacy on each individual note, photo, video, or status, and more, lives on the Profile page (and Home page) itself. We mention this under Publisher and Wall later in this chapter, but more details about how to specify privacy for each and every post you make to Facebook are featured in Chapter 7.

The Privacy control

Despite the relatively complicated set of privacy options on Facebook, actually setting the privacy on any given item is relatively simple. Wherever you can set the privacy of a piece of information on Facebook, you see a small gray lock icon. Clicking it allows you to choose one of the audience options from the drop-down menu list: either Everyone, Friends and Networks (if you're a member of a network), or Friends. Choosing Custom lets you get extremely specific about who can see your content. We talk about this a little later. Figure 5-1 shows the Privacy control, just after someone has clicked on the gray lock icon, and set the privacy of something to Everyone.

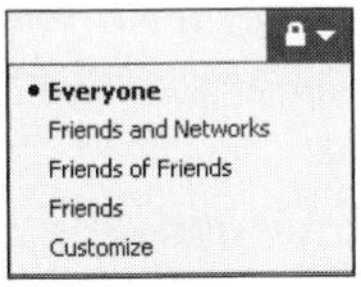

Figure 5-1:
The Privacy
control.

Profile Privacy page

The Profile Privacy page allows you to control the visibility of the static information that lives on your Profile. This includes what shows up in the left column of your Profile and the Info tab of your Profile. You can access these settings by clicking Settings on the big blue bar on top, and the selecting the Privacy tab on the left.

There are four distinct sections on the Profile Privacy page itself that cover most of the privacy-related options you have for the static information on your Profile. Check them out in Figure 5-2:

✔ **Profile:** The Profile section allows you to control who can see what on your Profile. In this section, you can control who can see your Basic information, including your current city, gender, and hometown; your interests, including your activities, favorites, political and religious affiliations, and your relationship status; your education and work information; your connections and groups; videos and photos of you; and every part of your contact information including phone numbers, e-mail and physical addresses.

Within the Profile settings you also have the capability to set a privacy default for your Publisher, the box at the top of your home page and Profile from which you can set your status and post links. (Chapters 2 and 7 talk more about the Publisher.) When you set your default to a particular audience, all posts you make through the Publisher will be visible to that audience. If you usually want to publish to just your friends, set this setting as the Publisher Default to Friends by selecting Friends from the drop-down menu. If you want to publish to most of your friends except your co-workers, you can do that by selecting Custom from the drop-down menu and selecting Friends, Except Coworkers. (*Note:* For this to work, you have to make a co-worker's Friend List first. Friend lists are described in Chapter 4.) You can always override the default on the publisher itself if you have a particular post that you want to share more or less broadly than your default.

✔ **Search:** The Search section controls who can find you in a search for your name on Facebook. This section also controls whether your public search listing gets indexed in outside search engines. In addition, you can decide what ways people can interact with you after they find you in a search. For example, you can decide that strangers can't Poke you, but they can add you as a friend.

✔ **News Feed and Wall:** News Feed is the constantly updating list of stories about your friends' actions on Facebook. News Feed appears on your friends' home pages. The Wall is a list of your recent activity on Facebook that appears on your profile. This section lets you decide what kind of actions generate stories in your profile and News Feed stories in your friends' News Feeds. This does not cover the set of stories that go on your wall or your friends' News Feeds through the Publisher. Those stories are covered by the Publish default, which is described in the preceding Profile section. The News Feed and Wall setting specifically lets you control whether or not stories are published when you write on friends' walls, comment on a piece of content, change your profile info, such as adding or removing a favorite band, or add a friend.

When people arrive at your profile, the Profile tab privacy level will override any more open levels of privacy you set for individual pieces of content. For example, if you posted a Status asking for restaurant recommendations in a new city, and set the level to Friends of Friends, but your Wall is only set to Friends, then friends of friends arriving at your Profile won't see your Wall, and therefore won't see that status. However, if the friend of friend conducts a search containing a word in your status, or a mutual friend shares a link to your status with a friend of friend, that person *will* see it, because although you've restricted visibility of your Wall, you've granted access to the individual piece of content if she finds it some other way.

✔ **Block:** *Blocking* someone on Facebook is more or less the digital equivalent to some combination of a restraining order and a witness protection program. For the most part, if you add someone to your Block list, he can't see any traces of you on Facebook.

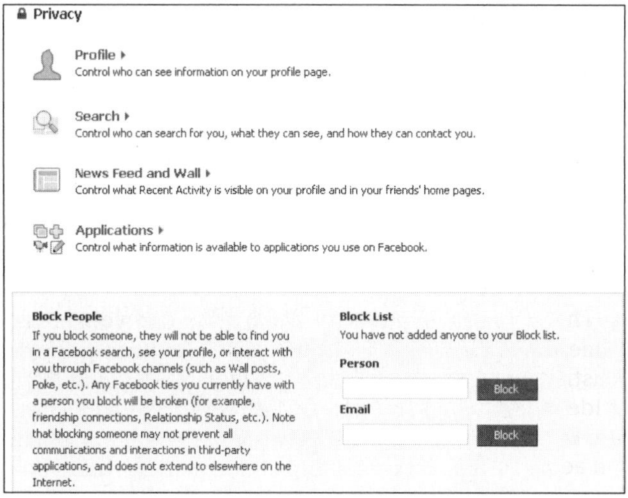

🔒 Privacy

Profile ▸
Control who can see information on your profile page.

Search ▸
Control who can search for you, what they can see, and how they can contact you.

News Feed and Wall ▸
Control what Recent Activity is visible on your profile and in your friends' home pages.

Applications ▸
Control what information is available to applications you use on Facebook.

Block People

If you block someone, they will not be able to find you in a Facebook search, see your profile, or interact with you through Facebook channels (such as Wall posts, Poke, etc.). Any Facebook ties you currently have with a person you block will be broken (for example, friendship connections, Relationship Status, etc.). Note that blocking someone may not prevent all communications and interactions in third-party applications, and does not extend to elsewhere on the Internet.

Block List

You have not added anyone to your Block list.

Person

[Block]

Email

[Block]

Figure 5-2:
The Profile
Privacy
page.

The Application Privacy page

Applications built on top of Facebook Platform are sometimes built by
Facebook and are sometimes built by other people. (For more information on
adding applications, see Chapter 13.) The Applications section of the Privacy
page controls what applications interact with your information as well as
what information they're allowed to interact with. For each application, you
can select a number of options that control the way in which that application
shares information with your friends:

- **Application Stories:** You have the capability to specify which people can
  view the content you post in a particular application. For example, if you
  use the Facebook Events application, you can specify whether there's
  a box or tab on your Profile that shows all the events you've attended
  or plan to attend, and then the Privacy option lets you decide who you
  want to see that box or tab. Here are the steps to setting the Profile privacy for applications — Figure 5-3 shows an example:

  1. Click the Settings link at the top of the page.

  2. Choose Application Settings from the drop-down menu.

  3. Click Settings next to a particular application.

  4. On the Profile tab of the dialog box that appears, you can set the
     privacy level of the box and or tab (if you have one) for that appli-
     cation using the Privacy drop-down list.

Figure 5-3:
Setting
application
privacy
preferences.

➤ **Feed Stories:** Choose whether an application can publish a story onto your Wall or into your friends' Home page when you perform an action. For example, if you're using the Blockbuster.com application, use this setting to decide if your friends can see when you add a new movie to your queue. The specifics of the privacy options for publishing stories vary from app to app. But most apps have settings that control feed stories in some way. Follow these steps to access those controls:

1. Click the Settings link at the top of the page.

2. Choose Application Settings from the drop-down menu.

3. Click Settings next to a particular application.

4. Click the Additional Permissions tab of the Settings dialog box shown in Figure 5-3.

5. From there, you can decide whether applications can publish to your Wall or your friends' streams.

➤ **Your information with applications:** You also control what information your own applications or the other Web sites you use in conjunction with Facebook can access. You can decide whether other sites you visit can use your Profile picture, birthday, contact information, and so on, in order to make your experience on their sites smoother. We get into more detail about these options in Chapter 13. You can access these settings in three steps:

1. Click Privacy Settings from the Settings menu in the blue bar on top. (The menu appears when your mouse hovers over the Settings link.)

2. Click the Applications link on the Privacy Page.

3. Select the Edit Settings tab.

Connecting and privacy

In Chapter 4, we talk about connecting to people on Facebook. Connecting with someone can be a way of extending a level of trust. When you find someone on the site with whom you want to connect, or when you're responding to someone who wants to connect to you, you can make a decision about how much of your information you'd like to share. Look at all the content on your Profile Privacy page you currently have set to Friends. Whenever you're considering becoming a Facebook friend with someone, think about the content you're sharing with friends, and make sure you're comfortable sharing with that person. Also look at all the content that you're sharing with Friends of Friends. Does the person you're considering adding as a friend have the kind of friends you can trust with your less sensitive information? If the answers to any of these questions make you uncomfortable, you either need to adjust your privacy settings, or rethink the friend request.

Network privacy

In Chapter 2, we talk a little bit about joining a network and how that is a way of affiliating yourself with other people who have something in common with you, such as attending the same school or working for the same company. When you join a network, you're usually saying, "I choose to trust people who have this thing in common with me to see more information about me." It is often the case that many students are perfectly comfortable sharing their phone numbers with other students, but they wouldn't want just anyone in the world to see their phone numbers. The same may be true of people who share a work network with one another.

Facebook takes Network-level privacy pretty seriously: It's difficult for anyone who doesn't legitimately belong in a school or work network to join one, so many people find the Friends and Network privacy option the ideal balance between sharing information with their friends as well as a wider audience. The people in one's network may not be friends yet, but they are a pretty trustworthy bunch, if you trust your co-workers, or your classmates. For this reason, there are some pieces of generally pretty privacy information you may share on your Profile, such as your e-mail or physical address, or phone number, that you'd find value in sharing with an audience wider than your friend group, as long as it's a trusted audience. Many students share their dorm room phone numbers with their entire school, making it easier for classmates to contact one another for questions, for example. Facebook employees are wary about sharing their personal numbers to a wide audience, in case a stranger uses them instead of going through Customer Support channels. However, employees are perfectly willing to share their phone numbers with the entire Facebook company network because it makes doing our jobs much easier.

Custom-made privacy

All relationships in real life are not created equal. You share different stories with your family than with your co-workers. The photos you show your closest friends may not be the same ones you put up on the refrigerator. For that reason, the *Custom* privacy option allows you to both include and exclude individuals or groups of "friends" from being able to see parts of your Profile and your content. Find the Custom option for any piece of content by clicking the little lock wherever you see it, and selecting the last option on the menu that appears, Custom (edit). The Custom Privacy dialog box shown in Figure 5-4 pops up and enables you to configure the audience of your photo, or note, or address, in many different ways:

✔ **Limit the visibility of a piece of content to all your friends plus a subset of your networks.** Leah shares her contact information with her friends and the Facebook network because she knows most of her co-workers. She does not share her contact information with the Brown network (where she went to school) because she doesn't want her information in the hands of that many strangers. Open the Custom Privacy dialog box and select All Friends, along with whichever specific networks you'd like to share. (***Note:*** This is only relevant if you are in more than one network.)

✔ **Target a piece of information to just one network.** Leah uses two e-mail addresses — one for work, and one for her personal life. She has both listed on her Profile, but she's set the visibility of her work e-mail address to the Facebook network, and the visibility of her personal e-mail address to her friends. Set the visibility in this way by making sure All Friends is unchecked from the Custom Privacy dialog box, and selecting the network with which you'd like to share.

✔ **Limit the visibility of information to a subset of your friends.** In Chapter 4, we give all the details for making Friend Lists, groups of friends that have something in common. These lists can be used in conjunction with privacy to show a particular list something you don't want other people to see, or you don't think other people care about. Say you're having a housewarming party and want all your local friends to know about it, but don't want to bother friends who don't live nearby. You can mention your party on your Profile and limit the visibility to your list of friends who live in your city (assuming you've made such a list. If you haven't, you can make one now by reviewing the steps in Chapter 4.). To do this, simply uncheck the All Friends box in the Custom Privacy dialog box, and select the friend list(s) you want to invite.

✔ **Restrict certain people from seeing your content.** Conversely, sometimes you have information you're comfortable sharing with the majority of your friends, but you don't want certain people knowing about it. Many people keep a list of friends called "Limited" or "Acquaintances" that consists of all the people they've met, but aren't quite comfortable inviting into their homes, for example. After creating such a list, you can announce your housewarming party on your Profile, and then set the visibility of the announcement to All Friends. Then, in the Except box at the bottom, type the name of the list you'd like to exclude. You can also exclude someone by name. Figure 5-4 is an example of Leah sharing something with everyone of her friends that works at Facebook except Carolyn: Maybe Leah's organizing a practical joke for everyone to play on Carolyn when she gets into work.

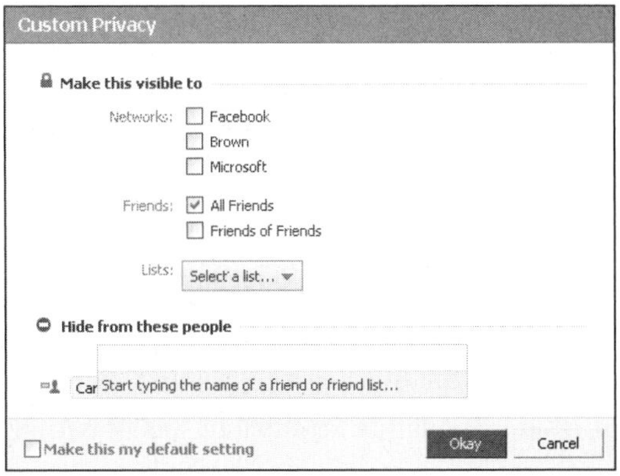

Figure 5-4:
Setting
custom
visibility.

Custom Privacy

🔒 Make this visible to

Networks: ☐ Facebook
☐ Brown
☐ Microsoft

Friends: ☑ All Friends
☐ Friends of Friends

Lists: Select a list... ▼

⊘ Hide from these people

=👤 Car Start typing the name of a friend or friend list...

☐ Make this my default setting   Okay   Cancel

 Anyone who is in a Friend List that is excluded from seeing something —
whether that's a photo album or your Wall on your Profile — will never be able
to see that content. If someone is on two lists, one of which can see something
and one of which is excluded from seeing it, that person won't be able to see
it. In order to verify that you've set your privacy correctly for a particular
friend, navigate to the Profile Privacy tab under Settings. There you see the
option to view your Profile as a specific friend sees it. Type the friend's name
in the box and hit enter, in order to verify that the way she sees your Profile is
the way you intended.

Taking Personal Responsibility for Safety

No one wants anything bad to happen to you as a result of something you
do on Facebook. Facebook doesn't want that. You don't want that. We, your
authors, don't want that either. We are trying, right now, to keep it from happening by telling you about these options and explaining how they work.
Facebook tries to keep it from happening by giving you all these privacy
options in the first place. You're the third piece of the pie, or the puzzle, or
whatever. In order to ensure your own safety on Facebook, you have to make
an effort to be smart and safe online.

So what *is* your part? Your part is to be aware of what you're putting online
and on Facebook by asking yourself a few questions:

Is what I'm putting on Facebook legal or illegal?

Would I be embarrassed by someone in particular finding this information?

Will the audience with whom I'm sharing this information use it in a way I trust?

You need to be the one to choose whether displaying any given piece of information on Facebook is risky. If it's risky, you need to be the one to figure out the correct privacy settings for showing it to the people you want — and not to the people you don't.

Your part is equivalent to the part you play in your everyday life to keep yourself safe: You know which alleys not to walk down at night, when to buckle your seatbelt, when to lock the front door, and when to toss the moldy bread before making a sandwich. Add these to your list:

> I use my Facebook privacy settings wisely.

> I am careful about what information I expose to lots of people.

Remembering That It Takes a Village to Raise a Facebook

Another way in which you (and every member of Facebook) contribute to keeping Facebook a safe, clean place is in the reports that you submit about spam, harassment, inappropriate content, and fake Profiles. Facebook assumes that your friends aren't putting up bad stuff, but when you're looking at content of people you're not directly connected to, you should see a little Report link beneath it. This is true for Photos, Profiles, Groups, Links, Applications, Pages — more. When you click one of these links, you see the Report page. Figure 5-5 shows an example of someone reporting an inappropriate photo. (Photo not pictured, for obvious reasons — sorry.)

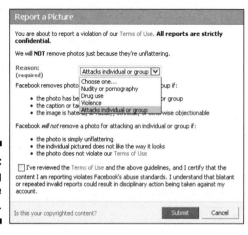

Figure 5-5:
Reporting
inappropriate
content.

The various Report options that you see may vary, depending on what you're reporting (a message as opposed to a photo, for example). These reports are submitted to the Facebook user operations team. The team then investigates, taking down inappropriate photos, disabling fake accounts, and generally striving to keep Facebook clean, safe, and un-obnoxious.

When you see content that you don't like — for example, an offensive group name or a vulgar profile — don't hesitate to report it. With the entire Facebook population working to keep Facebook free of badness, you wind up with a pretty awesome community.

After you report something, Facebook's User Operations team evaluates it in terms of violating Facebook's Terms of Use. This means pornography, fake Profiles, and people who send spam get taken down, disabled, or warned, respectively. However, sometimes something that you report may be offensive to you but doesn't violate the Terms of Use and, therefore, will remain on Facebook. Due to privacy restrictions, User Operations may not always notify you about actions taken as a result of your support, but rest assured that the team handles every report.

Peeking Behind the Scenes

Facebook's part in keeping everyone safe includes a lot of manpower and technology power. The manpower involves responding to the reports that you and the rest of Facebook submit, as well as proactively going into Facebook and getting rid of content that violates the Terms of Service.

The technology power that we talk about is kept vague on purpose. We hope that you never think twice about the things that are happening behind the scenes to protect you from harassment, spam, and pornography. Moreover, we hope that you're never harassed or spammed, or *porned* — the unofficial verb form meaning "being assaulted by accidentally seeing unwanted porn" — but just so you know that Facebook is actively thinking about user safety and privacy, we talk about a few of the general areas where Facebook does a lot of preventive work.

Protecting minors

Again, we keep this section purposefully vague to avoid becoming *Gaming Facebook's Systems For Dummies*. In general, we want you to note that people under the age of 18 have special visibility and privacy rules applied to them. For example, users under the age of 18 don't have Public Search Listings created for them. Public Search Listings enable people to be found in outside search engines, such as Google. Facebook decided never to expose minors in this way. Would anything bad have happened if Facebook had decided otherwise? Probably not, but better to be safe than sorry.

Other proprietary systems are in place that are alerted if a person is interacting with the Profiles of minors in ways they shouldn't, as well as systems that get alerted when someone targets an ad to minors. Again, with reference to the personal responsibility part, as a teenager (or as the parent of a teenager), you are responsible for understanding privacy and safe behavior on Facebook. Facebook tries to prevent whatever it can, but at the end of the day, you have to be a partner in that prevention.

You must be at least 13 years old to join Facebook. No one younger than that can have an account without violating the Terms of Use.

Preventing spam and viruses

Ah, spam, that delicious little can of . . . something once meat-like? Male-enhancement medications? Prescription drugs delivered to your door? "Please sir, send me $ and I promise to return $$$." Everyone can agree that spam is the bane of the Internet, all too often sliming its way through the cracks into e-mail and Web sites — and always trying to slime its way into Facebook as well, sometimes in the form of messages to you, or Wall posts, or groups of events masking as something its not to capture your precious attention.

The spam reports that you provide are incredibly helpful. Facebook also has a bunch of systems that keep track of the sort of behavior that spammers tend to do. If you haven't read this yet, hop to Chapter 2 for the scoop on CATPCHAs, the first line of defense against spammers creating multiple dummy accounts (the bad kind of dummy) that can be used to harass people unwanted ads. The spam systems also keep track of those who message people too quickly, friend too many people, post a similar link in too many places, and other such behaviors that tend to reek of spam. If you end up really taking to this Facebook thing, at some point you may get hit with a warning to slow down your poking or your messaging. Don't take it too personally, and just follow the instructions in the warning — this is the spam system at work.

Part II
Sharing Your Life on Facebook

The 5th Wave   By Rich Tennant

"Mr. President, North Korean President Kim Jong-il just sent you a SuperPoke."

In this part . . .

One thing you hear repeatedly in this book is this idea of sharing. Facebook is about sharing your real life with the people you care about. This part focuses on giving you knowledge of the tools you use to share yourself on Facebook, and the tools you use to share in the lives of your friends.

Between your personal Profile and the applications that you choose to use, there are hundreds of ways to connect to family and friends — both old and new.

Chapter 6

Building Out Your Profile

Your Facebook Profile is more than just a bunch of information — it's an ongoing, ever-evolving story of you. Did you ever have to respond to a writing prompt that asked you to write page 73 of your 248-page autobiography? Your Profile page is the page you are working on right now, except your autobiography is a complete multimedia presentation, pulling your words, your photos, your friends' thoughts, and postings together. All of those things together tell the reader both who you are and what's important to you. Your Facebook Profile is not about altering who you are but rather representing yourself. It is both the introduction of you and your way of sharing yourself with the people who matter to you. What do you want people to know about you? What do you want your friends to find out about you?

In Chapter 2, we cover the basics of your Profile, Profile picture, education, and work history. In this chapter, we talk about how to write the story of you in the language of Facebook.

Figure 6-1 shows your entire Profile. The Profile has basically two columns. The skinny column on the left displays the basics about you. The larger column on the right has a few tabs. These tabs are actually the most important parts of your Profile, so we begin with those before moving on to the pieces in the left column.

Figure 6-1:
An entire
Profile.

"Wall" You Need Is Love

The *Wall* is the focus of your Profile. It's what your friends see first when they get to your Profile, and it's also where they leave public messages for you. When you go to a friend's Profile, checking out the Wall is the quickest way to find out what they've been up to recently. Figure 6-2 shows a sample Wall.

The first thing to remember about the Wall is that it's by you as well as about you. You have control over what stays in your Wall and what you put there, but your friends have the ability to help you tell your story. This aspect of the Wall makes it really interesting. Think about all the things you learn about a friend the first time you meet his parents, or all the funny stories you hear when your friend's significant other recounts the story of how they met. These are the types of insights that your friends may casually leave on your Wall, making all of your friends know you a little better.

Figure 6-2:
Carolyn's
Wall shows
a snapshot
of her life
right now.

The Wall can feel a bit overwhelming at first — it has so many different photos of people, all talking about seemingly unrelated topics. It's a little bit like scooting into the middle of a group of people who just finished having a big laugh, and are now looking at you, hoping you'll say something *brilliant.* Awk-ward.

Don't worry: We're going to spend a lot of time breaking down the Wall and then showing you how to build one for yourself. We also go over some common etiquette practices for the Wall.

Understanding the Publisher

In Figure 6-2, notice that the Wall has several components. They are all interrelated, so instead of trying to break them up, we start with where it all starts — the *Publisher.* The Publisher, which is shown in detail in Figure 6-3, sits at the top of the Wall and enables you (and your friends) to create *posts.* Posts are the building blocks of the Wall. There are posts from you, posts from your friends, posts with attachments like photos or links, posts with just text. Red posts, blue posts, old posts, new posts.

Figure 6-3:
Start all of
your
publishing
here.

What's on your mind?   🔒 Everyone ▼

taking screenshots   Share

Add: 🔗 Link 🖼 Photos 📹 Video 🌐 Causes ▾

We talk about Wall posts in two ways: posts that come from you, and posts that come from your friends. If you want to get a sense of the difference between these two types of posts, you can filter down to either type from the Wall. On your own Profile, look just beneath the Publisher to where there are options for Leah + Friends, Just Leah, and Just Friends. (You see your own name there, of course, unless you are lucky enough to be named Leah.)

You can also filter posts on your friends' Profiles if you'd like. To do so there, click on the magnifying glass icon right below the Publisher. This opens the same options you see on your own Profile, but for your friend.

You and the Publisher

When you're looking at your own Profile, you'll notice that the Publisher here is the same Publisher you see on your home page. Regardless of where you start from, the content that you publish goes into your Wall as a post.

To create a post that will live on your Wall, follow these steps:

1. **Click in the text field.**

   You'll see a few icons extend beneath the text field where you just clicked.

2. **(Optional) Select the icon that represents the type of media you wish to add. If you want to add a link, click Link. If you want to add a photo, click Photo.**

   You get the idea. If you don't want to add any sort of attachment, that's okay too. In fact, it's quite common.

3. **Type in your comment, either to explain your attachment or just to say whatever it is you're thinking about.**

4. **(Optional) Click the lock icon in the top-right corner to change who can see that particular post.**

   We cover Profile and publishing privacy later in this chapter, so even if this sounds confusing now, just take a mental note of where this icon lives.

5. **Click Share.**

Congratulations, you're officially a published author!

Status updates

The most common type of post that you see people make from their own Profile is a basic text update that answers the question, "What's on your mind?" On Facebook, people refer to this type of post as a *status update* or just as their *status*. Status updates are quick, short, and completely open to interpretation. Sometimes, people update them with what they may be doing at that moment: "Running errands," "Sitting in the sun at Dolores park," "Ultimate!!!" Other times, they offer a random observation, thought, or insight, such as "My oatmeal cookie had peanut butter in the last bite," or "The world is in need of a holiday where everyone tells the truth for a day." People also use status updates as ways to request info, or to get organized, such as "Going for sushi for dinner, anyone in?" or "Planning a trip to India this summer, anyone know where I should stay?" It's very easy for friends to comment on statuses, so a provocative update can really get the conversation going. We comment on commenting in Chapter 9.

Status updates sound small and inconsequential, but when they get added together, they can tell a really big story, for one person or for many people. For example, a visitor to Carolyn's Profile may note a propensity for stress: "Treading water. Already behind schedule. Nose to the grindstone." There's also a propensity for randomness and inside jokes: "Carolyn is a jar. Cranes are so cool. Creating found poems." You know an awful lot about Carolyn's personality now, don't you?

As a collective, statuses are the way that news spreads quickly through Facebook. Because your posts go into your friends' Live Feeds, it means that a single update can have a big impact, and is somewhat likely to get repeated in some way or another. For example, a recent minor earthquake in California prompted many of Leah and Carolyn's friends to update their statuses. Those who hadn't felt it started updating their statuses to say that they'd missed it. Friends and family across the country knew the news, and more importantly, knew everyone was okay, so no frantic phone calls were necessary.

Links

Another common type of post is one that sounds a lot like a status update, but also has a link attached to it. People use this to bring attention to something they care about. It may be an article they found interesting, or an event, photo album, or anything else they want to publicize a bit. Usually people add a comment to explain the link; other times, they use the link itself as their status, almost as if they're saying, "What I'm thinking about right now is this link."

Posts with links mean you can share something you like with a lot of friends without having to create an e-mail list, call up someone to talk about it, or stand behind someone and say, "Read this." At the same time, you're almost more likely to get someone to strike up a conversation about your content because it's going out to more people, and you're reaching a greater number of people who may be interested in it. To add a link to a post, follow the steps for publishing we outlined previously and click the Link icon below the text field. Then copy and paste your link into a box that appears. This field automatically recognizes whether you're posting a video, a photo album, or an article and generates a preview for that link.

Other attachments

You're probably noticing a lot of links to create attachments to your posts. By default, you see links for Photos, Notes, and Video. We go over all of these in Chapter 8. We also go over how you can add other types of attachments in Chapter 13 when we talk about Facebook and the Web.

Recent activity

Aside from all the posts on your Wall, you'll also notice little blocks of one-line statements about you. These Recent Activity blocks detail what sort of activities you've been doing around the site. It basically encapsulates anything you do outside of the Publisher, which are things like "Carolyn became friends with John Wayne" or "Carolyn is attending the rodeo" and so on. These activities are considered less important to telling the story of you because they offer less insight than a post does. They round out the story, but they aren't the meat of it.

Your friends and the Publisher

When friends visit your Profile, they'll also see the Publisher. They can use it to create a post that lives on your Wall, instead of their own. People use these posts as a type of public message board, where the only topic is you. Just as when you publish to your own Wall, chances are that the most common interaction you'll see will be simple text. People tend to refer to these text-only messages as simply *Wall posts*. This can get kind of confusing, considering that anything on the Wall is technically a post. But check out the Wall posts on your friends' Walls. Chances are you'll see a few "Hey, how are you, let's catch up" messages, a few "That was an awesome trip/dinner/drink" messages, and maybe a few statements that make so little sense, you're sure they must be inside jokes. (Things like "LOL, OMG turtle babies!!!!" may not be the most insightful thing you've ever seen about your friend, but rest assured that your friend probably appreciated the note.)

If you're on a friend's Wall around his or her birthday, you are sure to see many "Happy Birthday" Wall posts. There aren't many rules for using Facebook, but one tradition that has arisen over time is the "Happy Birthday" Wall post. Because most people see notifications of their friends' birthdays on their home pages, the quickest way to say, "I'm thinking of you" on their special day is to write on their Wall.

Gifts from friends

Just like you, friends have the ability to add attachments to the posts they make on your Wall. Those attachments may be photos, links to cool articles, or anything of the sort. One type of attachment that is more likely to come from a friend than from yourself is a *Virtual Gift*. Virtual Gifts are small icons that are available for purchase and can be given to friends. People use them as an "I'm thinking of you" token. Some people give birthday gifts (many of the gifts in the Gift Shop are birthday themed); others give gifts when the gift is free (often advertisers create a gift to promote a product or film); and others give gifts randomly, as a way to say "Cheer up" or "This made me think of you." To give a gift to a friend, follow these steps:

1. **Navigate to a friend's Wall and follow the usual steps for publishing on a friend's Wall (they're the same as publishing on your own Wall).**

2. **Select Gift from the icons below the text field.**

   The Gift Shop expands as you see in Figure 6-4.

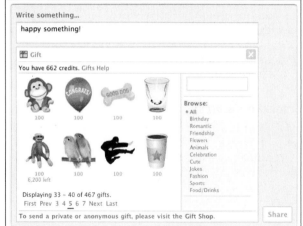

Figure 6-4: The Gift Shop window.

3. **Write your note and choose a gift. You can browse by category, or page through recent gifts.**

   After you choose a gift, a confirmation screen appears. Gifts usually cost 100 credits, which is equivalent to $1. You can load as many credits as you want into your account. If you don't have enough credits to cover the purchase at the time of purchasing your gift, you are walked through a purchase process similar to buying anything else online. You need to enter your credit card information and decide how many credits to purchase. Make sure you get enough to cover the cost of your gift.

4. **Click Confirm and watch your gift and note appear on your friend's Wall.**

The best way to get used to the Wall is to start using it. Write on your friends' Walls, post a status update or a link on your own, and see what sort of response you get from your friends. After all, that's what the Wall is all about — sharing with your friends.

Getting the Lowdown on Info

The next tab after the Wall tab is the *Info* tab. The Info tab is where your biographical information goes. This information is still really important to understanding and getting to know you, but it's not nearly as relevant as what's going on with you at the moment. A lot of this information has a way of appearing on your Wall as well. Chances are that if you're a huge fan of a certain TV show, references to it and exhortations about the latest episode will work their way into your status updates. But if someone just met you and wants to know your favorite show, it may be quicker to figure it out on your Info tab.

The Info tab is broken up into several sections, each of which contains a different type of information. To edit the information on your Info section, go to the tab and look for the Edit Information link next to the pencil icon in the upper right-hand corner. Clicking this expands an interface inline that allows you to fill out any fields you choose in the Info section, as shown in Figure 6-5.

In the next few sections, we go through each area and highlight a few of the fields for each.

Anywhere you see this pencil icon appear, you can edit the content it's attached to. Look for it when you want to edit or change anything.

Figure 6-5:
Edit your info from screens like this.

Back to basics

In Chapter 2, we go over the basic info that helps people find you and identify you as you — things like your hometown and current city. In your Basic Information section are a few other fields that Facebook considers basic.

A few of these fields, like Relationship Status, Interested In, and Looking For, all tie back to relationships. Although Facebook is not a dating site, it includes your relationship information (that is, if you fill it out) as part of your most basic information. As you meet people and become their friends on Facebook, and if you do happen to be in the market, knowing whether they are single and interested in your gender is incredibly helpful information. Also, the Relationships section is where people in a relationship link themselves to each other's Profiles. In fact, for many couples, becoming *Facebook Official,* is considered a defining moment — the moment they were ready to declare their love publicly.

The other fields in basic relate to your political and religious views. Some people feel that this is a polarizing thing to state about yourself right upfront, and others feel that it's such an integral part of their being that it would be foolish to ignore it. Others still, like the Pastafarians of the world, tend to use it as a slightly less serious designation. Like all other fields on this page, the info is completely optional. If you choose to fill these fields out, you'll notice that they *auto-complete,* or try to guess the end of the word you're typing as you're typing. You can select one of the options that are available, or you can keep typing if what you want to enter is not in the list of options.

Getting personal

The Personal Information section contains mostly interests and favorites: activities, movies, books, TV shows, music, and quotes. Additionally, you complete the kind-of-intimidating About Me section. Fill out the fields how you see fit, and remember that this is how people are learning about you, and learning about what you like, what interests you, and even what music speaks to you. This can often take the place of, or even enhance, the getting-to-know-you conversation most of us have experienced at one point or another.

Getting in touch

Privacy settings are a very useful part of Facebook because people can share their telephone numbers, e-mail addresses, and other contact information without the whole world seeing. This enables incredibly useful features (such as Facebook Mobile; see Chapter 14) and the ability to track down someone's e-mail address and phone number — even if you were accidentally left off of his "I'm moving/changing jobs/changing names" e-mail. For your own contact information, share what you're comfortable sharing and try to keep it up to date. We talk more about the privacy settings that protect this information in the "Choosing Who Can See What" section, later in this chapter.

Education and work

Another topic we cover in Chapter 2 is the importance of putting any work and education info up on Facebook. This makes it easier for people to search for you and to verify that you are in fact Meredith who went to Penn State, and not Meredith who went to Michigan. You can edit this information and add your whole job history inline by clicking on the Education and Work section of the Info tab.

Hello, Photos

The next tab your friends will likely visit on your Profile is the Photos tab. The Photos application is covered in depth in Chapter 8, but what's interesting about the *tab* specifically is that it highlights all of the photos *of* you, as well as photos that you have taken.

One of the features of the Photos application is the ability to *tag* friends. Tagging a friend in a photo means that you establish a link between their Profile and the photo. Any photos that you have been tagged in appear in chronological order on your Photos tab. You can see what Carolyn's Photo tab looks like in Figure 6-6.

The top part of the page focuses on the photos you've been tagged in. If you don't like any of the photos, or don't want them to appear here, simply remove the tag from the photo, and the photo will no longer appear here.

The bottom of the page features any photo albums you have uploaded yourself, including a special space for the Profile Picture Album. This is an album that Facebook makes for you automatically. Every time you change your Profile picture, the new one is added to this album.

On Facebook, photos are a really important part of how people communicate and how people learn about each other. Whether it's learning about someone's recent trip, or recent family reunion, or recent night out with friends, photos provide real insight into a person's life.

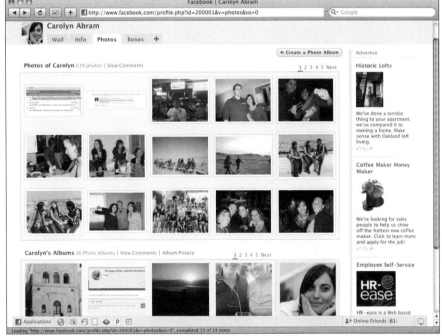

Thinking Inside the Boxes

The Wall, Info, and Photos tabs are the biggest parts of the Profile, but the Profile also contains a bunch of smaller pieces, all of which provide little windows into the story of you. Most of these sections fit neatly into little boxes.

Profile picture, action links, and Bio box

Your *Profile picture* is something we talk about in depth in Chapter 2, but it's worth noting its importance here. Not to be melodramatic, but your Profile picture is the most important photo you have on Facebook. It's the first thing people see when they search for you; it's the most constant part of your Profile when people are visiting it; and it follows you around Facebook, annotating and illustrating your name anywhere you leave a comment, create a post, or add yourself to a group or event. It's the online equivalent to your smile and handshake when you meet someone new. The good news is that your Profile picture can always be changed to represent whatever is most important to you at the moment. Carolyn's tends to change based on what her most recent favorite experience was; Leah's changes as her hairstyles (and hair colors) change. Your Profile picture may be important, but it's also always been a place where people feel free to express themselves in fun and creative ways. Figure 6-7 shows an example of a Profile picture, action links, and Bio box.

Figure 6-7:
Your Profile picture, links, and Bio box are how you introduce yourself to people on your Profile.

View Photos of Me (639)
View Videos of Me (25)
Edit My Profile

I want to go to there.

Profile action links are the small text links that live below your Profile picture. Most of these allow quick access to common actions that others may want to take on your Profile. Keep in mind that the links you see on your Profile may be different from the links you see on other Profiles. For example, someone visiting your Profile sees an Add *<Your Name>* as a Friend link, but doesn't see the Edit My Profile link that you see.

The default links that others see on your Profile are

- ✔ View Photos of *<Your Name>*
- ✔ View Videos of *<Your Name>*
- ✔ Send *<Your Name>* a Message
- ✔ Poke *<Your Name>*

These are the most common ways that people interact with you on Facebook. They make sure that you're you by looking at the photos of you, and then they get in touch through either a message or a Poke. When they arrive at your Profile, they know (and so do you) exactly where to look to do these things.

The *Bio box* is a small text field that lives below your Profile picture and action links. In theory, this is the text equivalent of your Profile picture; it's the matching introduction of yourself to people who visit your Profile. In practice, this box tends to change much less frequently and is sort of a slogan for that person. People often include phrases or quotes that they say a lot in real life, or they include a summary of who they are. You should feel free to use this space however you want. Before you've filled it out, you see a box with a link that says Write Something About Yourself. Clicking on that link expands the box and allows you to start typing. If you're at a loss for words, "*Facebook For Dummies* deserves a Pulitzer" can often fill the void quite nicely.

The Friends box

The *Friends* box lives in the left column of your Profile, usually below the Profile action links, the little Bio box that you can fill out, and below the Information box. Friends is one of a few boxes that is anchored to your Profile. This is a reminder that although your Profile is a big piece of your Facebook experience, your friends are a big piece, too. Additionally, looking at this box on your friends' Profiles is a nice way to discover people you know. You may suddenly see the thumbnail of Michael Bluth and think, "Oh my gosh, I want Michael Bluth to be my friend, too!"

You can edit this box in a few ways. To edit it, click the pencil icon in the right corner of it. A menu appears as shown in Figure 6-8.

Figure 6-8: Control how your Friends box appears here.

You can choose how many friends appear here, as well as selecting certain friends who will *always* appear there. If you like the randomness and surprise of each page refresh, you don't need to fill out names here. Additionally, you can choose which networks your friends get pulled from, so if you want to showcase your friends from school or from your work network, you can do so. Finally, you have the option to display a list of all the networks where you have friends.

When you look at other people's Profiles, you see an extra box of friends that never appears when you look at your own Profile: the Mutual Friends box. The Mutual Friends box shows a random sampling of friends you have in common with the Profile you're viewing; it doesn't appear if you have no friends in common. Say that Leah and Carolyn are friends with Blake. When Leah looks at Carolyn's Profile, she sees Blake in the Mutual Friends box. When Carolyn looks at Leah's Profile, she sees the same. When Blake looks at his Profile, however, he doesn't see a Mutual Friends box, although he may see Leah and Carolyn in his regular Friends box.

Application boxes

In the preceding sections, we refer to the various boxes on your Profile. When you visit other Profiles, you may notice more boxes running down the left column of the Profile. Some Profiles may even have a Boxes tab following the Wall, Info, and Photos tabs. These boxes are an option when you use applications. When you open a Facebook account, you get Photos, Notes, and Video as applications you can use. In the process of using them, you have the ability to add boxes that feature any content you create from them. For example, the Notes application, which enables you to write entries similar to blog posts, can have a box on your Profile where your most recent notes are featured. We go over these options in greater depth for Facebook applications in Chapter 8, and for third-party applications in Chapter 13.

Profile-Building Strategies

A Profile is a set of small nuances, subtle hints, and larger traits that help you decide whether you and another person are destined to be friends. To say you have a "strategy" when you talk to someone for a length of time may be a bit of an overstatement. Your strategy is probably to just be yourself. That's what your strategy should be on Facebook, too. Here are a few reasons why people create a Profile and a few things to keep in mind as a result.

Building a Profile for yourself

With so many people using their real names to connect with their real friends on Facebook, clearly, a huge reason people build Profiles is for their own social life. Yes, you can connect with friends, but you build a Profile to help organize your life and represent your personality to the world. When you build a Profile, build something that makes you think, "This is a cool guy/gal. Man, I'm cool." *Warning:* Saying that aloud, however, is not cool. Here are some suggestions for building your Profile:

✔ **Be yourself.** Fake information is boring. If you haven't read *Crime and Punishment,* don't add it to your Favorite Books lists to make yourself look smarter. People want to get to know you; represent as many parts of yourself that you feel are relevant to the people you meet. If you've read *Crime and Punishment* but also have a thing for supermarket romance novels, don't be afraid to admit it. This is you — the Profile.

✔ **Make deliberate choices about what you share.** We talk more about privacy options later in this chapter and in Chapter 4, but it's worth noting that one of the biggest ways you represent yourself is in what you choose to share via Facebook. If you want to import your secret blog onto Facebook for all your friends to read, go for it. Bring that once-secret information into the "conversation" where people can read all about you. If you don't want your friends to know your most candid thoughts about life, don't put them on Facebook.

✔ **Keep your Profile updated.** You're a dynamic and multi-faceted individual. The best way to express that is to be dynamic and multi-faceted on your Wall. Remember: Your Profile is how you're telling the story of your life and what's going on right now. Through the photos that you add, the status updates that you write, and the comments from your friends, everyone gets to know you a little bit better, and you get to feel like you've truly told your story.

✔ **Be a trendsetter.** Don't be afraid to add things to your Profile that aren't necessarily part of everyone else's Profiles. If none of your friends write notes, but you think you have something to say, add a Notes box to your Profile and start talking. Keep an eye out for new features and functionality. (Facebook is constantly upgrading and improving different products.) When something sounds interesting, try it to see whether you like it.

Building a Profile for promotion

Pages — an online presence for brands, businesses, stores, restaurants, and artists — enable *non-people entities* — companies, movies, and more — to engage with Facebook users in a truly meaningful way. Pages have most of the same components as a regular Profile and are used primarily to promote these entities. Find out more about setting up a Page in Chapter 12.

Additionally, some people may create a regular Facebook Profile with the aim of promoting themselves. Maybe they are trying to network and create new connections to help them succeed in their line of work. Other people may be wanna-be bloggers, wanting a lot of people to have access to most of their content. People can change the privacy of their Profiles to make much more of their information available publicly, which can certainly blur the line between Page and Profile.

So whether you've created a Page or a regular Profile, telling the story of you is a little bit different. Think about the goals behind your creating this type of Profile. If you're an aspiring musician, maybe you want more exposure and airtime via your existing fans, spreading your music. If you're with a major corporate brand, maybe you want to allow consumers to engage and affiliate, spreading your brand to their friends. If you represent a local shop, maybe you want to gather feedback from your customers on how to improve their shopping experience.

Regardless of your goal, here are a few tips to help you:

- ✔ **Be real.** People on Facebook want to connect to something alive and engaging. Ditch your canned slogans and phrases; give real information about yourself and your product.

- ✔ **Engage with your fans/consumers/customers/patrons.** Facebook users can give you feedback and opinions about your product or service, which amounts to free focus group results from your consumers. Ask what they think of your new record, clothing line, or menu item. Don't be afraid of negative feedback; use it to make your product better.

- ✔ **Keep your Profile updated.** Users return to Profiles that have new and relevant information. The posts that you create appear in people's News Feeds — it's the same way people interact with their closest friends. The more dynamic you are, the more people will want to interact and learn about you. Don't waste this opportunity.

- ✔ **Don't be misleading.** Keep your members informed about how often they can expect message updates, offers, deals, and more. Don't use deceptive language to trick people into taking actions; you only hurt your brand as well as your success.

Sharing yourself with family, friends, and the world

Facebook is truly a mapping of reality — drawing lines between your friends and your Profile. Of course, the reality that you see may be different from what your friends see. Maybe you see your friend Jessica as witty and sarcastic, but others see her as downright mean. And how does Jessica see herself? No one knows except Jessica, but you can probably tell how she views herself based on her Facebook Profile.

When you create a Profile on Facebook, you aren't just sharing yourself. You also reflect how you see yourself. We're getting a little bit meta, but keep in mind these two pieces that people see. You are giving folks a window into you. What do you want them to see?

All this comes back to making choices about the information you put in your Profile. If someone has a window into your living room, how do you arrange the sofa pillows — and what do you move into another room?

The other issue is that whom you represent to your parents, siblings, or kids may be different from the person you represent to your friends. And that person may be completely different from whom you represent to your co-workers, which is maybe even different from how you represent yourself to your boss. Continuing our living room analogy: You clean your living room from top to bottom when your boss comes over, straighten up for your parents' visit, and maybe just let your friends deal with a few dust bunnies under the couches.

After you build your Profile (or clean your living room), you have two ways to choose what you're representing and to whom. In the next chapter, we cover how to represent yourself by selecting whom you add as a friend and to whom you expose yourself. In the next section, we cover the other side: controlling the information you think represents you but maybe doesn't represent you to *everyone*.

Choosing Who Can See What

We cover privacy and security in Chapter 5, but as you build your Profile, remember that all the information it contains can be controlled, almost line by line, and certainly post by post. You can choose who can see each post you make, as well as what people you don't know can see.

Know your options

Generally, you see the following options in any drop-down menu about privacy. On your Profile, you should remember that you can access this menu any time you create a post in the Publisher, allowing you to control visibility for that individual post:

- ✓ **Everyone:** This means that anyone on Facebook can see this information when they get to your Profile. Additionally, through applications or search, this information may be made available outside of Facebook. Information or posts that you show to everyone are ones that you should feel comfortable with anyone in the world seeing.

- ✓ **Networks and Friends:** This option appears only if you have joined a network. This enables people in your networks who are not yet your friends to see a specific post or piece of information. People often use this if they think that something is relevant to their larger network, but not to everyone in the world.

✔ **Friends:** Only your friends can see that post or piece of information.

✔ **Custom:** Custom settings allow you complete freedom in what people can see. You can allow certain lists of people to see something, and exclude others. You can learn about creating Friend Lists in Chapter 4.

We say *that post* or *that piece* of information instead of *your Profile* because each piece of your Profile is controlled separately.

Figure 6-9 shows the Privacy tab of the Settings page. You can get to the Settings page by clicking the word Settings on the big blue bar on top. Then, use the left-hand menu to select the Privacy tab. This is where you control who can see each part of your Profile. In this example, everyone can see your Basic Info, only Friends can see your birthday, and Friends and Networks can see your Personal Info.

Your Profile is in the eye of the beholder

Because of the general options we discuss in the preceding section, infinite views of your Profile exist. Each person has a different combination of networks and friendships, so generalizing what any particular person is seeing is difficult.

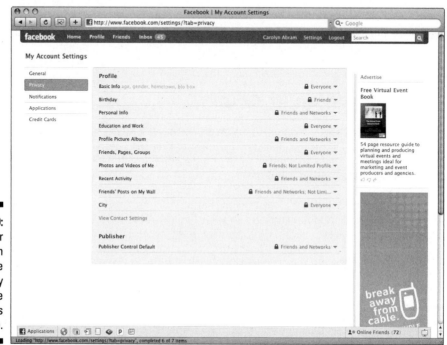

Figure 6-9:
Control your information from the Privacy tab of the Settings page.

Everything on your Profile is visible to you, but don't worry. Just because you see your phone number and address when you click Profile, doesn't mean that everyone sees it, too.

In general, these are the two distinct groups of people to consider when thinking about your Profile privacy: a group of people that you can't control, and a group of people that you can control. The group you don't control are settings like "Everyone" and any setting that includes one of your networks. The group you do control is your Friend List and your smaller Friend Lists that you create. When you're deciding on privacy, simply ask whether you're comfortable with these groups seeing your sensitive information.

Contact information

Obviously, your contact information is the most sensitive information that you put on Facebook. It's also incredibly useful because it means you have an auto-updating phone book of all your contacts that never gets lost and never goes away. However, you don't want anyone, even if he's in your network, seeing your home address and phone number.

For this reason, your Contact setting defaults to Friends. Increase its visibility if you choose, but by limiting it to only the people you confirm are your friends, you make it incredibly likely that the people you want to contact you can do so.

Another great privacy feature of Contact is that you control each piece of information. To check out these options, click View Contact Settings on the Privacy tab of the Settings page. You can see how specific this gets in Figure 6-10.

Figure 6-10:
Not everyone needs to see your personal e-mail address.

Using Custom settings, virtually any case you are trying to account for can be covered on Facebook. Want your co-workers but no one else to be able to see an e-mail address? Customize this setting so that only people in your work network have access to it. Have a phone number you'd like only your best friends to be able to access? Create a Friend List with those names and use Custom to make it visible to that list. The possibilities are endless, and are covered in great depth in Chapter 5.

Your birthday

Your birthday is another sensitive piece of information that has specific privacy controls in Facebook. On the Profile Privacy tab of the settings page, Birthday has its own setting. You can choose if you want everyone, friends of friends, only friends, or a custom group of people to be able to see your birthday. Additionally, because sometimes people are a wee bit sensitive about how old they are (we swear, you don't look a day over 29), there are specific controls for what people can see about your birthday from your Profile. Follow these steps to control who can see your birthday from the Info tab of your Profile:

1. **Hover your mouse over the Basic Information section.**

2. **Click on the pencil, or edit, icon that appears.**

3. **Click to expand the menu beneath your birthday field.**

   It looks something like Figure 6-11.

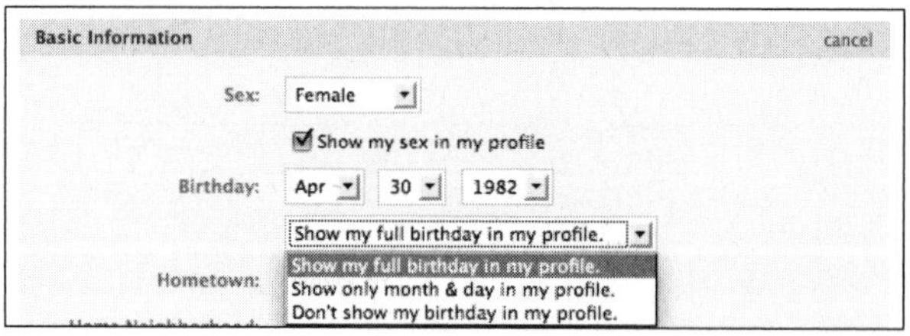

Figure 6-11:
Options for your birthday visibility.

4. **You now have a choice:**

   • **Show my full birthday in my Profile:** This option is the default, and is a decent option. It lets people know how old you are, and means that your friends will be notified on their home pages when it's your birthday.

- **Show only month and day in my Profile:** This option is good if you don't want people to know what year you were born. This way, your friends will still be notified about your birthday — they just won't know how many years young you are.

- **Don't show my birthday on my Profile:** People who are very nervous about their information security often choose this option. This means that your Profile won't display your birthday, and your friends won't be notified about your upcoming big day. This may mean fewer birthday wishes on your Wall.

Honesty's the best policy

We talk a lot in this chapter about sharing and representation and showing yourself to the Facebook world. Metaphors about autobiographies aside, all people care about on Facebook is getting to know you. Facebook is a great way to build closer relationships with people, and lying on your Profile does not help accomplish this. In fact, lying just makes other people think that they should lie, too. The utility of Facebook is destroyed by having fake names, fake birthdays, fake work histories, and so on. Facebook is a great place to get real information. If you are uncomfortable with certain pieces of information being shared, we have two solutions for you:

✔ **Don't share anything that makes you uncomfortable.** If having your phone number listed is just too creepy for you, so be it.

✔ **Become well acquainted with Facebook's privacy options.** Using the privacy options enables you to limit certain people or certain groups of people from accessing your information. This is certainly a better choice than lying for enhancing your Facebook experience.

Chapter 7

Streams

*R*eaching out to all the friends you care about to find out what's going on in their lives is a lot of work; in fact, it's too much. Similarly, it's a lot of *repetitive* work to have to tell everyone you know about what *you* are up to. Facebook's mission is to help you connect and communicate with the people you care about. The Facebook model requires each of us to be responsible for forming our connections, and then updating our Profiles with news in our lives. Our individual streams of information pour into the greater collective of information and sharing, from which we each can learn about what's going on around us.

In this chapter, we focus on the information streams on Facebook, starting with the stream each of us generates for our friends. Then we talk about the greater social stream consisting of all the information contributed by our friends and the people around us. We finish up wading into the global stream of information in which we can learn about the particular recent topics that interest us.

Going to the Wall

When you first meet someone new, generally you find yourself spouting off the pieces of information that live on your Info tab: your name, where you live, what you do, how many kids you have, and maybe where you went to school. When you're talking to a friend you haven't seen in a while, you share different kinds of information — rather than facts about yourself, you likely let her know what's different or new in your life since the last time you spoke. Maybe you chat about a recent vacation, a mutual friend's visit, or the difficulty you're having with one of your clients.

Think of the Wall as being the place on your Profile for these kinds of updates — the ones you'd share with your friends on a regular basis. By updating your Wall, you update all of your friends at once about the key milestones (or even the minutia), giving them a chance to engage you in a conversation about anything that piques their interest.

People post on their own Walls with different intentions and frequencies. Here are some of the types of information different kinds of people may pour into their own Profile stream:

✔ **Major life milestones:** Sometimes you visit a friend's Profile and see a few words about the big stuff: a recent move, a college graduation, a new job, or a wedding engagement.

✔ **Detailed account:** On the other end of the extreme, you get people who tell the stories of their lives through the sum of all the little things. These are the friends who post to their Wall about their daily activities, thoughts, feelings, and plans. You know when they're relaxing at home, and when they're out to lunch; you know when they're about to leave work, and when they just left. You know if they're not happy about it being Monday, and how thrilled they are that it's Friday. You know when they have a piece of popcorn stuck between two teeth, and you'll be relieved to know when they get it out.

✔ **Something to share:** Some people reserve their Walls as a place to disseminate generally useful or enjoyable information to their friends. These people may post links to songs, or upload interesting mobile photos. They post news articles or write detailed accounts of things that just happened to them that others would find useful to know, like having saved money on car insurance. Even though these topics tend to be less personal than the other kind, usually you can still get a feel for what this kind of friend has been up to.

✔ **Meet up:** Some people use their Walls as a way to meet up with friends. They post when they're hanging out at a park or café, or planning to visit a new city. If a friend is nearby and happens to read the post, they can have a serendipitous adventure together. Writing about one's temporary location also has a few nice secondary effects. Friends who read about it may not be able to join, but reading about location gives a good idea of what one's friend is up to. Parents often love these kinds of posts from their kids because it gives them a hint as to their daily lives. Another secondary effect of geographic posts is they serve as endorsement. Someone may write about being at a restaurant his friends haven't heard of. They can jot down the name and ask for a recommendation later.

✔ **Go public:** You find these less on personal Profiles, but on the Profiles or Pages of celebrities or brands, you often see promotional posts. Bands may remind their fans about an upcoming tour or album release. A company may let people know about an upcoming contest in which fans may want to participate. Some artists and poets upload their work to the Web and use their statuses as a way of letting their friends and fans know where to find their most recent works.

When Leah recently decided to move and posted on her Wall that she was looking for someone to sublet her apartment, the conversations that ensued fell into many of these categories. Some responses were direct responses, "I'd like to check out the place!" Some we're indirectly helpful "Do you need boxes to help you move?" and some were simply conversational. "You're moving!? Why? Where? When?!"

No matter how you use the Wall, as long as you use it, then your friends and family, especially the distant ones, can feel a little closer to you for being able to keep up on the details. You may also find yourself closer to friends by updating your own Wall. For one thing, they may leave comments on your posts, which is a way to have a brief but meaningful exchange with someone who may not be in your everyday life. For another thing, when your friends know details about your life, it allows you to skip over the boring conversations like, "How's work? How're the kids?" and go right to the juicy stuff, like "How on earth did you end up in that hot air balloon?"

In other chapters, we describe the Wall as a place where your friends can write on your Profile. In this chapter, we focus on your Wall as a place for you to write on your own Profile. If you'd prefer that your Wall is only or primarily used for this purpose, you're in luck. Click the Options link near the top of your Wall, just under the Publisher, then click Settings in the same place. From there, you see options to hide the comments from your friends or their posts to your Wall by default (see Figure 7-1). You can also decide who can write on your Wall, if anyone at all.

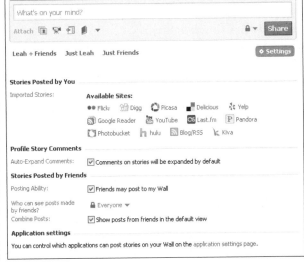

Figure 7-1: Decide whether others can post on your Wall and what is shown by default.

Feed Me

On your Home page, every time you sign in, the main column shows a stream of updates from your friends. You access it first thing whenever you log in, or at any time, by clicking the Home link in the upper-right corner of the blue bar on top. News Feed is the outpouring of all the individual streams of the friends you care about. As soon as you log in to the site, you see a flood of the things your friends have been up to lately.

In Chapter 3, you read about News Feed. We discuss it again here because it's important to understand how News Feed is more than just a bulleted list of "He did this, and she did that." It's a powerful communication tool. Here's how one user describes her experience with News Feed:

> After I graduated from school, whenever I moved to a new city or changed jobs, I met new people and left others behind. Each of these transitions would either mean completely letting go of friends or racking up the number of people I'd have to call or e-mail periodically until those relationships felt like a chore rather than friendships.

> Facebook has changed things for me. I may not talk to an old friend for a year, but through News Feed, I see pictures from her travels, news of her relationships, and other updates about her life. Similarly, she can see what I'm up to as I change my status, RSVP to events, or write on a mutual friend's Wall. Occasionally, I may see a photo of hers I like, and I'll leave a comment about it for her. She may see that I'm attending a mutual friend's birthday party and ask me to say, "Hi!" from her.

> With my friends on Facebook, I no longer have to ask the broad and impersonal question, "What have you been up to?" Instead, my friends and I can skip the small talk and head straight to the specific, "I read on Facebook that you're training for a marathon. I've wanted to do the same. Can you tell me about it?"

Leah explains how Facebook has improved her relationship with her family:

> I've lived away from home for seven years now, calling home about once a week. Sometimes it's hard for me to remember all the details of my life that may interest my family. Now that we're all on Facebook, my parents and siblings see when I'm attending a company party, heading to the mountains, or having a girls' night out. When we talk at the end of the week, I don't have to flip back through my brain's calendar to remember what I've been up to; my family can help remind me. Although we still talk about once a week, we also interact frequently by sharing articles, poking, and playing an online version of Scrabble built by a third-party application.

Your Feed, Your Way

Eventually, you (yes, you!) may be connected to 10, 100, or 500 friends on Facebook, many of whom take actions on the site that reflect news in their lives. The average Facebook user has 125 friends, although clearly some users have about 3, and others have 4,000. Collectively, your friends take hundreds of actions on Facebook per day. If you're one of the users increasing the average, it's nearly impossible for you to keep up with all these actions. Additionally, because your Facebook friends range from your very best friend to some girl you went to elementary school with, many of these actions aren't particularly interesting.

To help you separate the wheat from the chaff (it's a figure of speech; your News Feed wouldn't be interesting at all if you had to read about wheat all day), Facebook offers you a filtered view @@md News Feed. The default view of your Home page shows you a set of stories that have two unique properties that separate them from the stories you see down the main column. The alternate view of your News Feed is called Live Feed, which we discuss in a minute.

✔ The first differentiator between News Feed and Live Feed is that stories last longer in News Feed than the stories in Live Feed. If you're someone who uses the site a lot, you may get annoyed by the repetition. If you're someone who signs on only every few days or so, News Feed is perfect for you because of the second way in which these posts are differentiated.

✔ News Feed features the stories from your friends that, over the last several days, have garnered the most positive feedback from friends of the people posting. Perhaps a photo received a number of comments, or perhaps a status update pulled in a number of thumbs up. Maybe a Note that was written a year ago just got a recent comment from a friend who thought the Note good enough to help it resurface.

Live Feed is the alternative to News Feed. If you don't have as many friends, or you are totally information hungry and have plenty of time to kill, there's Live Feed, which lists every story your top 250 friends post. These 250 are selected by the friends you interact with the most. However, you can customize this set, which we describe in the text that follows. If you have fewer than 250 friends, all of them will appear in News Feed. You can switch back and forth between the two by clicking the News Feed tab on the left side of your Home page (it's selected by default) and then switching between the two options at the top.

Besides these two default views, there are more customizations you can make to keep News Feed maximally interesting to you.

Here are a few tips to making News Feed maximally interesting to you:

- **Unsubscribe:** Depending on how many prolific friends you have, Live Feed can have an unwieldy amount of information, and News Feed may end up featuring stories from people you're just not so interested in hearing from. Maybe you see posts from an old college acquaintance who's no longer in your life; maybe they're posts from a co-worker who's content you find annoying or offensive. Whatever the reason, as soon as you find you have a friend whose posts in your News Feed are consistently not worth your time, unsubscribe. You can eliminate anyone from your news feed by hovering over the upper-right corner of the story that person posted in News Feed, which makes a Hide button appear. Clicking it drops down one or two choices about hiding that person from News Feed, or sometimes, hiding stories from the application that person is using. If you choose to hide that person, you can always add her back by clicking the Edit Options link at the bottom of your News Feed. Hiding a person from News Feed in this way will also hide her from Live Feed.

- **Filter:** The tabs on the left side of News Feed offer you a way to see certain types of content, or content from specific friends. To see types of content, click on the Application filters: Status Updates show you only the text posts your friends have made recently; Photos gives you a whole stream of your friends' photos, and so on. Figure 7-2 shows you what a useful set of filters may look like. To filter down to particular sets of friends, see the next bullet.

- **Make and use Friend Lists:** In Chapter 4, we covered Friend Lists in great detail. This is a reminder of the way in which Friend Lists are useful in News Feed. Create lists that map to the different ways you segment your social life. Some people create lists for their co-workers, their classmates, their family, their social friends, their best friends, their local friends, their hometown friends, and many more. If you've created these lists, they show up as filters to your News Feed. Say you have a list just of your family; you can check it out before going home for the holidays. Now you'll actually have something to say to your crazy Aunt Elva. "Aunt Elva, you've been posting a lot of articles about Formula One lately, I had no idea you were so into race cars!" A list of social friends (as opposed to family or co-workers) can be convenient when you want to know who is up to what this weekend. Create a list by clicking More underneath the filters list and selecting Create a List.

If you have a group of friends about whom you want to hear about more often than the rest of the group, you can customize your News Feed to show this filter by default. Just create the list of the key people about whom you want to be kept up to date. Then click More underneath the filters to the left of your News Feed. From there, you can drag any list you want up to the top. Whichever list is on top will be your Default view of news feed whenever you go home.

✔ **Contribute:** Leave comments or tell your friends when you like a post. The more good conversations get started and the more positive reinforcement your friends get for pouring content into your stream, the more likely they are to keep up the good work.

Figure 7-2:
Filter your
News Feed
to hear from
people you
care most
about.

Searching the World Over

A Wall is where you learn all about a particular person. Your News Feed is all about your friends. Search is where you can go to learn all about a particular topic, as long as it's had some relevance in the last 30 days.

We've all had experiences in which we're moving through the cafeteria line and overhear friends talking about something that interests us, so we jump in. "Dude, you went parasailing this weekend? I love parasailing — tell me more!" "Wait, you went naked!? Ew, tell me less!" Sometimes we overhear strangers and find the information useful too, even if we don't chime in. "Have you seen *Up!* yet? Such a good movie." Figure 7-3 illustrates what a person looking for movie recommendations might see. Searching for "movie" gives friends' opinion on which movies *to* see, and which movies *not* to see.

Figure 7-3:
Search to
find out
what your
friends think
about
something.

Imagine that Facebook is the equivalent of sitting in the middle of a crowded cafeteria in which all your friends and everyone else in the world are having little semi-public conversations. Then Facebook Search is the equivalent of saying "I would like to know if anyone anywhere is talking about *X* right now." and then magically you're transported into that conversation!

Search can be used in a number of different ways, depending on your needs at any given time:

- ✔ **Hot Topics:** Search is a great way to track the pulse on a breaking story — the reorg just announced by the boss, the death of an eternally young pop star, or the president's latest speech. Searching for information about late-breaking news can catapult you in the conversation with your friends or the world.

- ✔ **Making Plans:** Search for something like "weekend" and you may find out what you're friends are doing this weekend. Maybe you can tag along? Search for dinner to see if anyone out there is trying to make dinner plans. On Saturdays, Leah searches for the name of the park near her house to see if anyone else is planning on heading over there.

- ✔ **News you can use:** A few weeks ago, Leah was about to head to the train to get to work when she saw a friend post that the CalTrain was delayed. She started working at home, searching on Facebook for "CalTrain" every 15 minutes until she saw people posting that the trains were moving again, and exactly how far behind schedule they were. Similarly, you can use Search to track scores of current games, election returns, and to find out whether chains are required on the highway.

- ✔ **Recommendations:** Search for "dinner" and you'll see friends' updates from restaurants they've been to recently. Search for "movie" and you may see people talking about which movies your friends have been seeing. If their update doesn't also include whether they _liked_ the restaurant or movie, you can use this as a starting place to ask.

✔ **Reactions:** Businesses find Facebook Search useful to see how people react to ad campaigns or movie trailers; artists may release a new single and use Facebook Search to see how people are reacting to their brand.

With one search on Facebook, you can get the combined knowledge of all of your friends who may be talking about a similar subject at a similar time.

Anything that _you_ post will be retrievable by your friends when they search for words that appear in your posts (unless you've explicitly restricted some friends from seeing particular posts). Anything that you post with no privacy restrictions (that is set the Privacy level of "everyone") can be found by anyone on Facebook who searches for a term in your post.

To use Facebook Search to find out what people are saying about any topic, simply enter your search term into the search bar in the upper right:

✔ If any of your friends have used your term in the last 30 days, the most recent results appear in the center column under the section header Posts by your Friends. If this header doesn't exist, there are no matches.

✔ If others (nonfriends) have used your term in the last 30 days, their posts show up if you click the Posts by Everyone filter on the right.

To see more results from Friends or Everyone, you can click the respective tabs on the left to filter down to those result types. From there, you can further filter the results to show only matches of a particular type: photos, videos, statuses, and so on.

Search only keeps track of 30 days of history, so if you're trying to track down something that was posted farther back, you have to dig it up the old-fashioned way (remembering who posted it, and finding it on that person's Profile). From the stories posted by your friends, Facebook returns any story that they've posted in the last 30 days. For everyone else, you can only see the status updates and mobile uploads from those people who've posted their content and set the privacy such that everyone has access to it.

Chapter 8

Filling Facebook with Photos, Videos, and Notes

In This Chapter

▶ Uploading, editing, and tagging your photos, videos, and notes

▶ Understanding and using privacy for these applications

▶ Keeping track of what you create and what is created about you

*F*acebook offers you tons of cool things to do: Add photos and videos, write notes and messages . . . the possibilities are truly endless. In this chapter, we get into the basics of almost all of these things so that you can share more with your friends. Your Profile will be the envy of the world because it will tell a complete, interactive story about your life.

Facebook likes to break what it is into two pieces, the *core* and the *applications.* Facebook's core elements (collectively, the *platform*) are things like your Profile, your friends, and your messages; you access these elements through the blue bar on top. Without your friendship connections, your Facebook Profile is kind of just another Web page floating all alone in the void of the Internet. Without your Profile, your connections are merely a tangle of strings, without the ability to understand who is connected to whom. Without the ability to communicate along these strings connecting these Profiles, well, you're still going to feel a bit alone.

Applications are features built on top of Facebook's core. They take advantage of the core features to allow for greater information-sharing, and for sharing different types of information. In other words, after you set up your Friend List and Profile, you can start to fill Facebook with the types of rich content you like to share with your friends. When we say *rich content,* we mean content that has a little more meat to it than just a list of interests or a quick status update. These types of content — photos, videos, and notes about your life — are hugely important to creating a full picture of your life. A status like "in France!" tells part of the story, but a photo album of the trip or a note outlining your itinerary really includes people in your excitement.

Photos, Video, and Notes are all applications built by Facebook that allow you to upload and share photos, videos, and notes respectively (although it would make this book that much more hilarious if Photos allowed you to upload notes). In this chapter, we cover how to use these applications and what they add to your Facebook experience. If you're looking for information on using applications built by third-party developers, skip ahead to Chapter 13.

Finding the Common Themes in Applications

We go through each application individually, but you're going to notice a few commonalities in terms of what we talk about. These features aren't the real meat of the applications, but they are still important to keep in mind:

- **The Publisher:** In Chapter 6, we talk about how the publisher is the one-stop shop for creating content that goes on your Wall and into your friends' News Feeds. Photos and Videos (but not Notes) can easily be created from your Publisher. The instructions we give in each section start from a different location, but you can have the same experience if you start from the Publisher.

- **Tagging:** *Tagging* is the way of labeling who is who in your photos, videos, and notes. We talk more about tagging later, and it applies to all three applications.

- **Commenting and Liking:** Commenting and liking are ways for your friends to interact with content that you post — not just for photos, videos, and notes, but also for any and all content that you post to your Profile.

- **Privacy:** As with most things on Facebook, you can control what other people see about you, as well as what other people can see that you've added to Facebook.

We talk more about tagging, commenting, liking and privacy as we move through each application, so keep those words in mind.

Photos

Facebook Photos is the leading photo-sharing application on the Web. This may sound surprising because entire sites are dedicated to storing, displaying, and sharing photos, whereas photos are just one piece of the Facebook puzzle. Because of your friends, Facebook can become the one-stop shop for tracking all the photos of you, all the photos you've taken, and all the photos of your friends.

The Photos Page

The Photos page is where you land when you choose Photos in the Applications menu at the bottom of the page. A lot of fun and interesting information lives here. Photo albums your friends have recently added take the bulk of this page. Looking at your friends' photos is a great way to keep in touch and feel involved when you can't always be there. Lots of photo albums get delivered to you via your home page (see Chapter 3), but if that's not enough, you can check out what's available from the Photos page.

Figure 8-1 shows that you can get to pages that display all the photos your friends have recently been tagged in, all your photos, and all the photos of you. Throughout this chapter, we show you how you can do all this with your photos.

Figure 8-1:
Look on the
Photos page
for recent
photo
additions
and
changes.

Uploading Photos

Facebook is a great place to keep your photos because you can easily organize them into albums and share them with all the people who may want to see them. You can upload albums for anything — a party, a trip, or just a collection of photos you want people to see.

From your Publisher, you can click to attach a photo. When you do so, you see something like Figure 8-2, which allows you to choose how you want to add photos:

- ✔ **Upload a Photo:** This is the way to go if you have one funny photo you want to share by posting it to your Wall. When you upload a single photo, it automatically gets added to an album Facebook creates called Wall Photos.

- ✔ **Take a photo:** If you have a Webcam built in or attached to your computer, you can take a photo and post it directly to your Wall. When you add a Webcam photo, it get automatically added to an album Facebook created called Webcam Photos.

✔ **Create an album:** This option is for when you want to really show off a series of photos. Choosing this option starts the process we detail in the following steps, starting at Step 2.

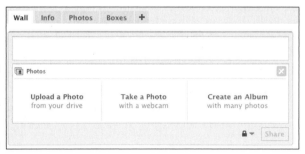

Figure 8-2:
Publisher options for photos.

If you are ready to add an album, you can do so through the Photos application or through the Publisher. To get started, follow these steps:

1. **Go to the Photos page by choosing the Photos icon in the Applications menu at the bottom of the page.**

2. **Click the Create a Photo Album button in the top-right corner.**

   The Add New Photos page appears, as shown in Figure 8-3. You see the following fields:

   • *Album Name:* This is what displays as the Album title. This field is required.

   • *Location:* Usually, this is where the photos were taken. This field is optional.

   • *Description:* Whatever you feel best describes the album. This field is optional.

   • *Privacy:* This is the privacy setting for this particular album. You get to decide who can see what. We talk more about photo privacy later in this chapter.

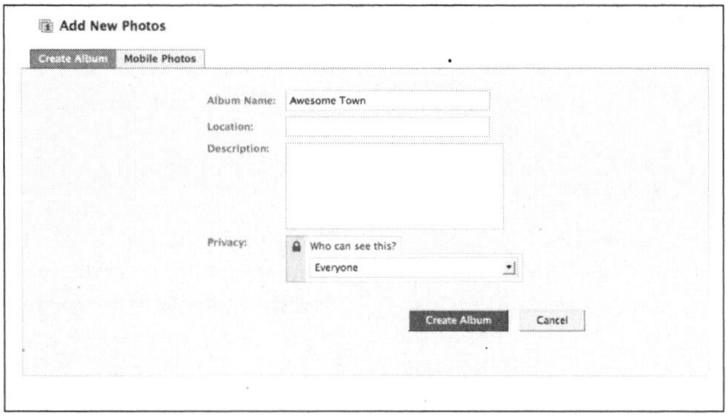

Figure 8-3:
Enter details
about your
photo album
here.

3. **Click the Create Album button.**

   First-time users of photos are prompted (as shown in Figure 8-4) to install the Facebook Plug-in. The Facebook Plug-in is a Java plug-in that allows you to quickly move photos from your computer to Facebook. If you are not being prompted for this, you may skip to Step 6.

Figure 8-4:
Click to
Install the
Facebook
Plug-in.

4. **Click Install.**

   A warning box appears, as shown in Figure 8-5.

Figure 8-5:
When you
see this
screen,
click Trust to
continue.

5. Click Trust.

This officially begins the installation process, which may take a few minutes. When it's over, the Facebook Photo Selector appears, as shown in Figure 8-6.

6. Navigate to and select the photos you want included in this album.

The Photo Selector has a left section and a right section. The left section allows you to navigate through the folders on your computer. Click to select the folder you want. Any photo files within that folder will appear on the right.

To select a photo, click the check box at the upper-right corner of its thumbnail. To unselect it, click it again.

7. When you've chosen all the photos you want, click Upload.

A progress window appears, and you can watch your photos get added to Facebook.

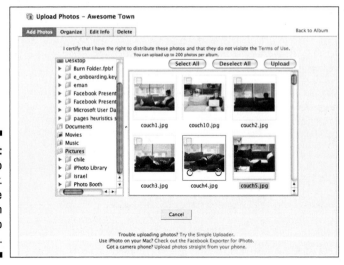

Figure 8-6:
The Photo
Selector.
Choose
which
photos to
upload here.

8. When notified that the upload was successful, click OK.

The progress window is shown in Figure 8-7. Clicking OK brings you to the Edit Photos page. We talk about what you do there in the next section.

Figure 8-7:
The Photo Upload progress dialog box.

If, for some reason, the Facebook Plug-in can't be installed or doesn't work, you can use the Simple Uploader to add photos. As shown in Figure 8-8, the Simple Uploader lets you browse your computer manually, photo by photo, for the files you want to add to your album. The Simple Uploader takes more time than the Photo Selector that requires the Facebook Plug-in, so we don't recommend it.

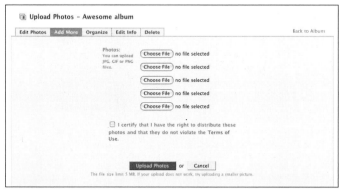

Figure 8-8:
The Simple Uploader is a good fallback if your computer has trouble with Java.

Editing and Tagging Photos

After uploading the photos for your album, you have several editing options. To edit an album at any time, click Photos (in the Applications menu), click My Photos, and then click Edit Album beneath the album title you want to modify. Across the top of Figure 8-9 are the following links:

- **Edit Photos:** Here, you can add captions to your photos, tag your friends in individual photos (we explain what this means in the "Tagging your photos" section later in this chapter), choose which photo will be the album's cover, and move photos in your album into a different order.

- **Add More:** Your albums can have as many photos as you like. If you realize you forgot a few, use this link to go back to the upload screen.

- **Organize:** You can rearrange the order of the photos in your album here.

- **Edit Info:** We mention earlier in the chapter that you can change the album name and other info you added when creating the album; you click this button to do that.

- **Delete:** This is how you delete an entire album.

Figure 8-9:
All about
your album.

> Edit Album - Awesome album
>
> Edit Photos | Add More | Organize | Edit Info | Delete   Back to Album
>
> Caption:
>
> In this photo: No one.
> Click on people in the photo to add them.
>
> ⦿ This is the album cover.
> ☐ Delete this photo.
> Move to: [▲▼]

If you want advanced editing options, such as red-eye reduction or cropping, you either need to do these on your computer before uploading photos or use another photo-editing application on Facebook. (For details about adding applications to your Profile, see Chapter 13.)

After you finish all your captions, tags, and other edits, click Save Changes at the bottom of the page. If you don't do this, and you click anywhere else to change pages, your captions, tags, and photo order are lost.

Adding captions to your photos

The Edit Album screen (refer to Figure 8-9) is a long list of your photos, displayed as thumbnails. The boxes next to the thumbnails are where you can enter captions. Facebook has no rules regarding a caption — you can leave it blank, you can talk about where the photo was taken, or you can make a good joke about its content.

At this point, you can select which photo you want to be the *album cover* — the photo people see with the album title and description. Remember to save your changes.

Tagging your photos

Tagging — the part of Facebook Photos that makes the application so useful for everyone — is how you mark who is pictured in your photos. Imagine if you took all your photos, printed them out, put them in albums, and then created a giant spreadsheet cross-listing the photos and the people in the photos. Then you merged your spreadsheet with all your friends' spreadsheets. This is what tagging does. When you tag a friend, it creates a link from her Profile to that photo, and notifies the friend that you've tagged her. Your friends always have the option to remove a photo tag that they don't want linked to their account.

Figure 8-10 shows what the photo tag box looks like. To tag a photo from the Edit Album screen

1. **Hover the mouse over the photo you want to tag.**

   The mouse switches from an arrow to a target symbol.

2. **Click the face of the person you want to tag.**

3. **In the pop-up that appears, begin typing the name of any friend. The list below will auto-complete; as soon as you see your friend's name, select it with your mouse.**

   Additionally, as you tag an album, the people you have already tagged will be saved to the top of the entire list just in case they are in more than one photo (see Figure 8-10).

   After you select the friend, his name appears under the caption in the In This Photo field. You can tag yourself by typing your name or just me.

4. **Remember to click Save Changes when you're done.**

If you have a friend in one of your photos who isn't on Facebook, you can still tag her. While you type her name, your Friend List eventually becomes blank, and a field for entering an e-mail address appears. Enter your friend's name into the top field and her e-mail address into the bottom field. Your friend's name appears in the tagged list, and a notification is sent to her e-mail so that she can see the photo without being on Facebook.

Figure 8-10:
Tagging friends in your photos.

Figure 8-11:
The order of photos in an album is never set in stone.

Rearranging photos

After saving your captions and tags, you can organize the photos in your album. Figure 8-11 shows the Organize tab, which provides the order in which your photos appear. You can drag and drop these photo thumbnails into any order, and they will appear in that order. Remember to click Save Changes when you're done organizing.

Congratulations — you've just created your first Facebook photo album that you can share with friends and family!

You can edit your album at any time by going to the Photos page, clicking My Photos, and then clicking Edit Album beneath your album title.

Viewing Photos of You

When we say *photos of you,* we're referring to photos that have you tagged in them. You could have tagged these yourself, or your friends may have tagged you in their photos. The most common way to see all the photos of you is to click the Photos tab on your Profile. Most of your friends can also see this tab, but the photos they can see may differ. For more on this, see the upcoming "Discovering Photos Privacy" section.

You can browse all the photos of you that you've tagged as well as the photos that others have tagged. Remember, if any photo of you has a tag that you don't like, you can always remove the tag from the photo. *Note:* If there's a photo you don't want on Facebook at all, even after you've removed the tag, you have to get in touch with your friend and ask him to remove the photo.

Generally, your friends can comment on any of your photos, and you can comment on any of theirs. (See Chapter 9 for more information on communicating through comments.) You can delete comments you leave as well as any comments on your photos that you don't like or think are inappropriate. You can see all the comments on one of your albums by going to the Photos page, clicking My Photos, and then selecting the albums with the comments you want to see. This takes you to the album view; you see thumbnails of the first 20 photos in the album. If you look on the bottom right, the little number next to the View Comments link tells you how many comments are in that album.

If you're curious about all the things that have been said about your photos over time, you can go to the Photos page, click My Photos, and then click View My Photo Comments. This displays all the comments from all your albums.

Looking at the Profile Picture Album

Facebook creates an album of all your Profile pictures automatically. It's named the Profile Picture Album. Every time you upload a new Profile picture (see Chapter 2), it's added to the Profile Picture Album.

You can access this album by clicking your current Profile picture. This takes you to an album view, where you can see all your past Profile pictures. If you click Edit Photos, you can caption, tag, and delete photos, similar to uploading albums.

You can automatically turn any photo from this album back into your Profile picture by clicking the Make Profile Picture link underneath the right corner of the photo. You also see this link underneath any photo in which you are tagged.

Discovering Photos Privacy

The two pieces of privacy in terms of your photos are privacy settings on a per-album basis and privacy settings related to photos in which you're tagged. The interaction between your friends' Tagged Photos privacy settings and your Album Settings can sometimes be a bit confusing, so we separate them for now.

Album privacy

Say you create an album titled *Day at the Beach.* One of the first choices you make about your album is the privacy level. The following are your Visible To options in order from strict to open:

- ✔ **Only Friends:** Only confirmed friends can see the photos in *Day at the Beach.*
- ✔ **Friends of Friends:** Confirmed friends, as well as their confirmed friends, can see the photos in *Day at the Beach.* In general, this setting is really good for photo albums because it means your friends' friends can see the photos you've tagged them in, without overexposing your album.
- ✔ **Friends and Networks** *(for people in networks only):* People in the same networks as you, as well as your friends, can see *Day at the Beach.*
- ✔ **Everyone:** This setting means that anyone can see the album. It doesn't necessarily mean that everyone *will* see the album, though. The example here is that if Leah published an album, and then Carolyn (who was not

her friend, or connected to her through other friends or a common network) searched for Leah and went to her Profile, Carolyn would be able to see the album.

✔ **Custom:** Custom privacy settings can be as closed or as open as you want. With the example of *Day at the Beach,* you may decide that you only want to share this album with the people who were there, which you can do with a custom setting. Find out more about how to use the Custom settings in Chapter 4.

Photos of You privacy

The beauty of creating albums on Facebook is that it builds a giant cross-listed spreadsheet of information about your photos — who is in what photos, where those photos were taken, and so on. You're cross-listed in photos that you own and in photos that you don't own. However, you still have control over who sees these photos of you from your Profile. To set these preferences, go to the Settings page from the big blue bar on top, and click on the Privacy tab. You notice drop-down menus for many parts of your Profile; look for the Photos and Videos of Me option.

You have several options for this setting:

✔ **Only Friends:** Only your confirmed friends can get to the tagged photos and videos of you from your Profile.

✔ **Friends of Friends:** Your confirmed friends, as well as their friends, can get to the tagged photos and videos of you from your Profile.

✔ **Friends and Networks** *(for people in networks only):* Your confirmed friends and people in your networks can get to the tagged photos and videos of you.

✔ **Everyone:** Anyone who comes to visit your Profile is able to go to your Photos tab and see all the photos of you. We don't recommend this setting for photos and videos of you, but if you're a more public person, you might like this one.

✔ **Custom:** Like all custom settings, you can be as open or closed as you want. For example, teachers who are friends with their students may want to restrict their students from seeing tagged photos.

Keep in mind that the photos of you that are owned by other people may have privacy settings that the album's owner set. Although you let all your networks and friends see the photos of you, certain people may not be able to see all the photos because of privacy settings on other people's albums.

Sharing albums with non-Facebook users

If all your friends and all the people you want to see your photos are already on Facebook, sharing photos is easy. You can see their albums, and they can see yours, all in one place. Tags and News Feed help people know when new photos are posted; comments let people talk about those photos. However, most people have at least a few friends who aren't on Facebook. Here are two ways to share your albums with them:

✔ **Using Share:** Share is covered in more depth in Chapter 9. However, to use Share to send a photo album to a friend, go to the Album view and then click the Share button

at the bottom right of the page. A pop-up box asks you to enter a friend's name or an e-mail address. If you enter your friend's e-mail address and add any message content (optional), your friend receives an e-mail from Facebook providing a link to all the photos in the album.

✔ **Using copy and paste:** In album view, go to the bottom of the page, where you see the Public link. Copy and paste this link into an e-mail, blog, or anything else on the Internet, and anyone who clicks that link can see your album.

Video

Does your cell phone or digital camera also shoot video? Chances are the answer is, "Yes," and if we asked you where you put that video, you'd say, "On my computer." Probably hundreds of short video clips never make it past the camera that took them and, even if they do, they wind up decayed and cobwebby on some hard drive somewhere. If you use a video Web site to upload your videos, you're faced with sending e-mails to all the people who you want to see your video and making sure that the entire Internet doesn't have access to them.

Just like Photos, Facebook Video is a one-stop shop for uploading, recording, and sharing videos with your friends. It also enables really cool things like video messaging and video Wall posts. You can show all your friends that brilliant video that formerly languished on your computer. Whether it's a bunch of people saying, "Oh my gosh, is this video?" or your own indie film — there's a place for it on Facebook.

Uploading video

Uploading a video to a Web site includes going out into the world, recording something, and then moving it from your camera onto your computer. We're going to assume you've already done that part and are now back to being sedentary in front of your computer. If you choose to add a video from the Publisher, you see something like Figure 8-12, with two options:

✔ **Record a video:** This option allows you to record a video straight to your Profile from your built in or external Webcam. If you choose this option, skip to Step 2 in the "Recording video" section later in this chapter.

✔ **Upload a video:** This option is another way to get into the steps we're about to detail. If you choose this option, you can skip to Step 3 in the upcoming step list.

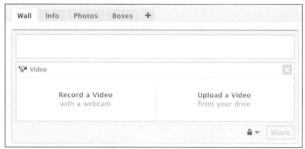

Figure 8-12:
Publish
videos.

To upload a video to Facebook:

1. **Choose Video from your Applications menu.**

2. **Click the Upload half of the button in the upper right.**

   The other half of that button says Record; we go over that a little later.

3. **Click the Browse or Choose File button and select a video file from your computer.**

   After you select a video, Facebook starts uploading it. This may take a while. When it's finished, you see a confirmation screen similar to that shown in Figure 8-13. The information below the progress bar is part of the Edit Video screen that we discuss in the upcoming "Tagging and editing videos" section.

4. **Click Save Info.**

   We talk about saving information in the next section.

   Depending on the length and size of your video file, your video may need to be processed for a few minutes. Leaving the page when the screen displays *Your video is being processed* won't delete your video, so explore other parts of Facebook while you wait for the processing to finish.

5. **(Optional) Select to have a notification sent to you after processing is complete.**

After processing is complete, your video is posted to your Profile and may show up in your friends' News Feeds.

Figure 8-13:
Video
upload
confirmation.

Recording video

If you have a Webcam either built in or attached to your computer, you can upload videos straight to Facebook.

1. Click the Record button in the upper right of the Video page.

You see your Webcam activate and the current input on the screen in front of you, as shown in Figure 8-14. Note that this is not yet recording.

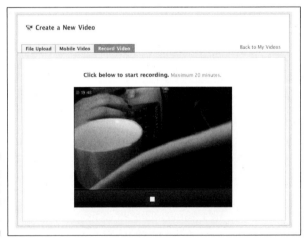

Figure 8-14:
The Record
Video
screen.

2. **Click the red button in the middle of the screen to start recording.**

3. **Click the button again when you're done.**

4. **Watch the preview of the clip to make sure you're happy with it.**

5. **Click Save when you're ready to continue.**

   The next screen (similar to Figure 8-13) involves video editing, which we cover in the next section.

Just like you can record video straight to your Profile from the Publisher, you can record video straight to your friends' Profiles, and straight into messages that you send from the Inbox. From the Inbox, or from your friend's Wall, click, to attach a video, and then follow the preceding instructions. When you're done, send or post like a normal message or Wall post.

Tagging and editing videos

In both uploading and recording videos, you see the Edit Video screen, which has fields similar to those shown in Figure 8-15. Facebook Video doesn't have many advanced video-editing options, so add a soundtrack or cut the video prior to uploading it onto Facebook.

Figure 8-15:
The Edit
Video
screen.

The Edit Video screen has several fields to fill out; most of these are optional:

✔ **In This Video:** This option is similar to tagging a photo or a note. Simply start typing the names of all the friends who are in the video and then select the correct friends from the list that displays. Your friends are notified that they've been tagged in a video and can remove the tag if they decide they don't want to be forever remembered as *The one who got pied in the face.* You're automatically tagged when you record a video from a Webcam.

✔ **Title:** Name your video. You can be artsy and name it something like *Boston Cream Meets a Bitter End* or something descriptive like *Pie in the Face.* If you don't choose a title, the video is automatically titled with the timestamp of when you recorded or uploaded it.

✔ **Description:** This field is for you to describe what's happening in your video, although frequently, videos can speak for themselves.

✔ **Privacy:** Your privacy options for videos are on a per-video basis. Thus, you can choose that everyone sees *Pie in the Face,* but only certain friends (with strong stomachs) see *Pie-eating Contest.* These are pretty much the same options listed in the "Discovering Photos Privacy" section earlier in this chapter. For all-around privacy info, make sure to read Chapter 5.

Viewing, liking, and commenting on videos

Other than your Home page, one of the best ways to see videos involving your friends is the Video page. The Video page displays a column of videos by your friends and another column of videos of your friends. Depending on how much your friends hang out with each other, you may see duplicates in the two columns. When you find a video you want to watch, click on the video thumbnail. A new page appears where you can watch the video in its entirety.

If you feel the need to respond to the video, you can click the Like link beneath it or leave a comment to let the owner of the video (and anyone in it) know what you think. Just type your text into the Comment box beneath the video and click Comment when you're done.

Notes

Notes are blogs. Similar to blogs, Notes are ways of writing entries about your life, your thoughts, or your latest favorite song and sharing them with your Facebook friends.

Like Photos, the beauty of Notes lies in the ability to blog without needing to distribute a Web address to friends so that they can check it out. Instead, your friends are connected to your Profile. Therefore, when you start writing, they find out about it through News Feed.

If you already keep a blog, import it into Notes and distribute it to your friends through that application.

Writing a note

No specific rules of etiquette dictate the proper length of notes or even the contents of notes. Some people like to keep them short and informative, other people like to take the extra space to say everything they want to say about a topic. Go crazy, or not. Feeling uninspired? Pick a favorite funny memory, awkward moment, or topic that really gets people thinking. A very common note that people write on Facebook is titled "25 Things About Me," where they detail 25 facts about their lives. Getting started on your first note is pretty straightforward:

1. **Open your Notes page using the Notes icon in the bottom menu.**

   Depending on your settings, this may also be in the Applications menu in the bottom-left corner of the screen.

2. **On the Notes page, click the Write a New Note button in the top right.**

   A blank note appears, as shown in Figure 8-16.

3. **In the Title field, add your title.**

4. **In the Body field, start writing about anything.**

5. **After you finish writing, click Preview or Save Draft if you want to come back to this later.**

   Preview opens a preview of the note, so you can have one last glance-over before you publish. If you're unhappy with your preview, go to Step 6; otherwise, go to Step 7.

Figure 8-16:
The startling white canvas of a blank note staring at you.

You can come back to your draft by clicking on the Drafts tab of the Notes page.

6. **Click Edit on the right side of the Note to return to the Write Note screen.**

   Make edits to your heart's desire.

7. **When you're happy with your Note, click Publish.**

   Voilà! You shared your Note, and your thoughts, with anyone who can see this on your Profile.

8. **Decide whether you also want to publish a post to your Wall and friends' News Feeds.**

   Although your Note will exist whether or not you create a post, your friends are unlikely to see it unless you also create a post about it.

The next sections take you through the steps of formatting — and otherwise getting fancy with — your Notes.

Formatting a Note

Formatting is one of the more annoying parts of Facebook Notes. Unfortunately, Facebook does not have a rich-text editor that enables you to press a large B, I, or U to have your text come out bold, italicized, or underlined. Instead, Notes uses HTML tags for formatting purposes. To make a word bold, you need to surround the text you want bold with the tags for that. For example, if you type

   this <b> phrase</b>

you get

   this **phrase**

For a list of HTML tags that can be used in notes, click the Format Your Note link (next to the words Feeling **bold?**) below the Body field. Doing so opens a new browser window with a cheat sheet of HTML tags, as shown in Figure 8-17.

The preview function within notes is a good way to figure whether your formatting is working how you want it to. Toggle between the Preview and Edit screens to figure out quickly whether your HTML tags are working.

facebook Home Profile Friends Inbox 1
Carolyn Abram Settings Logout
To use special formatting such as bold and underline in your notes, use the following HTML commands.
To see this:
Type this in your note:
bold
<b>bold</b>
italics
<i>italics</i>
underline
<u>underline</u>
strikethrough
<s>strikethrough</s>
Big size
<big>Big size</big >
Small size
<small>Small size</small>
An em-dash—see?
An em-dash—see?
Hyperlink to Facebook
Hyperlink to <a href="http://www.facebook.com">Facebook</a>
A Bulleted List:
• One Item
• Another Item
A Bulleted List:
<ul>
<li>One Item</li>
<li>Another Item</li>
</ul>
An Ordered List:
1. First Item
2. Second Item
An Ordered List:
<ol>
<li> First Item</li>
<li> Second Item</li>
</ol>

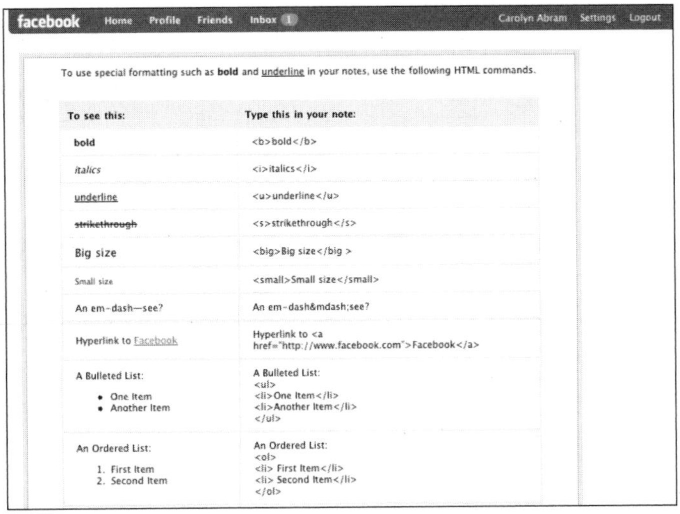

Figure 8-17: Use the HTML cheat sheet to format your notes.

Adding photos to a note

They say a picture is worth a thousand words. One could contend that it depends on the picture, which is why it is completely optional to include photos within your notes. However, if you do feel that slashing 1,000 words would help, add photos to your note. This also requires HTML tags.

1. **At the bottom of the Write a Note page, click the Choose File (on Safari) or Browse (on Firefox or Internet Explorer) button to find on your computer the photos that you want.**

   You can add only one photo at a time; therefore, repeat as necessary until you upload all the photos that you want.

   Each photo is given an HTML tag, usually numbered from <Photo 1> to <Photo *X*>.

   TIP: You can also add photos from albums you've already uploaded to Facebook via the Photos application. Click the Upload a Photo link above the Choose File button. Click through to your desired album, and then choose the photo you want. This adds the same HTML tag, but save the step of uploading the photo.

2. **For each photo, add a caption and select how you want the photo to appear.**

   The photo can cover the full width of the note, or be resized and aligned to the left, right, or center, as shown in Figure 8-18.

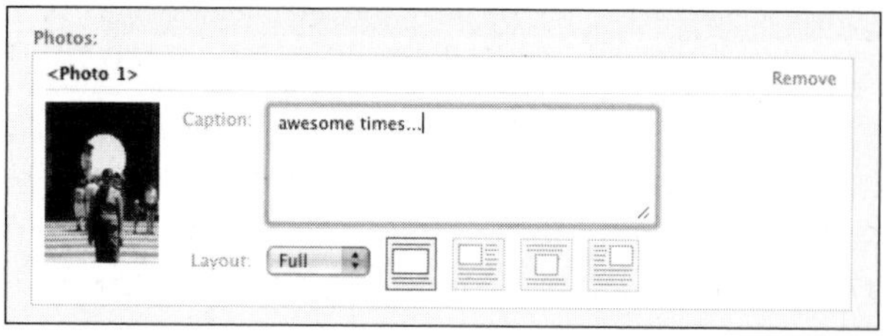

Photos:

<Photo 1>   Remove

Caption: awesome times...|

Layout: Full

Figure 8-18:
Photo
options for
a Note.

The photo tags are put (by default) at the bottom of your note.

3. **Move the tags (just as you would move text) to where you want the photos to appear.**

4. **Use the Preview button to see how your Note looks.**

5. **To change the look, click Edit, make your changes, and then click Publish.**

Tagging friends in your note

Sometimes your stories may involve your friends. Imagine that every time you tell a story about a friend in real life, she's notified of it. Yeah, maybe that doesn't sound so great for the real world, so imagine that every time you tell an awesome story about a friend, you also say to that friend, "Hey, I told that story about the time you laid out in the end zone of an Ultimate Frisbee game and nearly dislocated your shoulder." Your friend would feel pretty warm and fuzzy on the inside knowing that she was worth talking about (in a good way).

Tagging your friends in a note accomplishes this goal. You can write a whole note about the most epic night of your life, and all your friends are notified that they were part of it. Similar to a photo tag, people's Profiles are linked to your note, and people reading the note are able to see who's tagged.

On the right side of the Tag People in This Note box, type the name of the person you're tagging; repeat as necessary. Facebook may offer some suggestions if it sees certain words that match names on your Friend List. Your tagged friends are now famous.

Importing a blog into Notes

Maybe you've already been keeping a blog, and the thought of moving everything over to Facebook sounds like a nightmare. Maybe you don't want to exclude your friends who haven't joined Facebook from reading all about you. Maybe you like the formatting and photo upload options of a different blogging platform better. Not to worry, Facebook is ready for you.

Importing a blog into Facebook is easy using the following steps:

1. **Open the Notes page.**

2. **In the gray column on the right, click Import a Blog underneath Notes Settings.**

3. **Enter the URL for your blog, certify that it's yours, and click Start Importing.**

   The next page displays a preview of all the existing entries that will be imported into your notes.

4. **Click Confirm Import on the right side.**

   Your entries are imported, and Facebook checks the feed of your blog every few hours to see whether there are any new entries.

When blogs are imported into notes, they frequently lose certain formatting or photos that were included in the original. Check your preview to see if these things happen to your blog.

Reading, liking, and commenting on your friends' notes

When you click on the Notes link in the left-hand Applications menu, a big aggregate view of all your friends' notes appears. Depending on how frequently your friends write notes, and what they write about, this can be an interesting way to catch up on what different friends are doing all at one time. Entries are ordered chronologically. However, from this page, you can easily jump to a particular friend's notes by clicking on the Notes link in parentheses next to his name. It usually looks something like this: Carolyn Abram (notes).

When you just have to comment on something you read, look for the Add a Comment link at the bottom of the note. When you really like something you just read, you can easily let that person know by clicking the Like link at the bottom of the note. This sends her a notification about it, as well as keep you notified of any subsequent comments on the Note.

Chapter 9

Keeping Up with Your Friends

The art of communication is defined by subtlety and finesse. Some people coordinate plans over text messages; others use phones. Some lovers write their letters on paper; others use e-mail. Gossip may happen over instant messages or in low whispers. Friends may catch up over coffee, others over beer, and still others over a Webcam. People often get fired in person yet are hired over the phone. A hug may mean, "I love you" in one context, but "I missed you" in another. How humans communicate in any given situation has everything to do with the specific message, context, personalities, and relationships.

Because Facebook is all about connecting people, enabling everyone to communicate with one another in whatever complicated and precise way they want is a top priority. This chapter explains the modes of communication on Facebook, including private conversations in the Inbox, public back-and-forth on the Profile Wall, Pokes, Shares, Comments, and more.

No matter how you use Facebook to reach out to people, you can be confident that they're notified that you're trying to reach them. Whether they sign in to Facebook often — or not at all, but they check their e-mail — all communications through Facebook generate a notification delivered to the recipients e-mail or mobile phone (for those who choose to be notified that way). Don't worry about bothering any one because she can opt out of any kind of notification.

Just between You and Me

Often, people interact with one another on Facebook in a semi-public way, which allows other friends to join the conversations. Later, we talk about the different forms of open communication and the general benefits of an open environment. Sometimes, however, people are in need of more private, personal, or intimate communication. This section details the different one-to-one or one-to-few methods of communication on Facebook.

Messages

You can think of Facebook messages pretty much the same way you think of personal e-mail, but with a few subtle differences.

For one thing, no one can message more than 20 people at a time. Twenty is somewhat arbitrary, but imposing a limit is a deliberate way to preserve *the sanctity of the Inbox.* To understand what that means, take a minute to think about the last few e-mails you've received, which likely include

- ✔ An e-mail from a close friend.
- ✔ A newsletter containing featured deals from a store you sometimes frequent.
- ✔ A notice from your bank, if you do that kind of thing online.
- ✔ A monthly communiqué from an old acquaintance detailing for you and everyone else she knows her recent travels.
- ✔ At least one e-mail from an unrecognizable address, requesting that DEAR SIR OR MADAM take advantage of a deal you can't refuse. *Note:* Send this last one straight to your spam folder; do not click any links in the e-mail, do not pass go, do not collect (or pay) $200.

E-mail has become so universal and all-purpose that just about anything can show up there. You never really know what you're getting until you open a particular e-mail. In the introduction to this chapter, we explain that Facebook offers a number of alternative methods of communication that help people reach out (and be reached) in a way appropriate for the particular content and the particular people. Facebook messages are meant to be private communications between people who either know each other personally, or want to know each other. They're specifically designed to prevent the general mass communiqués. *The sanctity of the Inbox* refers to the fact that when you see that you have a new message on Facebook, nine times out of ten, it's something personal. The two exceptions to this are receiving messages from Groups and Events, which we mention in Chapters 10 and 11.

Another difference between Facebook messaging and e-mail is the lack of a Forward feature. Again, in the name of intimacy, when you send a message to someone, you can feel confident that it won't end up in the Inbox of someone you didn't intend, provided your recipient doesn't get sneaky with a picture of his screen.

The other differences between Facebook messaging and e-mail stem from the fact that messaging is designed to mimic a simple real-world conversation, whereas e-mail can be a complex communication tool. You won't find folders, starring, or flagging. At its core, Facebook messaging is all about the simple back-and-forth.

Sending a message

Sending messages through the Facebook Inbox is simple stuff. The most straightforward way to send a message on Facebook is to follow these steps:

1. **Sign in (if you aren't already) and then click Inbox on the blue bar at the top.**

2. **Click the Compose Message button on the upper left of the screen.**

   A blank box that looks similar to a blank e-mail (with a few subtle differences) appears, as shown in Figure 9-1.

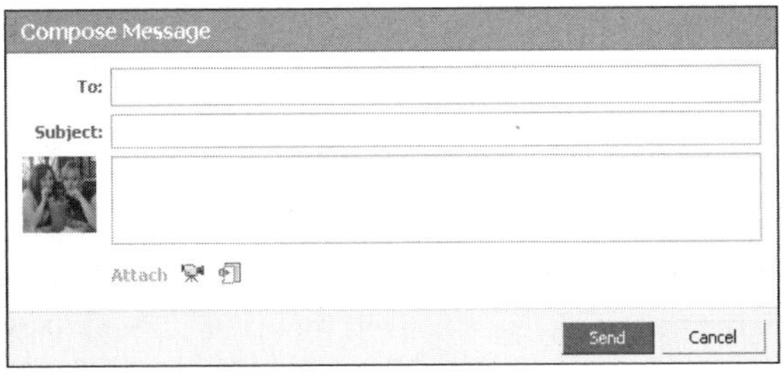

Figure 9-1:
Composing
a message
from the
Facebook
Inbox.

Compose Message

To:
Subject:
Attach
Send   Cancel

3. **Start typing a friend's first name.**

   As you type, you see a drop-down box listing possible matches. When you see the name you're after, you can either click it with your mouse, press the down arrow until the name is selected, or keep typing until the correct name is highlighted in dark blue; then press Enter. If you accidentally select the wrong name, press the Backspace key twice or click X next to the name you're trying to delete.

   To send a message to a friend who isn't a Facebook user, type the full e-mail address and then press Enter.

4. **(Optional) To add another recipient, just start typing the next name or e-mail address; you don't need commas, semi-colons, or anything else to separate the names.**

5. **Fill in the Subject line just as you would in an e-mail.**

   Some people choose to leave this field blank, but we don't recommend it. Blank subjects make it hard for your recipients to find your message again after reading it the first time.

6. **Fill in the Message box with whatever you want to say.**

   Before you send it, we recommend rereading what you've written — Facebook doesn't offer a spell checker on the site. Beneath the Message box, you see the Attach options, which you can ignore for now; we explain those in the upcoming "Sharing is caring" section.

7. **Click the Send button (beneath the Attach options) when your message is complete.**

   If you ever change your mind about sending the message, before hitting Send, click Cancel.

To reply to a message that is just between you and one other person, simply fill in the box underneath Reply and click Send. To reply to a message between you and more than one other person, you have two options. To reply to everybody, fill in the box at the bottom of the message labeled Reply All and click Send. If you want to reply to only a particular person in the conversation, clicking Reply next to that person's name and Profile picture opens a Compose Message window addressed to that particular person with the subject already filled in. Again, you just have to fill in the Message box and click Send.

Some Internet browsers have a built-in spell checker to scan any text that you enter into a Web site. Firefox, for example, puts a dotted red line under any word you enter that its spell checker doesn't recognize. If you happen to be someone who is, what we politely refer to as, *spelling impaired,* you may want to find a browser you like with spell check functionality. Carolyn and Leah both use and recommend Firefox.

Receiving a message

If you find sending a message on Facebook exciting, you should try receiving one. Remember that you can navigate to your Inbox from any page by clicking Inbox on the blue bar at the top. Before you find anything interesting there, you have to inspire one of your friends to send you something.

Post something (see Chapter 6) something inquisitive or provocative to your Profile, as long as you have enough friends who are active on Facebook. Writing a good post usually triggers a message or two. When she posted "*Leah is anticipation incarnate,*" she received several messages from friends taking wild guesses about what she was so excited about, including, "You're psyched for the weekend?" and "You can't wait for our Frisbee game?" One friend told her flat out, "The anticipation is over, here's the message you were waiting for."

Before we walk through the particular experience of receiving a message, it helps to understand how the Inbox is arranged. While you receive Facebook messages, your Inbox fills with rows; each row corresponds to a particular thread. You may be asking, "What do you mean by thread? What does thread have to do with messages? Do I have to sew a button onto one? No one said anything about sewing on Facebook." *Message threads* are best explained by examples.

Say your sister sends you a message on Facebook, then you reply, and then she replies. All three of these messages are considered part of the same thread because they're spawned from the same initial message and between the same people: you and your sister. When you look at your Inbox, you don't see two separate rows for each message your sister sent; you see one row encapsulating the entire thread. When you click that thread's subject, you see, from oldest to newest, all the messages exchanged on that thread: her first one, your reply, and then her reply.

The point of collapsing messages into a thread is to help keep your Inbox clean and easy to read. If it didn't work this way, then when you and your sister messaged each other all the time, your Inbox would eventually fill up. To find older messages from her or anyone, you'd have to keep paging back through the Inbox (or use Inbox search). Your mousing finger doesn't appreciate such abuse. By collapsing messages, whole conversations are kept together, allowing you to see more conversations at one time in your Inbox.

To get a little more complicated, say, Leah, Holly, and Carolyn are friends trying to make plans. The exchange may go something like this:

1. **Leah writes a message to Helen and Patricia.**

2. **Helen replies to Leah and Patricia, and then Patricia replies to all in response.**

   All three of these messages — Leah's initial one and Helen and Patricia's subsequent replies — are considered part of the same thread — a single row in the Inbox — because they're all in response to the same initial message and the participants (Leah, Helen, and Patricia) are the same. By clicking the Subject line of the thread from the Inbox, each person sees all three messages from oldest to newest, as shown in Figure 9-2.

Figure 9-2:
Expanded
view of a
three-way
message
thread
containing
three
messages.

3. **Helen wants to say something privately to Leah about Patricia's response, so she clicks Reply to the right of Leah's name and sends only Leah a message.**

Although this message was a response to the thread, a new thread is created in Leah's Inbox because it has a different set of participants: only Leah and Helen. Separating threads when the audience changes helps you keep track of who *exactly* received which messages. See Figure 9-3.

Figure 9-3:
A collapsed
view of
two thread
examples on
Facebook.

When you sign in to Facebook, you know you have a message waiting for you if you see a number next to Inbox on the blue bar at the top. The number corresponds to the number of unread threads you have. In the second example, where both Patricia and Helen replied to all, Leah would sign in and see *Inbox (1)*. Even though she received two new messages, when she navigates to her Inbox, only one thread has unread messages in it, hence the Inbox (1). Unread threads have light blue backgrounds (refer to Figure 9-3). Click the subject of the thread to open and read the messages.

Anatomy of a thread

In this section, we define a thread in the context of Facebook messaging, demonstrate how they work, and illustrate why they make your messaging life less complicated. Here, we deconstruct a thread:

✔ **Action Check Box:** At the top of the Inbox, you see four buttons: Unread, Read, Report Spam and Delete. To use these buttons, first select a check box at the left of any thread. You can mark types of thread — all in view, all unread messages, or all read messages — by using the Select options at the top of the Inbox. Then, clicking the Read button, for example, puts all checked off threads into an already "read" state. Clicking Delete removes all the selected threads permanently. Note that you can't delete a thread permanently. If someone sends a message in reply to the thread, it returns to your Inbox in full. When you open the thread, however, only the new message shows, and you have to click the Show Deleted Messages on This Thread link to see previously deleted messages.

✔ **Profile Picture:** The picture on the left of a row in the Inbox is that of the person who most recently sent a message on that thread.

✔ **Sender Names:** The names next to the Profile picture are the authors of the most recent messages on that thread. If you are one of those authors, you'll see the word "You" instead of your own name. The first name in this list always matches the picture.

✔ **Date and Time:** Shows when the last message on the thread was sent.

✔ **Subject:** The subject is entered by the first person to send a message on a particular thread.

✔ **Snippet:** Underneath the subject line is the first line of the most recent message. This can be extremely helpful if the sender forgot a subject line, or the message is so short that you can read the whole thing before having to click into the message at all.

Messaging non-friends

In the "Sending a message" section earlier in the chapter, we mention that you can share with friends on Facebook or people not on Facebook via their e-mail addresses. You can also message a person who is on Facebook but not a friend (if that person's privacy settings allow it). This is particularly helpful when you encounter someone on Facebook whom you'd like to say something to, but you're not sure whether you want to add her as a friend yet, or ever. Here are a few examples:

✔ **Identification:** You search for an old friend and find three people with the same name. One Profile has a clear picture of someone who is definitely not your friend. The second person has a Profile picture of someone in the distance climbing a mountain, which could be your friend, except that you notice that person is in the Dallas network and you're sure your friend has never lived in Dallas. The third Profile doesn't have a picture, just a placeholder silhouette. (If that turns out to be your friend, you should recommend he read this book, especially the section in Chapter 2 about setting up a Profile.) From the search results page, you can click Send Message next to the person with the placeholder Profile picture and ask whether you know each other.

✔ **Friend of a Friend:** Here's a story: "Last week my friend had a birthday, and I wanted to send him a present. He was about to move into a new house, and I didn't know the address. I knew the name of the girl he was moving in with, so I found her on Facebook and sent her a message; she sent me the address." For most features on Facebook, you need to be someone's friend or at least in someone's network in order to interact with them in any meaningful way. However, sometimes you have legitimate reasons to contact someone who really doesn't belong in your Friend List. For these interactions, Facebook messaging is perfect.

✔ **Getting to Know You:** Pretend you've just joined a new company and you know very few people. Or, to really experience this example, go join a new company. Say you can use Search to find people who work for the same company you do who you'd like to get to know or ask a question, and send them a message on Facebook.

You should keep in mind three things when messaging non-friends:

✔ **You can message only one non-friend at a time.** You have two ways to do it:

  • By navigating to that person's Profile and clicking Send *so-and-so* a Message from underneath his Profile picture.

  • From the search results page, by clicking Send Message next to the person you want to message.

In the earlier "Messages" section, we said you can message up to 20 people — that applies to only your Facebook Friends and people whose e-mail addresses you already have.

✔ **Some people message non-friends to get a date.** If you're successful here, congratulations! We hope you lovebirds have fun — be safe and invite us to the wedding. Generally, though, we don't recommend using Facebook for this purpose. Unlike some other Web sites, most people aren't on Facebook to find dates. Before you message someone for this purpose, be sure that the Looking For field on that person's Profile strongly indicates openness to romantic inquiries.

Messaging a non-friend should be treated with caution. If you message non-friends too often or too many people report your message as solicitous or unwanted, your account is automatically flagged in the Facebook system. You receive a warning first, but if you continue to repeat the offence, your account may be disabled. Remember earlier in this chapter when we mentioned the sanctity of the Inbox? If every person on Facebook could message everyone else, Inboxes would start to fill with impersonal or unwanted messages, eventually making the Inbox too messy to be functional.

✔ **When you message non-friends, those people receive the ability to message you back, even if you've disabled the ability for strangers to message you.**

Sharing is caring

Have you ever read something on the Web that reminded you of a friend? Or that you thought would appeal to someone in particular? Or that related to a conversation you were *just* having? Or that made you laugh so hard you couldn't wait to find someone to tell? If you're any kind of Internet user, then the answer to those question are "Yes," "Yes," "Yes," and "Oh my gosh, yes." (If you answered them aloud in a public place, you may have caused some head-turning.)

For all those times, Facebook offers Share. *Share* allows you to send a link, a preview, or sometimes a whole piece of content easily to any friend whether that friend is on Facebook or not. If you're thinking e-mail is effective enough for sending this kind of Web content, we're willing to bet you've never tried Share.

In this section, we detail several different ways to share on Facebook. In most cases, clicking one button opens a Compose Message window (see the earlier section, "Sending a message") with the photo, video, or link of the Web page you're currently looking at automatically included in the body of the message.

Sharing from the Inbox

In some ways, sharing from the Inbox is the most difficult way to share because it requires more clicks and some copy and paste action, but it's most similar to what you're probably used to in e-mail:

1. **Copy a link to the page you want to share with someone.**

2. **Click Inbox on Facebook.**

3. **Click the Compose Message button in the upper left.**

4. **Paste the link into the Message box.**

   You can also click the link icon next to the word Attach beneath the message field, and put the link in the field that opens.

Although this is just as much work as sharing a link via e-mail, it's way cooler. When you paste the link into the Compose Message window, the window expands to show a preview of the page you're about to share. The preview includes the title of the page you're sharing and a snippet of text swiped from that page. If the page you're sharing has any images on it, you'll see one of those, too. This is exactly the preview of the page your recipients see when you send the message.

You can change any element of the preview that isn't accurately descriptive of the page you're sharing. You can select a different image by clicking the arrows underneath Choose a Thumbnail. (***Note:*** A *thumbnail* in computer-speak refers to a little version of a larger picture. In this case, Facebook grabs the biggest image from the page you're trying to share, shrinks it, and uses that thumbnail for the preview.) If no picture is actually representative of the content, you can check the No Picture box. You can also edit the title or the snippet of text in the preview by clicking right on the text itself.

If the page you're sharing features a video, a page on YouTube (www. youtube.com), for example, then the actual video shows up in the preview. Here, *preview* is an understatement because you and your recipient can actually play the video straight from the preview without leaving Facebook.

Share buttons on Facebook

Perhaps you've already noticed the little Share links all over Facebook. They show up on albums, individual photos, notes, events, groups, marketplace listings, News Feed stories, user Profiles, and more. They help you share content quickly without having to copy and paste. You don't even have to go into the Inbox.

If you're looking at content on Facebook that you want to show someone, simply click the Share link near it. The Share link actually serves two separate purposes. When you click it, you see two tabs: Post to Profile and Send a Message. Here, we cover the Send a Message tab. You can read about the Post to Profile tab in Chapter 7.

After you click the Share button, a small Share window opens. Click the Send a Message tab, and the Share preview appears with the subject, description, and thumbnail image already filled in for you. All you have to do is fill in the To line. Again, these can be friends on Facebook or the e-mail addresses of those not on Facebook (yet). Optionally, fill in the Message box, and click Send. In Figure 9-4, Leah is preparing to share a photo with Carolyn.

Figure 9-4:
Sharing
a photo
through
Facebook.

Sometimes you share something with someone on Facebook, and he can't see it because of the privacy settings of the content you're sharing. Here's an example: Say you see some photos a friend posted of her recent trip to India. You have another friend (they don't know each other) who is traveling to India soon, so you click the Share link on the album and send it to him. If the first friend has set the privacy of the album so that only her friends can see it, your second friend won't be able to see the album. The second friend receives the message, but instead of the preview, there's a note that the content isn't visible because of privacy settings.

You can't really know beforehand whether someone will be able to see the content you're sharing, but if the two aren't friends with each other, be prepared for your second friend to write back asking you to describe what you were trying to share. Although this can be frustrating at times, especially because there's no good way to work around it, it's helpful to remember the rules are in place to help everyone maintain control over their own content, which ultimately is a good thing.

The Share buttons on the Web

Facebook offers plenty of interesting stuff, but the rest of the Web presents a lot of engaging material as well. Facebook allows (and encourages) Web sites to add Facebook Share buttons near interesting content. For example, next to every article on www.nytimes.com is a Share link. The same is true for www.youtube.com. Clicking Share on these sites offers you a few Web sites' sharing capabilities, including Facebook's. If you click Facebook, you get the same Share pop-up (refer to Figure 9-4) that you do when you click Share buttons on Facebook. Tens of thousands of Web sites have placed Facebook Share buttons on their content to make it easier for you to spread the information love.

The Share bookmarklet

Although it's convenient that many Web sites have Share buttons built right in, you don't actually need any of them for super-simple, one-click sharing. You can add a special Share link to your browser's bookmarks folder, and no matter where you are on the Internet, you can share the page just by clicking that Share bookmarklet. The easiest way to add the Share bookmarklet to your browser is by following the instructions on the Share Bookmarklet page (located at www.facebook.com/share_options.php). After you're done, you'll either have a Share button in your Browser's toolbar, or a link to Facebook Share in your browser's bookmarks or favorites. This all depends on which browser you use (Firefox, Internet Explorer, Safari, and so on, and how it's configured on your computer). After you've added the Share bookmarklet, try it. Head to any Web page you like and click the Share on Facebook link from your bookmark list. (On Internet Explorer, you need to click Favorites first, and then Share on Facebook. On Firefox, you just need to click Share on Facebook from your Bookmarks Toolbar.) Just like all the Share buttons, the bookmarklet recognizes when you're sharing videos or music to make them easy to play directly from the recipient's Inbox.

Chat

Sometimes you've got something to say to someone, and you've gotta say it now. If that someone is not sitting right next to you, the next best thing is if she's ready to send and receive instant messages through Facebook Chat. Chat allows you to see which of your friends are online right at the same time you are, and then enables you to send quick messages back and forth with any one of those people, or have multiple simultaneous conversations with different friends. You'll find Chat in the bottom-right corner of the blue bar: Click the word Chat to see what wonders lay beneath.

Anatomy of Chat

In this section, we detail each component of Facebook Chat so that you can be chatting up your friends in real time, in no time.

- ✔ **Online friends:** When you look at the Chat button, you see a number next to the word Chat. This is the number of your friends who are online in front of their computers right now, signed into Facebook. Clicking anywhere on the Chat button opens the list of all those friends. Next to each you see an icon. A green dot means that person has been using Facebook in the last few minutes. A crescent moon means the friend has his computer signed in to Facebook, but hasn't clicked anything in a while. Friends who don't appear in this list either aren't signed into Facebook, or have hidden themselves from Chat by going offline.

- ✔ **Search online friends:** Soon, if not already, you'll have a lot of friends on Facebook. To quickly find the friend with whom you want to chat, or to see if that friend is even online, click the Chat button, and then start typing that friend's name in the search box. As you type, you see the list of Online Friends narrow to only those with names who match what you've typed. After you see the friend you were looking for, click the name to start chatting. If you get a Could Not Find That Friend Online notice, it means that person has set her status to offline, or is not signed in to Facebook.

- ✔ **Friend Lists:** Friend Lists, which are covered in great detail in Chapter 4, can be quite useful in Chat as an organizational tool. Friend Lists are handy when you're not looking to talk to a particular person, but a friend who has an important characteristic in your life. Leah keeps her friends organized into lists such as Social Friends, Co-workers, and Best Friends. When she has a question about work, she quickly looks to the co-workers list to see who is online to ask. When she's looking for a dinner date, she looks to the Social Friends list. To create a list, click Friends List from the open Chat box. Start typing a new list name underneath Create a New List. When you click OK, you see the new list appear in your Online Friends and instructions to drag friends who are currently online into that list. You can edit Friend Lists more easily by going to the Friends page; again, this is covered in Chapter 4. From the same Friend Lists drop-down, check the Friend Lists that you want to see in chat. (Some lists you may have created for a different purpose, and won't make sense in Chat.) Any Friend List you create directly from Chat will automatically show up there. You can reorder your Friend Lists, if you're using any in Chat. Leah likes to keep her Best Friends list at the top; these are the people she chats with more frequently, so she likes to quickly see when they're online.

✔ **Online status:** The icon of the little man next to a green dot on the Chat button means that you are currently showing as online to some or all of your friends who are looking at their Online Friends lists. This is a signal to those friends that you may be up for chatting. If you're not, but want to continue browsing Facebook, click the Chat button➪Options➪Go Offline. The Chat button changes to reflect your Offline status. While you're offline, your friends can't send you an instant message, and you also can't see which of your friends are online. Clicking the Chat button again shows you the list, but it also brings you back online. Gotta pay to play!

If you've created some Friend Lists, you can selectively be online for people in some lists, and offline for people in other lists. Sometimes at work, Leah goes offline for her social Friend List, but stays online for her Co-worker list so that people who need to talk to her about work can contact her immediately. (Friends see her as offline so they'll either send her a message or call her later.) To use this feature, you first must have Friend Lists as described previously. Then click the Chat bar to display your online friends. Next to the title of the Friend List, you see a little slider that is either set to gray or green. Click the slider to switch the state from online to offline and back again for this list. Just as in the general offline case, if you go offline for a particular Friend List, you can no longer see who from that list is online.

✔ **The Chat window:** Time to get down to the business of actually chatting. To chat with someone, simply click their name in the Online Friends list. A little window pops up: Enter text at the bottom and hit Enter. Your friend sees an identical Chat window appear flashing in his bar on the bottom and hears a little sound. If he replies to you, you'll hear the sound too, and your Chat window will start flashing as well. If you're browsing Facebook at the same time you're chatting, you can always minimize the chat window using the standard minimize icon in the upper right corner of the Chat window. Clicking your friend's name opens the window up again. Clicking X closes the window. Your friend doesn't know you've done this, and, in fact, if you open a new conversation window to that friend, you see exactly where you left off. If you sign out of Facebook or go offline, your friend receives a notice that you've gone offline. You can have several Chat windows open or minimized at the same time.

✔ **Pop-out Chat:** You can also pop out Chat. Clicking Pop Out This Chat from the Chat Options menu opens up a new browser window that is dedicated to Facebook chat, basically sequestering the Chat functionality from the rest of Facebook. Pop-out Chat shows your Online Friends side by side with very large conversation windows with your friends. Larger conversation windows allow you to better focus on your conversations because they take up more of your screen and show you more of the conversation as it's unfolding. Pop-out chat also allows you to browse Facebook without being bothered by little Chat windows blinking all the time. You can always pop your conversations back into Chat by selecting Pop-in Chat from the Options menu.

If you close the Facebook window from which you popped out Chat, this automatically closes the Chat window too, even though it's in a different window.

✔ **Options:** Clicking Options in the Chat window allows you to make a few customizations. A few are mentioned previously, such as setting your online status, reorganizing your Friend Lists, and popping out Chat. From here, you can also Show Feed stories in Chat, which basically means that your friends see what other public actions you're taking on Facebook while talking to them. These can be great ways to keep the conversation moving. You can choose whether to play a sound when you receive new messages, which can be helpful if you don't always notice the blinking. And finally, you can decide whether you want to see your friends' Profile pictures alongside their names in your Online Friends Lists.

Poke

On most Profiles, you see the option to "Poke <*so-and-so*>!" As Facebook employees, probably one of the most frequent questions we're asked is, "What is *Poke?*" We're happy to tell you what it *does,* but we can't tell you what it *is,* other than to say Poke is the interpretive dance of the Internet; it can mean something different to everyone. In some cases, Poke is a form of flirtation. Other times, Poke may mean a genuine *thinking-of-you.* Some people do it just to say, "Hi." Leah's mother Pokes her when she hasn't called home in a while.

Pokes

You were poked by
Leah Pearlman.
poke back | remove poke

Say your wife Pokes you (maybe her Poke means *take out the trash, honey*). The next time you log in to Facebook, on the right side of your Home page, you'll see You Have Been Poked by <*insert your wife's name here*> and a little picture of a poking finger. You have the following options: Poke Back and Hide Poke. *Poke Back* means she'll see the same notice you got the next time she logs in (except with your name instead of hers). *Hide Poke* simply removes the notice from your Home page. If you sense the potential for an endless loop, you sense right.

Requests

Requests

1 friend request

The best way to explain a request on Facebook is by example. The most common type of request is a friend request. When someone finds you on Facebook and clicks Add <*your name*> as a Friend, the next time you log in, you'll see (on the right side of your Home page) that you have a request waiting for you. Other types of requests are invitations to attend events and join groups, or to join a game, and plenty more. Whenever you have a request waiting for you, it shows in this same location on your Home page. If you don't see the Requests section on your Home page, you have no pending requests.

Although sending a request is a private affair, often the response to the request is public. For example, if you request that someone add you as a friend, only that person will ever know about that request, until that person accepts your friend request; then others will see in their News Feeds that you two are now friends. Similarly, no one sees your invitations to join a particular group, but if you act on that request by joining, this information generates a News Feed story to your friends.

Unlike a message, you can't explicitly send a request. Requests are only generated in the context of other actions. For example, if you invite someone to an event (see Chapter 11), a request is automatically sent to that person. If you tag people in someone else's photo (see Chapter 8), a request is sent to the photo owner. If you specify that you're in a relationship with someone in particular, a request is sent to that person to confirm your claim. You also receive a request if someone wishes to join a closed group or event you administer. (For more about groups and administrators, see Chapter 10.)

Notifications

Sometimes rather than reach out *to* you on Facebook, your friends reach out *about* you. For example, say you attend a U2 concert with a friend. The next day, your friend may write a note about how mind-blowing he found the concert, and because you were there next to him having your own mind blown, he tags you in the note. (See Chapter 8 for details on Note tagging.) Your friend wrote the note about you, but he doesn't have to tell you he wrote the note about you because Facebook notifies you when you're tagged in a note or photo. It's a way of letting you know that someone's thinking or talking about you. When you have a tagging notification, you see a little red icon near the bottom-right corner of any page; the number inside the icon lets you know the number of new notifications you have.

 Clicking this flag shows you the last five notifications you've received; clicking See All takes you to the Notifications page, where you see all the notifications you've received for the last seven days.

Here are examples of other kinds of useful notifications:

- When someone tags other people in a photo you uploaded, tags you in note, or tags you in a photo.
- When someone has written on your Wall or on the Wall of a group or event that you admin.
- When someone leaves a comment right after you've commented on a photo, note, or posted item.
- When someone replies to a post that you made on a discussion board.
- When someone comments on one of your notes, posted items, photos that you've taken, or photos that you're tagged in.

You can actually receive an unbounded number of different kinds of notifications, thanks to a rich array of applications. Even if you don't have the Video application added to your Profile, you receive a notification when someone tags you in a video. If someone quotes you using the Quotes application, the notification shows here.

You can stop receiving notifications from any application. Just do this:

1. **Go to the Notifications page by clicking the Notification icon on the bottom-right corner of the page and selecting See All.**

2. **Click X next to the type of notification you no longer want to receive and choose Hide All, or in the column on the right, deselect the check box next to the application you don't want to hear from anymore.**

3. **To receive these notifications again (and see any you've received in the last seven days from that particular application), simply reselect the check box.**

Notifications is kind of an overloaded term on Facebook. The kinds of notifications we describe in this section are those you receive on Facebook when someone talks about you. (They all show on the Notifications tab in your Inbox when you log in.)

Email Notifications, however, refer to the e-mails you receive when anyone is talking about you or to you, as in all the preceding examples, including messages, pokes, and requests. These notifications ensure you know when something of interest is going down on Facebook — even when you're not logged in. To see the full set of notifications and to select which types of e-mail notifications you want to receive, click Settings on the blue bar and then click the Notifications tab. Select all check boxes you find relevant to you, and click Save Changes when you're done.

Public Displays of Affection: Comments, Publisher, and the Wall

So far, we've been talking about the kind of communication that takes place between specific people, in private. Private conversations are perfect for discussing topics relevant to only a few people, confiding in friends, or getting to know (and spending time with) someone specific. This section talks about a different kind of conversation; the kind you have among friends at a party where anyone may jump in or at a concert or bar where others may overhear. These conversations cover topics of potential general interest, unspecific to a particular group of people within the bounds of one's friends or networks. In the real world, we tend to have more conversations that are private. This is not because we're all gossips and secret-keepers: It's because the existing modes of communication, until now, have only facilitated private conversations. A phone call, e-mail, post card, or instant message, for example, always engages a specific set of participants. Facebook supports the aforementioned private conversations, but also offers new ways to communicate to enable the open conversation.

In this section, you read how Facebook allows you to have conversations in a public way that encourages any of your friends to jump in if the mood strikes. Facebook encourages openness by the way it allows more information to flow to more people, which deepens and strengthens relationships.

The writing's on the Wall

Have you ever thought someone was so great that you wanted to look at him and say, "You are *so* great," and then turn to the world and say, "World, isn't he *so* great?" That's the spirit of the Wall. Every user, you included, has a Wall on their Profile page where friends (or anyone else they've permitted) can write things to you or about you that the whole world can see. To write on someone else's Wall, simply navigate to that person's Profile. If it's not selected already, click the Wall tab next to the Profile picture, write your message in the box labeled Write something, and then click Post. When you write on someone's Wall, remember that this generates a News Feed story that any one of your friends may see.

The spirit of posting on someone's Wall is to say nice things about that person in public. In practice, different people in different situations do Wall-writing for different reasons. Some people use the Wall to have basic back-and-forth conversations similar to how other people use messaging. Others use the Wall as a place to comment on a change to someone's Profile. If you change your status to something intriguing like *<Your Name> is keeping a secret,* expect a friend or two to ask about it on your Wall. If you change your relationship status, add new favorite bands, or update your Profile picture, you'll probably get feedback on your Wall as well.

A Wall practice that is nearly universal among Facebook users is the "Happy Birthday!" Wall post. Assuming you leave your privacy set so that your friends can see your birthday on your Profile (you can hide the year), they will also see a reminder on their Home pages as your big day approaches. On the actual day, you can expect to receive Wall posts all day long wishing you a happy birthday. If this doesn't happen, either you need more Facebook friends or you need to buy this book for some of the friends you do have.

When you look at a friend's Wall, you'll notice something *very familiar.* In Chapter 2, 3, and just about every other chapter, we mention the Publisher — the box that lives on the top of your Home page and Profile, into which you can publish any piece of content for the world to see. When you look at other people's Profiles, you see the same Publisher, with only a few differences. The first difference is that the prompt is different. Your Publisher asks you "What's on your mind?" The Publisher on a friends' Wall asks you to "Write something . . ." The implication is "Write something for this person." The other difference is that in your own Publisher, you can attach different types of media from the applications you use. On a friend's Publisher, you can attach different types of media from the applications you use *or* the ones that friend uses. More on that in a minute. In Figure 9-5, you see an example of Leah just having written on Carolyn's Wall. You see a few different links and buttons (as shown in Figure 9-5). Here's how they work:

Figure 9-5: The anatomy of a Wall on a Profile.

> ✔ **Link** works just like the Attach button in the Inbox. (See the earlier "Sharing from the Inbox" section.) Click Link and then paste a link into the box. This puts a Share preview directly on your friend's Wall, along with any comments you add.

✔ **Photo** lets you upload a photo to your friend's Profile, or else snap a real-time photo from your Webcam if you have one. All the steps to uploading a photo to your friend's Wall are revealed when you click this button.

✔ **Video** works only if you have a Webcam on your computer. Click this button, and recording begins. If you're looking to tug at the heartstrings of the recipient, this is a great way to say hello in an absolutely endearing way.

✔ **Gift** takes you to a virtual gift shop where you can choose a fun or personal picture to have pasted on your friend's Wall. Most gifts cost $1 each, so if you receive one, someone cares about you at least $1 worth. (Actually, you can purchase 10 gifts for $5, so someone may only care about you 50 cents worth, but still.)

✔ **Share** is simply how you submit the text you wrote in the box on the Wall. If you change your mind after you've posted, click Remove right next to your Wall post.

✔ **Wall-to-Wall** is another way that Facebook makes communicating easy. Say you're looking at Friend A's Profile. On his Wall, you see a post from Friend B that doesn't make sense: "And what did she say after that?" This usually happens because B's post is a response to something A wrote on B's Wall first. In order to see the full flow of the conversation, click Wall-to-Wall. It shows you the recent Wall posts, in order, between A and B. Note that you only see this option when you can see the Profiles of A and B.

✔ **Remove** (not pictured in Figure 9-5) is an option you see only next to Wall posts you've written or ones that appear on your Wall. Note that if you write on someone's Wall and then delete it, by default she will still get an e-mail notification informing her that you've written on her Wall.

Note: For some of your friends, you may see a little drop-down arrow next to Gift. This means these friends use applications that allow you to add other types of media to a friend's Wall. To see what each of these applications do, we recommend clicking the arrow, clicking the application that interest you, and then following the instructions that pop up. You can't go too wrong on the Wall, because as soon as you post, you can always quickly hit Remove.

Care to comment?

Leaving comments is another form of public communication. You can leave a comment on a photo, a video, a note, or various other things just by writing in the Add a Comment box beneath the object (some objects have an Write a Comment link that you have to click first to see the box). Leaving comments has the double-nice property of informing the content author something about his work *and* attracting other's attention to the content when the comment shows in other people's News Feed.

Broader audience

Sometimes you have something to say, but no one in particular to say it to. For those times, use your Publisher — the big empty box at the top of the home page that asks you, "What's on your mind?" We've covered the Publisher in Chapters 2 and 3, but want to bring it up again here in the case of communicating with your friends because sometimes putting a message out there for the world to see can be the best way to get a conversation started. Sometimes people use their status to help connect in person: *Leah is at Starbucks if you want to join.* Sometimes, they use it to keep everyone informed of things they need to know: *Carolyn is off to Spain — don't expect her to reply to anything.* Often, it's a reflection of mood that may strike a chord with someone else, but you can't know who till you post: *Blake is happy it's Friday.* And sometimes, people write whatever they want for whatever reason:

> *Dustin loves comics about dinosaurs.*

> *Katie does breakfast for dinner.*

> *Ezra says pay attention to politics, people.*

When you post something, it shows on your Profile and in your friends' News Feeds, so remember: If you write something intriguing like *<Your name> is about to pop the question,* you'll probably hear about it from your friends.

Facebook in an emergency

Communicating on Facebook can be a lot of fun. It can also be useful, emotional, and enriching. However, sometimes, the ability to communicate on a wide scale with those you know can be critical.

On April 29, 2007, at Virginia Polytechnic Institute and State University (Virginia Tech), a lone gunman killed 32 students and wounded many more. While the story broke over television and radio, those with loved ones on the campus scrambled for information. Students across Virginia Tech who were not involved in the attack logged in to Facebook. To help reassure their friends and family that they were okay, the students set their statuses to something similar to *<so-and-so> is safe.* Thanks to reporters and word-of-mouth, news spread quickly that Facebook was the fastest way to confirm the safety of any particular Virginia Tech student.

Part III
Getting Organized

The 5th Wave   By Rich Tennant

"I know it's a short profile, but I thought 'King of the Jungle' sort of said it all."

In this part . . .

When we talk about organization, we aren't talking about cleaning up your desk so all the piles of paper sit at right angles to each other. No, we mean the idea of getting organized — around an idea, a common interest, or even a common time.

In this part, we go in depth into how you can use Pages and Groups to organize people around beliefs, favorites, and even around slogans. We also talk about how to organize your life (and the people in it) into conveniently planned events. The best part about organizing on Facebook is that it can often lead to organizing off Facebook.

Chapter 10

Creating and Joining Groups on Facebook

*H*umans are social animals. Although you spend plenty of time tweaking and massaging your Profile, the real value of Facebook lies at the intersections of its massive network: more than 200 million people in every country in the world meeting up with the people they care about for a virtual cup of coffee. Can you foot this bill? We'll get the next one.

The coffeehouses on Facebook are known as *Groups*. Every 30 seconds, a new discussion is started in one of more than 10 million Groups on Facebook, on topics ranging from The Beatles to global warming to Ottawa University's Class of 1958 reunion. If you can't find the Group you're looking for, you can create and host it yourself. Like everything on Facebook, you decide who can participate — from ten of your closest friends to everyone in the world.

Getting Going with Groups

Like Photos, *Groups* is a pre-installed application built for you by Facebook. You can access the application's Home page (Figure 10-1) by choosing Groups in your Applications menu in the Chat bar at the bottom of any page. This page shows you what's new in the Groups scene on Facebook, in terms of which Groups your friends have joined recently and which of the Groups that you participate in have been updated. You can also browse and search Groups or even create your own.

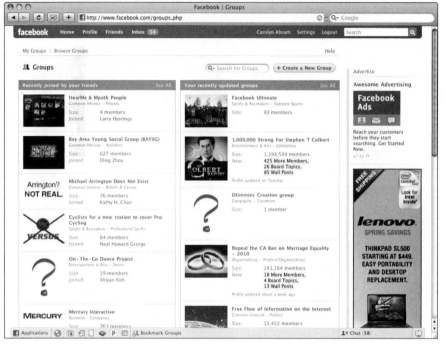

Figure 10-1: Find out what happened recently in the Groups you and your friends care about.

Joining a Group

The best way to understand a Facebook Group is to look at one from a member's perspective. We're using the Beatles Fans Around the World Group, where more than 100,000 fans congregate, as an example. To find this Group, just follow these steps:

1. **Type** Beatles Fans Around the World **into the Search box and press Enter.**

   Note that Groups on Facebook may share similar or even identical names. If you're having trouble finding it, the address is `www.facebook.com/group.php?gid=2204708817`. The Group is shown in Figure 10-2. (More information about searching for Groups comes later in the chapter in the section, "Searching Groups".)

2. **Click the Join This Group link under the picture at the top right of the page and become an insider.**

   (You can't see this link in Figure 10-2 because the monkeys who take our screenshots are already members.)

   If you don't want to frolic in strawberry fields forever, don't worry; we show you how to leave the Group when we finish.

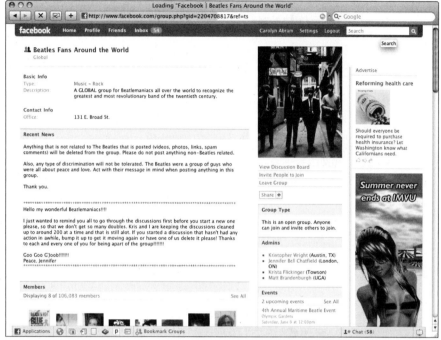

When you join a Group, your fellow members can't see your Profile unless they're your friends, your friends' friends, or in your networks (depending on your privacy settings). In other words, standard Facebook privacy rules apply; Groups don't influence them in any manner. The only indirect consequence of joining a Group is that the Group appears in the Groups section of your Profile (unless you've hidden that section) and the action of joining shows up in your Recent Activity on your Wall. Furthermore, a story about your joining the Group may appear in your friends' Home pages. None of these consequences occurs if the Group you join is secret, which is a concept we discuss in the upcoming section, "Creating Your Own Groups."

Anatomy of a Group

The first thing you see when you visit a Group is its Home page. Just as your Profile provides a summary of you (not to say that *you* could ever be summarized), this page provides an overview of what's happened in the Group recently, including snapshots of the most recent photos, videos, and member comments.

In **bold,** at the top of every Group's Home page sits the most important bit of information: the Group name.

Depending on privacy settings (see the later "Creating Your Own Groups" section for more on this), you may be able to see all of a Group's contents before joining it even though you can't post new content. That's the case with the Beatles Fans Around the World Group because the administrator has chosen the most flexible settings.

In many ways, a Group is similar to a Profile shared among its members. A Group's Home page is divided into a wide, left column and a thin, right column; each column contains a number of different sections. Each section is delineated by a blue title bar and contains the most recent content posted in that section, such as the last few photos or discussion topics. To see everything posted to a section, click See All on its title bar. A group administrator may decide to hide certain sections for his Group, although we purposely chose this Group because it contains all the possible sections.

From top to bottom, the left column offers the following sections:

- **Basic Info and Contact Info:** This section contains the basic details of the Group, such as a description that outlines its purpose as well as its type and subtype, which must be standard Facebook categories (see the upcoming section, "Creating Your Own Groups"). The type of Beatles Fans Around the World is *Music,* and its subtype is *Rock;* you can click either word to see other Groups belonging to the selected type.

    If the Group represents a real-world group (for example, the National Breast Cancer Foundation), the Information section may also contain the organization's contact information, such as a physical address or an Internet address. Because the administrator of this Group isn't an official representative of the band and has no public presence, he has decided to jokingly specify the address as *151 E. Broad St.* in homage to Paul McCartney's album, *Give My Regards to Broad Street.*

- **Recent News:** This section discusses recent events, such as a re-release of a classic Beatles album. This section appears only when the Group administrator provides recent news.

- **Members:** This section shows you other Facebook members who are part of the Group. If any of your friends are in the Group, they're listed first, followed by other people who belong to your networks (if you have any). This reflects the belief that the people close to you are always more interesting than strangers. *Remember:* Groups don't influence the basic Facebook privacy model, so you're not able to see the Profile of a fellow Group member unless she's already your friend, is a friend of your friend, or belongs to one of your networks.

    Beatles Fans Around the World has more than 100,000 members, which is impressive but far from the size of the largest Facebook Groups, which boast more than a million members (such as "When I Was Your Age, Pluto Was a Planet"). Of course, more than 500 distinct Groups about

The Beatles exist throughout Facebook, each with their own member base and personality. That's a prime benefit of it being so easy to create a Group on Facebook: One size need not fit all.

✔ **Discussion Board:** The home of lively conversations and debates between members, the discussion board is the nexus of a Group. Each topic in a discussion board represents a new area of the broader Group dialogue where particularly insightful or provocative topics can garner hundreds or thousands of responses. For instance, as you can imagine, the "What's your favorite song by the Beatles?" topic has kicked off quite a heated debate. We can't imagine why because the answer is *Hey Jude.*

✔ **The Wall:** This Wall may look a tad different from the Wall you are used to encountering on your friends' Profiles, but its purpose is the same — it is the perfect mechanism for casual, free-form commenting. In Beatles Fans Around the World, members often use the Wall to verbalize passionately their gratitude for 50 years of great music. They aren't trying to start discussions.

✔ **Photos:** As you might guess, this section contains photos that are of relevance to the Group. In this case, fans of The Beatles have posted more than 2,000 of their favorite photos of their beloved band. Only a selection of the most recent photos is shown on the Group's Home page, but you can click See All to view the rest of them.

In some instances, these photos are of Group members posing with the band long ago. Such photo sharing is a staple of many Facebook Groups. For instance, visit Facebook hiking Groups and you see members sharing pictures of their most recent conquests. Group members can leave comments on these photos just as your friends can comment on the pictures you post to your Profile.

✔ **Links:** This section contains links to types of content that don't belong under Photos or Videos. For example, a member named Michelle posts a link to a funny article that explains how to persuade your friends to like The Beatles, while another member named Daniel posts a link to his favorite video of The Beatles. (You may be wondering why he put that video in Posted Items rather than in Videos. He did that because he found the video on another popular video Web site called YouTube. He doesn't have the right to copy the video into Facebook Video, so he just points members to its original home.) Like virtually everything else in a Facebook Group, you and other members can comment on the items that people post.

✔ **Videos:** Like photos, videos enrich Groups by moving them beyond mere discussion. Here, fans of The Beatles tickle their memories with clips from the band's golden years. Viewing videos is very similar to viewing photos. The most recent videos are shown on the Group's Home page, and you can click See All to view the rest. To watch a video, click it. Group members can also leave comments on videos.

Whew. You'd think that'd be enough, but settle down: We've got another column to go! The right column contains information that may be interesting to members but is probably less important than the things we just discussed. It includes

- ✔ **A picture:** Group administrators can choose any picture they like to represent the Group on the Home page, but they have to be picky: They get only one.

- ✔ **Action links:** Just as your Profile contains a set of important actions (such as View Photos) underneath your picture, a series of action links follows the Group picture. These include View Discussion Board (which is a shortcut to the See All link of the Discussion Board section), and either Join This Group or Leave Group, depending on whether you're already a member of the Group. If the Group is *closed* (see the later "Creating Your Own Groups" section), you may join only with a Group administrator's approval, in which case the link reads, Request to Join Group. If you're the administrator of a Group, you see additional administrative options here.

  If the Group administrator chooses to allow it (the administrator of Beatles Fans Around the World has), you also see a link to Invite People to Join.

- ✔ **Share:** The Share links scattered throughout Facebook allow you to quickly share with your friends interesting content that you find, either by sending it to them in a message or by posting it onto your Profile. This Share button allows you to share a link to the Group (along with a preview containing the Group's name, description, and picture).

  If the Group is *open,* you may want to use the Invite People to Join link to send an invitation to join rather than a mere link. If the Group is *secret,* you can't share a link to the Group with anyone who isn't already a member because the Group's privacy settings don't permit it. (See the upcoming section, "Step 1: Group Info," for more information about open and secret Groups.)

- ✔ **Group Type:** This section displays information about the Group's privacy settings. As we mentioned, the administrator of Beatles Fans Around the World chose the most flexible settings possible in his effort to attract fans of the Beatles. This means he exposes the existence of the Group to everyone and allows anyone to see the Group, join it, and invite others to join. This latter set of permissions constitutes an *open* Group. A Group may also be *closed* or *secret,* as we discuss in the "Step 1: Group Info" section, later in this chapter.

- ✔ **Officers:** If a Group has any officers, the Officers section lists its names, primary networks, and titles. Because this concept doesn't really make sense in Beatles Fans Around the World (the administrator has not designated any officers), the section doesn't appear. For Groups that have real-world counterparts, like a school newspaper, the officers section can accurately represent the Editor-in-Chief, Business Manager, and so on. For Groups that are less serious (as many Facebook Groups are), you'll often notice officer designations like "Chief Dummy" and "Dummy-in-residence." See the upcoming "Managing your Group" section for more information about officers.

✔ **Admins:** The Admins section lists the names and primary networks of all the Group's administrators. Whoever creates a Group is automatically the administrator of that Group, meaning he writes the Group's information, controls its privacy settings, moderates its discussions, and generally keeps the Group running smoothly. He can also promote other members to administrators to grant them the same privileges. See the upcoming section, "Managing your Group member list," for help with promoting members to administrators.

✔ **Events:** You may not see this box if the Beatles Fans around the World has no upcoming events. If it does, you see not only the box, but the name of the upcoming event within it. Group admins can invite all members of a group to a particular event, which we talk about in the "Creating a Group Event" section at the very end of this chapter.

✔ **Related Groups:** This section displays a list of other Facebook Groups that you may be interested in based on the Group you're currently looking at. *Related* is a bit of a misnomer; Facebook builds this list by looking at the other Groups that members belong to, rather than looking for other Groups that offer similar content. As a result, the list often contains quirky Groups that are more reflective of the member's interests and personalities than of the Group's topic.

We've been referring to the administrator of the Beatles Fans Around the World Group throughout this chapter. Thanks to the Admins section, we can finally give him proper recognition! There's Matt, and as you see from the parenthetical note after his name, at the time of this writing, he hails from the University of Georgia (UGA is his primary network). There's also Kristopher, Krista, and Jennifer. Thanks guys!

A Group's Home page ends how it began: with a gray bar. The bottom bar contains a Report Group option that you can use whenever you encounter a Group you consider offensive. See the "Finding the Group for You" section, later in this chapter, for more information about reporting Groups.

Adding your two cents (or more)

The best way to get started with a Group is to contribute to the discussions that are already taking place among its members. Click a topic that sounds interesting in the Discussion Board section and dive in. ***Remember:*** You can click See All on the section title bar to see all the ongoing discussions for the Group rather than just the most recent ones displayed on the Group's Home page. If you don't see a topic that strikes your fancy, start your own by clicking Start New Topic.

After you reply to an existing topic or start your own, Facebook helps you keep up with the conversation in a number of ways:

✔ Facebook sends you a notification whenever someone replies to one of your discussion posts. By default, this notification arrives not just on Facebook but also via e-mail. You can turn this off if you don't want it; see Chapter 9 for more information on notifications.

✔ The Groups page (which you get to from the Applications menu) displays a list of your recently updated Groups in its right column. The yellow-highlighted text indicates the Group's content that changed.

✔ As always, your home page, especially your News Feed, is a great way to keep up with what's happening in your Facebook universe.

Finding the Group for You

Groucho Marx once said that he wouldn't want to be part of any club that would have him as a member. He probably wouldn't be happy about Facebook, which has millions of public Groups that would readily accept him, you, or anyone else who'd like to join. This section helps you pinpoint the Groups that cover your interests, whether you search for specific Groups, browse Groups, or check out Groups that your friends like.

Searching Groups

If you already have a topic in mind, the following is the fastest way to find Groups that cover it:

1. **Click within the Search box.**

   The Search box sits on top right corner of the big blue bar on the top of every Facebook page.

2. **Enter the name of a Group you wish to find, such as** Cat Lovers, **and press Enter.**

   The search results contain content from all over Facebook, such as Profiles, Groups, and Events.

3. **Look for the Groups category on the left side of the search page and click on any of the Groups in that space to learn more.**

To search only Groups and thus avoid Step 3, use the Search box at the top of the Groups page. The search results are the same in each case. To navigate to the Groups page, choose Groups from the Applications menu (in the Chat bar at the bottom of every page).

When an administrator creates a Group, she may restrict access to a Group by network (if she has one), or by changing the Group access type to *closed* or *secret,* as we discuss in the upcoming section, "Creating Your Own Groups." Facebook displays only the Groups that you have permission to see in the list of search results.

Narrowing your search

If you're having trouble finding the Group you're looking for, you can try refining your search by Group type.

To filter your Group search results, first make sure you are looking at *only* Group search results, and follow these steps:

1. **Click on the menu next to the word Show right above the search results.**

   By default, you are shown all group types.

   The menu displays different types of groups, such as Common Interest or Music.

2. **Choose the category type you are looking for.**

3. **Click the Filter Results button. This reloads the page and reveals an additional menu.**

   This menu has sub-types for the original category you chose.

4. **Choose any relevant sub-types and click Filter Results again.**

Filtered results can sometimes be a little funky because they rely on people to classify their groups correctly and people tend to take this classification not so seriously. Group search filter options are shown in Figure 10-3.

You can also narrow your search more quickly by adding words to your search phrase to make it more specific. For instance, searching for *Cats the musical* rather than *Cats* returns results that are more relevant.

Whether the search filters help, you can clear them and return to the original results list by clicking the original Groups filter on the left side of the Search page. You can also return the Group Type menu to All Group Types and click Filter Results again.

Figure 10-3:
The Filter
Groups by
Type
drop-down
list helps
you filter
your Groups
search.

Checking out popular Groups

When you go to the bookstore to find an interesting book, you're not at the mercy of the staff. Your friends, co-workers, classmates, and neighbors — who know you better than anyone — can guide your search by telling you which books *they* enjoyed. Groups are no different, so don't worry if you're having trouble finding good ones; your friends and networks are here to help.

Whenever you visit the Groups page, you see a running list of Groups recently joined by your friends in the left column. Your friends don't manually suggest these Groups to you; Facebook assumes that your friends join Groups that interest them and automatically pushes those Groups to you. To see all Groups recently joined by your friends, click the See All link on the column's title bar or the See All Recent Groups Joined by Friends link at the bottom of the list.

Reporting offensive Groups

If you stumble upon an offensive Group in your travels, you should report it to Facebook so that the company can take appropriate actions. To report a Group:

1. **Click the Report Group link on the gray bar at the bottom of its Home page.**

   You see a form like that shown in Figure 10-4.

2. **Fill out the report by choosing a reason for the report and include a comment that explains why you feel the Group should be removed.**

3. **Click Submit.**

Facebook removes all Groups that

✔ Contain pornographic material or inappropriate nudity

✔ Attack an individual or Group

✔ Advocate the use of illicit drugs

✔ Advocate violence

✔ Serve as advertisements or are otherwise deemed to be spam by Facebook

Many Groups on Facebook take strong stands on controversial issues, such as abortion or gun control. In an effort to remain neutral and promote debate, Facebook won't remove a Group because you disagree with its statements.

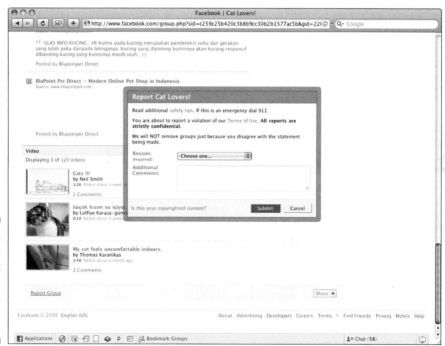

Figure 10-4:
If you find a Group that is offensive, Facebook is here to help.

Creating Your Own Groups

If you can't find the Group you're looking for on Facebook, or even if you can but you just want one with a different personality or member list, you're welcome to create your own. As a Group's creator, you're by default the *Group administrator,* which means that you write the Group's information, control its privacy settings, moderate its discussions, and generally keep it running smoothly. You can also promote other members of the Group to administrators to grant them the same privileges, and then they can help you with these responsibilities.

To begin creating a Group:

1. **Choose Groups from the Applications menu on the left-hand navigation bar to navigate to the Groups page.**

2. **Click the Create a New Group button at the top right of the page.**

Creating a Group entails at least one step — specifying the Group's name and other basic information — and you have the option of completing two additional steps: customizing how your Group appears to its members, and creating a member list. Facebook divides the process into three screens, one for each step, and highlights the current step at the top of the page. We discuss each step in depth in the next few sections. You can edit any property of a Group except for its name at any time after its creation, so don't fret too much about getting things just right your first time around.

Although you can't manually delete a Group that you create, Facebook automatically deletes Groups that have no members. If you're the only member, simply leave the Group and poof! — the Group is gone. If there are other members, you (as administrator) can remove them from your Group using the Members dashboard. See "Managing your Group" later in this chapter.

Step 1: Group Info

The Group Info step asks you for the following information about the Group. Some information may not be relevant or desirable for the Group you have in mind. You must enter the information designated as *required,* as shown in Figure 10-5.

✔ **Group Name (required):** Enter the name of the Group you wish to create, such as Beatles Fans Around the World. If you want people who you don't know to join your Group, choose longer, more specific names to help them locate it through a search.

✔ **Network:** This option is only applicable to people who belong to work or school networks. If you belong to one of these, you have the ability to limit accessibility to only people in that network. For example, you may want to limit people who can join your company's basketball team's Facebook Group to only people from your company. Use this drop-down to limit membership to a certain network. If not, your Group is visible to everyone, although you will be able to limit people from interacting in other ways that we cover later.

✔ **Description (required):** A brief overview of the purpose or mission of the Group. This is similar to an organization's charter and is one of the first things a user sees when looking at your Group and determining whether to join.

✔ **Group Type (required):** A broad category that describes the focus of your Group, such as Music. You must also choose a subtype that further narrows the focus, such as Rock.

✔ **Recent News:** Anything that's happened recently that may be of interest to the Group's members. For Groups reflecting real-world organizations, this may be information about recent organizational activities posted for the benefit of members who didn't participate (say, the outcome of a blood drive). For Groups uniting people with a shared hobby or interest, such as hiking, this may be pertinent news about the activity, such as the temporary closure of a popular hiking trail. *Remember:* You can update this information at any time.

✔ **Office:** If your Group represents an organization that operates on a work or school campus, you can enter the colloquial location of the organization's office here, such as Tressider Building, Second Floor. If your Group has a broader audience for whom such an intimate description would not be helpful, you can enter a more precise physical address in the Street and City/Town fields, as described later in this list.

✔ **Email:** The e-mail address of a person or organization that's pertinent to the Group. It isn't necessary (and may be undesirable) to list your own e-mail address here. As the administrator, your name is listed under the Admins section of the Group's Home page, and members always have the option to send you a Facebook message.

✔ **Street:** If the Group represents a real-world organization that has a physical office, you can enter its street address here.

✔ **City/Town:** If the Group represents a real-world organization that has a physical office, you can enter the city or town of the office here. Combined with the Street field discussed above, these constitute the most important parts of a physical address.

Figure 10-5:
You need
to enter
only four
basic bits of
information
to get your
Group up
and running.

Step 2: Customize

Figure 10-6 represents the customize page, where you can add your Group's representative picture, as well as edit what members will see and be able to do on your Group's Home page.

Here's what you can do:

✔ **Upload picture:** The photo you choose to represent your Group will be featured prominently at the top of it, as well as in search results across the site. For that reason, people frequently try to find a photo that best explains what the Group is all about. For members of Facebook Ultimate Frisbee, it's a team photo. For Beatles Fans around the World, it's a picture of the Beatles. To add this image, follow these instructions:

   1. **Click the Browse or Choose File button to open your computer's standard interface for finding a file.**

   2. **Navigate to (and select) the picture on your computer that you want to use.**

     The picture you choose must meet the file size and type requirements outlined on the page. If you're not sure whether your desired picture meets the requirements, select the picture and continue with these steps. Facebook notifies you if the picture you choose can't be used.

3. **Check the box to certify that you have the right to distribute the picture (it isn't copyrighted) and that it doesn't violate the Facebook terms of use (it isn't pornographic or otherwise offensive).**

4. **Click Upload Picture.**

✔ **Web site:** The address of a Web site that's pertinent to the Group. If the Group represents a real-world organization, such as the National Breast Cancer Foundation, this would typically be the organization's official Web address, such as www.nationalbreastcancer.org. If the Group brings together fans of a particular television show, this would often point to the television show's official home on the Web.

✔ **Options:** A mixture of options that control which sections appears on your Group's Home page and, where applicable, who can add content to them. We explain these sections in "Anatomy of a Group" earlier in this chapter.

- *Show Related Groups:* Shows a section that displays a list of other Facebook Groups related to yours. This is largely determined by looking at which other Groups your Group's members are likely to belong, so the listed Groups may not necessarily relate to your Group's topic. You cannot control what appears in this list, and the contents can change at any time.

- *Show Related Events:* One of the cool integration points of both Groups and Events is that a Group can host an Event, enabling easy inviting of all the Group members, and the appearance of that Event in this section, should you choose to enable it. You (and the other admins) control what appears here by creating these Events wherein your Group is the host.

- *Enable Discussion Board:* Shows the discussion board. Groups are typically used to host discussions among members, so you probably want to keep this enabled.

- *Enable the Wall:* Shows the Wall, which is typically used for informal, casual remarks from members. If you'd rather encourage the more structured, in-depth discussion usually found in the discussion board, you may want to hide the Wall.

- *Enable Photos:* Shows the photos section. If you decide to show this section, you may also decide who may add photos to it. By default, all members of the Group may add photos, but you can restrict this to administrators by selecting Only Allow Admins to Upload Photos.

- *Enable Videos:* Shows the videos section. If you decide to show this section, you may also decide who may add videos to it. By default, all members of the Group may add videos, but you can restrict this to administrators by selecting Only Allow Admins to Upload Videos.

- *Enable Links:* Shows the Links section. If you decide to show this section, you may also decide who may post links to it. By default, all members of the Group may post links, but you can restrict this to administrators by selecting Only Allow Admins to Post Links.

✓ **Access:** When you designate a network for your Group, you indicate the broadest set of people who are allowed to join it. You can further restrict this set via one of the three access settings that Facebook offers:

- *This Group Is Open:* This default setting allows that anyone can view the Group's content. Only members in the Group's network (which is everyone if the network is Global) can join the Group. Group members can also invite members of the network to join.

- *This Group Is Closed:* Anyone in the chosen network can see the basic Group information, but only members can see the photos, discussions, and so forth. People who want to join must request membership, and you, or another administrator, have the opportunity to approve or deny these requests.

- *This Group Is Secret:* People can join the Group only if you or another administrator invites them. They cannot request membership; they won't even know of the Group's existence because it won't appear in search results or on the Profiles of its current members. Therefore, only members can see the Group description, discussions, photos, and so forth. The Group's network has little effect here given these additional restrictions on membership.

Figure 10-6:
Make your
Group your
own.

When you finish customizing your Group, click Save at the very bottom of the page. If you have an open or closed Group, you see a prompt asking you if you wish to publish a post to your Wall (and, therefore, to your friends' home pages), as shown in Figure 10-7. Click Publish if you want your friends to see the Group.

Figure 10-7:
Post to your
Wall for
additional
distribution.

Now, pass go, collect $200, and proceed to inviting people to your Group.

Step 3: Members

The final step enables you to invite people to join your Group. Additionally, after you've sent invitations, you see a fourth tab, titled Edit Members, appear. You'll be able to manage your admins, officers, and members from here after people start to join.

Remember that if you designated your Group as open or closed, it's not necessary for you to invite people; they may discover the Group on their own via News Feed, the search feature, the Groups section on their friends' Profiles, or many other sources. However, if you chose to create a secret Group, these invitations are the only means through which someone can discover and join your Group.

If you decide to invite people to your Group, it takes just a few seconds:

1. **Invite your friends who are already on Facebook by selecting them from the *Friend Selector,* as shown in Figure 10-8.**

   The Invite Members page displays a *Friend Selector,* which is a grid of your friends. To select any friend, you simply have to click her face or name. If you know exactly who you're going for, you can start to type her name into field labeled Find Friends. The grid filters down as you type. Select your friends whenever you're ready.

When you invite a Facebook member to join your Group, he receives a Facebook request from you. Depending on his notification settings, he may also receive an e-mail from Facebook regarding your invitation. Note that Facebook doesn't send the invitation to your friend as soon as you select him in the list. Keep reading for instructions on actually sending the invitation.

You can double-check your member list by clicking the Selected view of the Friend Selector (found in the upper-right corner above your friends' faces). If you accidentally selected the wrong Blake Ross, you can undo it by clicking his face again.

2. **Invite friends who aren't yet on Facebook to join the Group by typing their e-mail addresses (separated by commas) into the box labeled Invite People Via Email below the Friend Selector.**

   Can't remember their addresses? No problem. Click the Import Email Addresses link to open a window that enables you to select their addresses from your e-mail address book, assuming Facebook supports your e-mail provider (it supports the most popular ones). This process is very similar to that outlined in Chapter 6. Forgot some folks? Enter more addresses into the box and click Add again.

3. **(Optional) Include a message with your invitation by typing it in the box below the invitee list.**

   Although optional, this adds a personal touch and makes your invitation more persuasive.

4. **Click Send Invitations.**

   The invitations are sent to the people on the list. Forgot some people? You can repeat these steps at any time.

Managing your Group

When you finish creating your Group, you may want to do a number of things as people start to join. Many of these steps appear as action links under the picture on your Group's Home page. These actions are visible and available only to you and other administrators; if you recall, you did not see these special links when viewing the Beatles Fans Around the World Group earlier in this chapter. This section outlines the additional power (and responsibility) you wield as a Group administrator.

Designating Group officers

Many Groups reflect real-life Groups or clubs that have members serving in various leadership roles. Administrators can mirror these positions in a Facebook Group by designating members as officers and assigning titles, such as Secretary or Treasurer. To promote members to administrators, see the "Managing your Group member list" section later in this chapter.

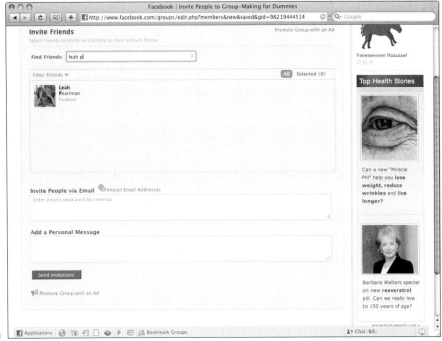

Figure 10-8:
Inviting
Facebook
friends to
your Event
is as simple
as selecting
them.

When your Group has officers, an Officers section appears on its Home page listing their names, primary networks, and titles. Group officers don't have the same privileges as administrators or any more administrative rights than regular members do.

To designate officers of your Group,

1. **Click the Edit Group link under the picture in the right column of your Group's Home page.**

2. **Click the Officers tab at the top of the Edit Group page.**

   You see two lists: a list of the officers (and their positions), followed by a list of non-officers.

3. **Promote a non-officer to an officer by clicking the Make Officer link next to her name.**

4. **When Facebook prompts you, enter a position (such as Secretary) for the officer-to-be.**

   You can enter any position you want, so it can be as silly or serious as your personality (and your Group's personality) dictates.

5. **Click Add to promote the member to officer or Cancel if you changed your mind.**

   A notification is sent to the member letting her know about the change.

6. **To change the position of an existing officer, click Edit next to his name in the Officers list. To demote an existing officer back to a regular member, click Remove Officer.**

Managing your Group member list

After you have members in your Group, you can use the Group member list to remove (and even permanently ban) undesirable members, promote your most trusted members to administrators, or demote your existing administrators (if any) back to regular members:

1. **Click the Edit Members action link under the picture in the right column of your Group's Home page.**

   A list of all Group members appears. Next to each name are two buttons: an X and a button that says either Make Admin or Remove Admin, depending on the admin status of each person.

2. **Use the link to the right of each member name that corresponds to the action you wish to take:**

   If you want to make someone an admin, click Make Admin. If you want to remove someone's admin responsibilities, click Remove Admin. If you want to remove someone, click the X. When you remove someone from a Group, you also have the option to ban her permanently. This is extremely useful in the case of a Group member who is harassing others or being abusive within the Group.

Messaging your Group members

Although you can use your Group's discussion board and its Wall to communicate with your members, there may be times when you want to guarantee that members read your message. Facebook messages are just the ticket because they appear in your members' Facebook Inbox, and (depending on notification settings) your members may receive an e-mail notification about them. (Because of Facebook restrictions on spam, this option may not be available to you if your Group has a very large number of members.)

To send a message to all members, click the Message All Members action link under the picture in the right column of your Group's Home page. You're taken to the standard Facebook Compose Message window. Complete the rest of the process as if you were sending a message to a single friend of yours, as outlined in Chapter 9. To your members, the message appears to originate from the Group rather than from you personally, and they're not able to respond to it.

Creating a Group Event

Your Group is open around the clock, but what if you want to gather your members in one place — either online or offline — at one time? For instance, you may wish to convene your Scrabble Lovers Group for a friendly tournament. (Although, have you ever witnessed a Scrabble tournament? They get intense.) In such cases, you may create a Facebook Event to host the details of the gathering and send the invitation to your members.

Although Facebook offers the Events feature to all of its users, it gives special capabilities to Group administrators for scenarios like this. By clicking the Create Related Event action link under your Group's Home page picture, you can create an Event that has the Group — rather than you personally — listed as the host in the Event and its invitation. Furthermore, you can easily add all of your Group members to the Event's invitation list by checking the Invite Members check box just above the Add Personal Message section. See Chapter 11 for more information about Events.

Chapter 11

Scheduling Your Life
with Facebook

Think about the worst birthday party that you ever had — the big kickball party during the hurricane when the clown was three hours late (and a little drunk) and none of your friends showed up because your mom (hands full with a torrential downpour and drunken clown) forgot to invite them.

Facebook can't do anything about clowns or the weather (as of publication time), but the invites would've happened if your mother used Facebook Events to plan the party. Facebook removes the hassle of hosting an Event — creating and sending the invites; managing the guest list — and allows you to focus on preparing the Event itself.

Not much of a party planner? No worries. Facebook also handles the planning of smaller, more impromptu Events. You can easily collect a crew for dinner or for Frisbee in the park. And if that still isn't enough, hundreds of Events in your area are on Facebook every week. This chapter shows you how to find the best of the best for this weekend.

Getting Going with Events

Like Photos and Groups, Events is an application built by Facebook and pre-installed by default. To access its dashboard, click the Events link in the Applications menu in the Chat bar at the bottom of any page. The Events page (shown in Figure 11-1) displays everything that's happening in the world of Events on Facebook. It's divided into the following four tabs:

- **Upcoming Events:** Lists upcoming Facebook Events that have you on their guest lists. This includes Events you were invited to and Events that you joined.

  Just in case you change your mind, even Events you said you aren't attending appear in the list. To change your RSVP, click the RSVP link on the right side of the Event listing. Click Remove to remove an Event permanently from your list (and yourself from the Event's guest list). See the "Anatomy of an Event" section for more information about this feature.

  To see more information about an Event, click its title to view the Event's Home page, which contains a detailed overview of the Event just as your Profile does about you. Facebook also embeds a summary of the most important information — the Event's tagline, host, type, location, and date; your RSVP; and which friends (if any) are attending — directly into the Event listing, as shown in Figure 11-2. Wherever you find an Event listing on Facebook — say, the Events browsing tool or a list of search results — this information displays.

- **Friends' Events:** Lists the Events that your friends are planning to attend. Each listing includes the names of the friends attending the Event. As always, click the Event title to view the Event's Home page. Click Add to My Events to add yourself to the Event's guest list and to your Upcoming Events tab. Doing so automatically specifies your RSVP status as Attending, although you can change this by visiting the Event's Home page.

- **Past Events:** Lists Facebook Events that had you on their guest lists, regardless of whether you attended them. Facebook doesn't delete an Event's Home page after the Event occurs. Instead, the Event's Home page, its photos, videos, and other media remain for posterity as a chronicle of what transpired.

- **Birthdays:** Although these aren't Facebook Events in the sense that they have an Event Home page, your friends' birthdays are important real-world Events that you don't want to miss. This tab lists all of the birthdays in the current month, as well as what age your friend is turning (if that information is available).

Anatomy of an Event

Events are represented on Facebook through its Home page, such as the one shown in Figure 11-3. A Home page evolves throughout the lifecycle of an Event. Before the Event takes place, it serves as an invitation and offers critical information for attendees, such as the Event's date and location. An Event's Home page also tracks who will or might attend the Event so that its host can plan accordingly. After the Event is over, the Home page serves as a water cooler for attendees to share their experiences in the form of photos, videos, and discussions.

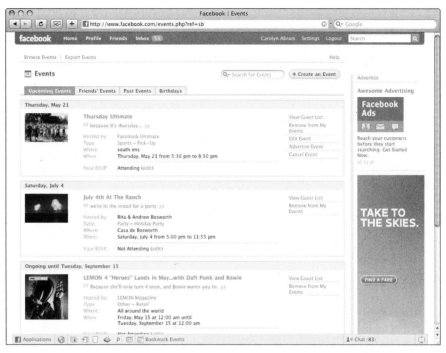

Figure 11-1:
The Events application's dashboard.

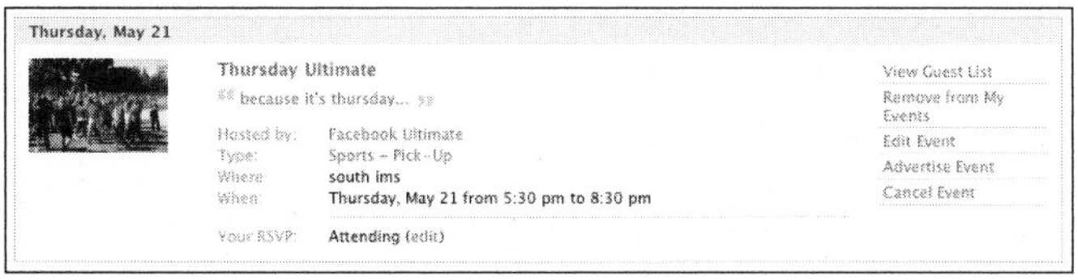

Figure 11-2:
An Event's listing displays a preview of the most important info.

An Event's Home page is divided into two columns, and each column is further divided into sections or boxes. Some boxes, such as photos and videos, contain only a snapshot of the most recently shared media; click See All in the title bar of these boxes to view a comprehensive list.

At the very top of the Event Home page, right below its name, is the Event's information. This area displays basic Event information, such as the name of the Event and the names of the individuals or organizations hosting it. It also contains the Event's *tagline* — a brief, catchy slogan, such as *A devil of a good time* for a Halloween costume party (but usually catchier). Most importantly, it contains the time and place for the Event. If the administrator specifies a street address, Facebook automatically displays a View Map link that provides directions.

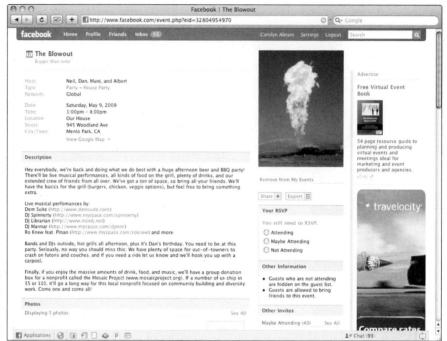

Below this information section is a series of boxes. As we explain each box, keep in mind that certain boxes may not appear on a certain Event's Home page, at the administrator's discretion.

The left column on the Event's Home page contains the following boxes:

- **Description:** A paragraph or two about the Event, courtesy of its administrator.

- **Photos:** Photos of interest to the Event's guests. The Photos box often remains empty until the Event takes place, after which attendees fill it quickly with photos from the Event. However, a Sweet 16 Event may include a series of photos showing the guest of honor growing up throughout the years. A wedding Event may include a picture of the real wedding invitation.

- **Videos:** As with photos, this box usually displays videos taken at the Event, but it may also contain related videos. For instance, a band hosting a concert may decide to share videos of its past performances.

- **Links:** Links to Web sites, photos, videos, and other content that exists outside of Facebook that's relevant to the Event. For instance, if a museum curator was showcasing an exhibit, he may include a link to his museum's Web site.

✔ **Confirmed Guests:** The list of people who RSVP as Attending the Event. The Confirmed Guests box lists your friends and people in your networks (if you are in any) before anyone else. Standard Facebook privacy rules apply, so you may not be able to view the Profiles of some guests.

✔ **Wall:** No page on Facebook would be complete without the Wall, a forum for casual discussion. Event guests usually leave well wishes here (for example, *Happy birthday!*) or their regrets if they can't attend.

The right column of the Event's Home page contains the following:

✔ **Event picture:** An Event administrator can choose a single picture that best represents his Event and display it prominently here.

✔ **Action links:** A series of important options kicks off the right column, including Add to My Events (if you aren't on the Event guest list), Invite People to Come, and Remove from My Events (if you're on the guest list). Unless you're an Event administrator, you have only the option of inviting other people if the Event is Open; see the "Creating Your Own Events" section for more information. If you're an Event administrator, this section includes additional options to edit the Event information, the guest list, or to cancel the Event.

✔ **Share:** The Share link scattered throughout Facebook allows you to share interesting content quickly with your friends, either by sending it to them in a message or by posting it on your Profile. The Share button allows you to share an Event link along with a preview containing the Event's name, description, and picture.

If the Event is open, you may want to use the Invite People to Come action link to send an invitation rather than a link. (See the upcoming "Creating Your Own Events" section for more information on open Events.) If the Event is secret, you can't share a link to the Event with anyone who isn't a member because the Event's privacy settings don't permit it.

✔ **Export:** Facebook enables you to export an Event in .ics file format (meaning that the file would have a file extension of .ics, the way many Word files have .doc at the end). Many popular calendaring programs, such as Microsoft Outlook, import .ics files; therefore, you can add your Facebook Events to your regular calendar.

✔ **Your RSVP:** Displays whether you're planning to attend the Event. Your RSVP can be Attending, Maybe Attending, or Not Attending. Your RSVP can be changed at any time by selecting a new option and choosing RSVP.

✔ **Other Information:** Displays other relevant information about the Event not important enough to include in the main column, such as whether guests may bring friends. The Other Information box doesn't appear if there's no additional information to display.

✔ **Other Invites:** Displays the people on the guest list who may attend, aren't attending, or who haven't responded (Awaiting Reply). The Other Invites section is shown in Figure 11-4.

✔ **Event Type:** Displays the type of the Event chosen by its administrator. Event types are Open, Closed, or Secret. See the "Creating Your Own Events" section for a description of these types.

✔ **Admins:** A list of the people who serve as administrators of the Event; therefore, they're in charge of writing the Event information and keeping guests up to date. Admins are usually (but not always) the hosts of the Event.

Figure 11-4:
The Other Invites box shows everyone on the guest list who hasn't responded.

Going to the After Party

When you get home from that birthday party or book club meeting, return to the Event page to post any photos or videos you shot. Click the Add link in the photo or video boxes and you're taken to an interface for adding photos and videos to the Event Home page. By default, you see prompts to add copies of photos or videos you've already added to Facebook, like what is shown in Figure 11-5. You can also choose to upload new photos or videos, or (if you have a Webcam), you can choose to record a video or take a video straight to the Event's Home page. Note that these features are only available if the Event administrator has turned them on. Keep an eye on your own home page to see when other guests post their photos and videos, which usually happens in one big flurry of activity a day or two after the Event. After all, there's nothing more rousing than a video of your book club in action.

Videos that you add to this event will be visible by anyone who can see the event.

📹 Add Videos to Facebook Ultimate

| Add from My Videos | Upload File | Record Video | Back to Facebook Ultimate

Select from My Videos

Figure 11-5:
Adding
videos to an
Event.

Add Selected Videos   Cancel

Finding the Event for You

With more than 200 million people on Facebook, it's no surprise that, at any given time, there are hundreds of Events in your area. Facebook gives you a number of tools to help you find the best ways to spend your weekend.

Searching Events

If you have an Event in mind, the fastest way to find it is to search.

1. **Click within the Search box.**

   The *Search box* is the text box in the top-right corner of every page, in the big blue bar.

2. **Enter the topic of an Event you want to find, such as** Dave Matthews Band, **and press Enter to begin your search.**

   The search results contain content from all over Facebook, such as Profiles, Groups, and Events.

3. **Click the Events tab at the top to retrieve only Event results.**

To search only Events, use the Search for Events box at the top of the Events page. The search results are the same in each case. To navigate to the Events page, click the Events link in the Applications menu in the Chat bar.

To filter your search results by date or type:

1. **Click the Show More Filters link next to the gray bar above the search results.**

2. **When the filter sidebar appears on the right, use the Date drop-down list to change the range of Events displayed.**

   You can show Events occurring on the present day, from now until tomorrow, within the next week, or within the next month.

3. **You can also use the Type drop-down list to filter the list to parties, sporting Events, and so forth.**

If the search filters don't help, clear them and return to the original results list by clicking the Hide Filters link, which appears in place of the Show More Filters link on the gray bar at the top.

Browsing Events

If you don't have a particular Event in mind, browse them at your leisure.

1. **Click the Events link in the Applications menu in the Chat bar at the bottom of any Facebook page.**

   This takes you to the Events dashboard.

2. **Click the Browse Events link at the top of the page.**

   Facebook displays (by default) a list of Events taking place within the next month that you have permission to attend, as shown in Figure 11-6.

3. **Use the options on the right sidebar to filter the displayed list by network, date, or type.**

To browse Events that are popular among your friends and networks, see the next section, "Checking out popular Events."

Figure 11-6:
Browse
Events to
find one that
suits your
fancy.

Checking out popular Events

Face it — nobody wants to go to *That Party*. The one where nobody shows up but you, and you're stuck reassuring the host that, "It's probably the weather, because, you know, who wants to go to a party when it's partly cloudy out, anyway?"

Fortunately, Facebook gives you an easy way to see which Events are popular among your friends and networks. The Friends' Events tab on the Events page shows you Events that your friends are attending soon that you can attend. Your friends didn't manually suggest these Events to you; Facebook simply assumes that your friends join Events that interest them and automatically pushes those Events to you.

Creating Your Own Events

Tired of being a *guest?* Ready to be in charge? Want to host your own Event, have complete control over the guest list, and almost single-handedly decide who among us is *in* and *out?* Follow these simple steps:

> **1. Take a cold shower.**

Now that that's out of your system, get down to business — the business of organizing and hosting fun Events. If you're planning an Event that's not happening for a few days or so, we recommended starting with the Big Events section. If your Event is more spur of the moment, or perhaps has already started, we recommend skipping ahead to the Quick Events section.

Big Events

Whatever actions have transpired before you log in to Facebook — a conversation about how awesome a surprise party would be, a sudden urge to give all of your friends free food in honor of the season — after you've logged in, creating an Event is easy. To begin, take the following steps:

> **1. Click the Events link in the Applications menu in the Chat bar at the bottom of any Facebook page.**
>
> This takes you to the Events dashboard.
>
> **2. Click the Create New Event button at the top right of the page.**

Creating an Event entails at least one step: specifying the Event's name and other basic information. You have the option of completing two additional steps if you want to specify an Event picture or guest list. (If you don't invite anyone to your Event but make it public, people can still stumble upon it, although it may be pretty lonely.) Facebook divides the process into three screens — one for each step — and highlights the current step's tab at the top of the page. We discuss each step in depth here. Any property of an Event (except for its name) can be edited at any time after its creation, so don't fret too much about getting things just right your first time through.

Step 1: Event Info

The Event Info step asks you for the following information about the Event (see Figure 11-7). In this first step, all the fields that are displayed when the page first loads are required (we note these in the following list). There are additional fields you will need to click to add, which we note as well.

- **Event Name (required):** The name of the Event you want to create, such as *Jenny's 21st Birthday.*

- **Tagline (click Add a Tagline):** A brief slogan for your Event, such as *Because she'll only turn 21 once.*

- **Location (required):** The name of the venue where your Event is taking place, such as Pete's Pizzaria. Some Events are online gatherings, in which case this can be a Web site address.

- **Street Address (click Add a Street Address):** The street address of the location where the Event is taking place. Once you expand this section, you will need to enter the address separately from the city or town where the Event is occurring. When you type in the city or town, the field tries to auto-complete as you type. If you specify the street address and town, Facebook displays a View Map link that your guests can click to get directions.

- **Start Time/End Time (required):** The anticipated timeframe for your Event, including date and time. Click the calendar icon to select a date more quickly.

- **Privacy (required, but will default to open):** Events have special privacy settings that allow you to control who can see Event Info, and who can RSVP to the Event.

  - *Open:* The default setting; allows anyone to view the Event's content. Guests can also invite other people to join.

  - *Closed:* Anyone may be able to view the basic Event information, but only guests can see the photos, the Wall, and so forth. People who want to attend must request an invitation, and you or another administrator have to approve or deny these requests.

  - *Secret:* People can join the Event only if you or another administrator invites them. They can't request an invitation because it won't appear in the search results. Therefore, only guests can view the Event's description, photos, and so forth. The Event's network has little effect here given these additional restrictions.

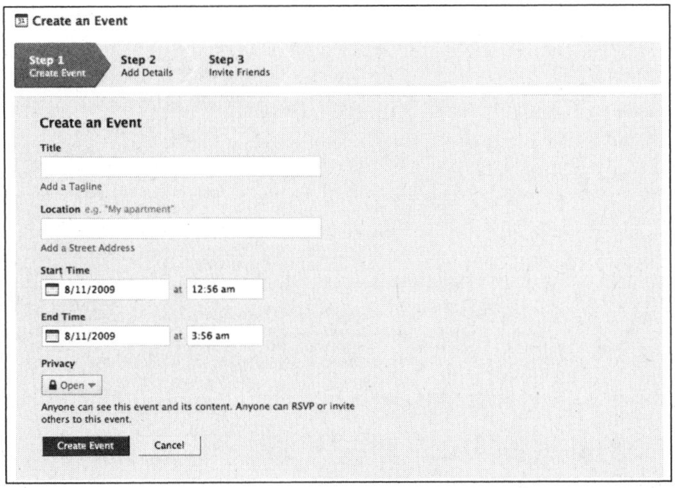

Figure 11-7:
Creating an
Event takes
just a few
minutes.

When you finish filling out these fields, click the Create Event button at the bottom of the screen to create the Event and move on to Step 2: Add Details. If you left any required fields empty or otherwise made an error, you remain on the first step, and a red box appears at the top explaining how to proceed.

Step 2: Add Details

Figure 11-8 represents the Add Details step, where you can add your Event's representative picture, as well as edit the information about the Event and what your guests will be able to do from your Event's Home page.

✔ **Add a picture:** Adding a photo to represent your Event makes it look pretty and inviting when your guests see the Event — both on the Event Home page and in invitation requests. Big, official Events often have their flier as the picture. To add an image, follow these instructions:

  1. **Click the Browse or Choose File button to open your computer's standard interface for finding a file.**

  2. **Navigate to (and select) the picture on your computer that you want to use.**

     The picture you choose must meet the file size and type requirements outlined on the page. If you're not sure whether your desired picture meets the requirements, select the picture and continue with these steps. Facebook notifies you if the picture you choose can't be used.

  3. **Check the box to certify that you have the right to distribute the picture (it isn't copyrighted) and that it doesn't violate the Facebook Terms of Use (it isn't pornographic or otherwise offensive).**

  4. **Click Upload Picture.**

✔ **Event Type:** The category of the Event, such as *Party* or *Meeting*. After you choose a type, you also need to pick a subtype, such as *Holiday Party* or *Business Meeting*. Facebook members create Events for gatherings as small and casual as happy hour or as large and formal as a wedding.

✔ **Description:** A brief overview of the Event, such as why you're holding it, what the attire is, and why you should come. The description is one of the first things a guest sees when looking at your Event and determining whether to attend.

✔ **Options:** A mixture that controls what guests can see on your Event, as well as what they can do from your Event's Home page.

- *Only allow admins to post content to the Event:* In the spirit of sharing and information flow, this box is deselected by default. In other words, this defaults to allowing your friends to upload photos, links, and videos to your Event. If you don't want them to be able to do that, select this check box.

- *Allow guests to bring friends to the Event:* Shows the Other Information section that indicates to guests that they can bring other people. Don't have enough chicken for everyone? Holding a party in an 8 X 5 box? You may want to leave this unchecked, or things could get ugly.

- *Show the guest list:* Displays the guest list, which includes everyone invited, not just the people who are planning to attend. As a suboption here, you can choose to show the guest list, but hide the people who said no, since you don't want people to know that in reality, no one's showing up.

When you finish customizing your Event, click Continue Save at the very bottom of the page.

Now, pass go, collect $200, and proceed to inviting people to your Event.

Step 3: Invite Friends

The final step enables you to invite people to attend your Event. Additionally, after you've sent invitations, a fourth tab, titled Edit Guest List, appears. You can manage your guest list from here after people start to RSVP.

If you designate your Event as open or closed, it's not absolutely necessary for you to invite people; they may discover the Event on their News Feeds, the Search feature, or many other sources. However, if you create a secret Event, these invitations are the only means through which someone can discover and attend your Event.

If you decide to invite people to your Event, it takes just a few seconds:

1. **To invite your friends who are on Facebook, select them from the *Friend Selector*, as shown in Figure 11-9.**

   The Invite Guests page displays a *Friend Selector,* which is a grid of your friends. To select any friend, simply click her picture or name. If you know exactly who you're going for, start typing her name into a field labeled Find Friends. The grid filters down as you type. Select your friends whenever you're ready. When you invite a Facebook member to attend your Event, she receives a Facebook request from you. Depending on her notification settings, she may also receive an e-mail from Facebook regarding your invitation. Note that Facebook doesn't send the invitation to your friend as soon as you select her in the list.

   You can double-check your guest list by clicking the Selected link in the Friend Selector (found in the upper-right corner above your friends' faces). This displays only the people you have already selected, so you can verify that you chose the right group of people. If you accidentally select the wrong Blake Ross, you can undo it by clicking his face again.

2. **To invite friends who aren't on Facebook to join the Event, type their e-mail addresses (separated by commas) into the box below the *Friend Selector.***

   Can't remember their addresses? No problem. Click the Import E-Mail Addresses link to open a window that enables you to select their addresses from your e-mail address book, assuming Facebook supports your e-mail provider (it supports the most popular ones). This process is very similar to that outlined in Chapter 4. Forgot some folks? Enter more addresses into the box and click Add again.

3. **(Optional) To include a message with your invitation, type it in the box below the Invite People Via E-mail box.**

This step adds a personal touch and makes your invitation more persuasive.

4. **To send the invitations to the people on the list, click Send Invitations.**

   Forgot some people? You can repeat these steps at any time.

Quick Events

Although taking the time to find an Event picture and invite your friends and coordinate all sorts of logistics is worthwhile for that extra-special day, what about all of the ordinary, run-of-the-mill Events that transpire every day? All of the coffee shops or park benches or dinners at your favorite cheap restaurant that would simply be better if you had a few friends along? Facebook makes these Events easy to plan by letting you create Events directly from the Publisher on your home page.

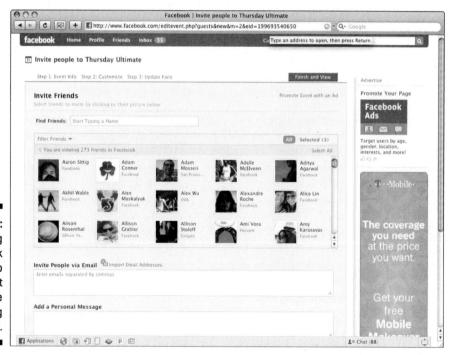

Figure 11-9: Inviting Facebook friends to your Event is as simple as selecting them.

The Publisher is the blank field that sits on top of your Home page and Profile page. From it you can post status updates, photos, videos, and Events.

To create an Event from the Publisher, follow the steps below:

1. **Click the What's on Your Mind? prompt within the Publisher.**

   You should be able to see icons denoting the various applications you can attach to your post.

2. **Click the Events icon, which looks like a tiny calendar.**

   Special fields expand, as shown in Figure 11-10.

3. **Fill out your Event's Title, Location, and Time.**

   You can also include a brief description of the Event in the blank space at the top of the Publisher. For example, your Event may read:

   Couldn't resist the berries at the farmers' market — all of you shall benefit.

   Title: Dessert Night

   Location: My place

   Time: June 31, 8:00pm

4. **Click Share.**

   The Event is immediately posted to your Wall and to your friends' Live Feeds. To you, it appears as shown in Figure 11-11.

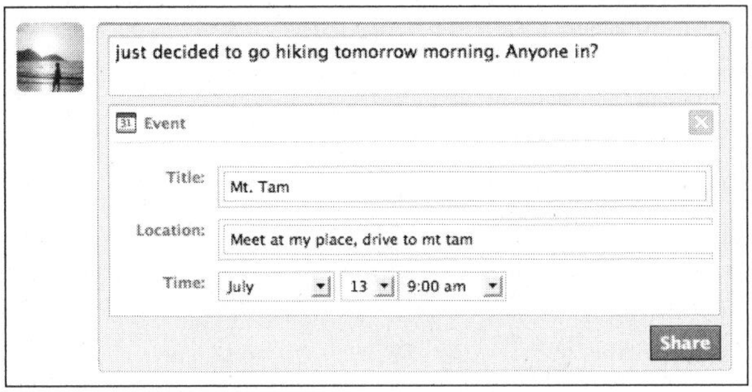

Figure 11-10:
Quick Event
creation
from the
Publisher.

You (the Event poster) can see a link to Invite Guests, but when the post with the Event appears to your friends, they see links to comment, like, or RSVP to it. So if your friends are avid Facebook users, chances are you'll see some responses pretty quickly. If you're worried they may not get to their Facebook accounts until after the plates have been licked clean, you can click the Invite Guests link beneath the post to directly invite people. Clicking this link opens the same Invite screen (but in a pop-up window) that you saw in the previous section.

Figure 11-11:
Now every
Event can
be a party.

You'll notice that if you click through to the Event, it has the same Event page described earlier in this chapter, just with more empty fields. If you have extra time, you can fill these out in the same way you would edit an Event you created way ahead of time, by clicking Edit Event below the picture.

When you create an Event from the Publisher, you don't have the same privacy controls that you have when you create an Event through the Events page. In other words, the Event you create here is open; you need to go into the Event to edit its privacy. It is definitely not the right choice for that surprise book party you're planning.

Managing your Event

You can do a number of things when you finish creating your Event and people start to join. Many of these steps appear as action links under the picture on your Event's Home page. These actions are visible and available only to you and other administrators. This section outlines the additional power you wield as an Event administrator.

Messaging your Event's guests

Rain delay? Halloween canceled? Keep your guests up to date about the Event by sending them a Facebook message. These messages appear in your guests' Facebook Inbox, and depending on their notification settings, they may also receive an e-mail notification.

To send a message to guests, click the Message Guests action link under the picture in the right column of your Event's Home page. You're taken to the standard Compose Message form with one addition: an Attendees drop-down list that allows you to indicate which guest list segment you want to message (everyone, those who are attending, may be attending, or haven't responded). Complete the rest of the process as if you were sending a message to a single friend. (If you need help with that process, see Chapter 9.)

Managing your Event's guest list

After guests RSVP to your Event, use the Event guest list to remove (even permanently ban) undesirable guests, promote your most trusted guests to administrators, or demote your existing administrators (if any) to regular guests.

1. **Click the Edit Guest List link under the picture in the right column of your Event's Home page.**

   The Guest List page is shown in Figure 11-12.

2. **Use the link to the right of each guest name that corresponds to the action you want to take.**

   For instance, to make a member an administrator, click the Make Admin link. As an administrator, the member has the same privileges discussed in this chapter as you do for this particular Event.

   You can also use the X to remove a guest from the Event. If you select this option, you can also choose to ban that person permanently so he may not rejoin the Event in the future. Banning someone is useful if the person is posting offensive content or otherwise stirring up trouble.

Figure 11-12:
The Guest List page is your one-stop shop for keeping tabs on your current guests and inviting more.

Chapter 12

Creating a Page for Your Business

*P*icture your town or city. Besides the occasional park or school, it's primarily made of buildings in which people live (like houses) and buildings in which people buy things (like stores). The world we live in is mostly composed of people and stuff that people need or want. People have real connections to all this stuff: the shops, the brands, the bands, the stars, and the restaurants and bars — everything that's important. These businesses have a significant stake in attracting and connecting with their fans, many of whom are on Facebook. Facebook is all about people and their real-world connections; the social map wouldn't be complete without these types of relationships.

Facebook offers a way for businesses to have a presence that's similar to (yet different from) the one users have. Any legitimate business, band, or public figure can set up a Facebook Page, which looks and behaves much like a user's Profile. Managers of a business can customize a Facebook Page to represent the business, informing and attracting customers. One primary difference between a business Page and a user's Profile is the default means of interaction, which reflects and accommodates the different type of connection that people have with businesses in real life. Another difference is the set of detailed statistics — *metrics* — that reveal how people interact with a particular Facebook Page. Businesses use these numbers to understand their return on advertising investment.

We spend a lot of time in this book explaining exactly what people get from having a personal presence on Facebook. In the first part of this chapter, we show you the potential value of having your business present on Facebook. After that, we explain the features and functionality of Facebook Pages, often by comparing and contrasting them with other types of presence on Facebook. If you have spent a lot of time on Facebook or read the first few parts of this book already, you have an advantage while following along. In the last part of this chapter, we walk you through the steps to get your Facebook Page set up and active to further fuel the success of your business.

Why Create a Facebook Page?

Before we can answer why you should create a Facebook Page, first think about other things you can do to achieve success for your business:

- ✔ **Offer a quality product or service.** Quality, differentiated products attract repeat customers and referrals.

- ✔ **Locate your business on a busy street or in a dense shopping area.** Highly trafficked locations translate to attention and accessibility.

- ✔ **Clean and decorate your shop, carefully design your Web site, or dress up for a performance.** Quality presentation gains trust from customers.

In the end, all of these are examples of things businesses do to achieve growth: namely, growth of a loyal fan base. Giving your business a presence on Facebook ultimately has the same purpose: namely, driving growth.

Then again, lots of things *can* drive growth. Handing out flyers on the street, placing coupons in a newspaper, or running a commercial during the Super Bowl may get you customers. The trick is to figure out which, of all possible promotional efforts, has the biggest bang for your buck. We think we know the answer.

Speaking of bucks, it's time to get the uncomfortable money stuff out of the way: Facebook Pages are free. All you need is access to a computer and the Internet, someone who knows how to use Facebook, and a little time. Setting up your business Page can take five minutes or several hours, depending on how advanced you want to get. If that sounds daunting, remember that it would take several hours to make, print, and distribute flyers — and even longer to create a Web site or film a commercial.

Following are several goals you may have for your business. Throughout this chapter, we show how Facebook Pages help you achieve each goal.

- ✔ **Engage your customers and fans** regularly and in compelling ways. When they think of your industry, they think of you. When they think of you, they feel like they know you. Even if you represent a large corporation, they feel like they understand the human side of the equation.

✔ **Provide customers and potential customers with an accurate source of information about the business,** such as an e-mail address, product details, or hours of operation.

✔ **Communicate new promotions, products, and updates** with as many customers as possible while alienating as few as possible.

✔ **Encourage customers to provide both positive and negative feedback** so you can continually improve.

✔ **Enable your customers to communicate with one another** about your business, product, or band in productive ways.

✔ **Impress your customers so much** that they come back again and again — and tell their friends to do the same.

Facebook Pages offers a suite of features that work together to help you achieve these goals. If you're in a position of promotional authority for a business and have even one of the preceding goals, you can find value in creating a Facebook Page. See an example of *The New York Times* Facebook Page in Figure 12-1.

Figure 12-1:
An example
of a
Facebook
Page.

Pages versus Profiles versus Groups

In real life, how people interact and communicate with their best friends, favorite bands, or local neighborhood associations is unique. Additionally, the needs of a person, versus a band manager, versus a group organizer in terms of connecting and sharing are also different. This is why people, businesses, and Groups all have unique types of presence on Facebook. The way people interact with these entities on Facebook reflects those real-world differences. Because Pages, Profiles, and Groups offer different features and functionality, we want to make sure that you understand each type of presence. Then, based on your specific business goals, you can pick the presence (or presences) best for your goals. Before we highlight the specific functionality differences on Facebook, first think about the real-world differences between people, businesses, and groups:

- ✔ **Communication:** Communication with a friend is usually a conversation, where you say something, and then she responds, and so on. And frequently, these conversations are very personal, with each member contributing equally. With a business, however, communication is often unidirectional: For example, your favorite band tells you about a new CD, or your favorite store announces a sale. Comparatively, communication within groups tends to flow among all members with equal authority, relevance, and interest to all members.

- ✔ **Access:** You are welcomed and encouraged to walk into a café or bookstore at any time during posted business hours. Quite the opposite is true of entering a friend's home unannounced. Additionally, a group usually meets at formalized meeting times agreed upon by all members (or a governing body) and at a venue accessible by all.

- ✔ **Information:** People are particular about which people know what information about them. Groups have varying degrees of privacy, depending on the group, but they generally fall into three buckets in which information is shared: only among members, only among members and the people they authorize, or the general public. With the exception of strategic future plans and some financial details, businesses usually want as many people to know as much about them or their products as possible.

These kinds of real-world differences determine the differences in design and functionality between a person, Group, and business presence on Facebook.

Table 12-1 details the specific differences between these types of presence on Facebook.

Table 12-1   Comparison of User Profiles, Groups, and Pages

Profiles	Groups	Pages
Have one administrator: you.	May have many admins, as arbitrarily appointed by the creator or other admins.	May have many admins, which are the appointed authority of the business.
Represent a real person.	With the exception of copyrighted material or hate speech, represent anything. Seriously.	Represent a real business or promotional entity.
Have friends. Friendships need to be confirmed by both parties. Only friends can see private information.	Have members. Member requests may be reviewed or automatic, depending on the Group's setting.	Have fans. Fan requests are automatically approved. The available information is the same for everyone.
Can send messages to other people, and up to 20 friends. If people are friends, they can always message each other.	Permit admins to message up to 500 members. Members can reply to the Group admin. Members must leave the Groups to opt-out of messages.	Allow admins to send bulk messages to all fans. People cannot reply to these messages and can opt-out of them.
The person behind the Profile may make choices about what — if anything — is globally visible.	Can restrict privacy to members, members and friends, or opt to be globally visible.	Can restrict privacy based on age, but are otherwise always globally visible.
Usually must approve all friend requests. Can opt to accept fans as well.	May choose to review membership requests, or accept automatically.	Automatically accept all fan requests.
Can block people for inappropriate behavior.	Can block people for inappropriate behavior.	Can block people for inappropriate behavior.
Can publish content, use applications, and customize with tabs and boxes.	Can publish content, use applications, and customize with boxes.	Can publish content, use applications, and customize with tabs and boxes.
Have no access to aggregate information about Profile views and interactions.	Have no aggregate information about the page views and interactions with the Group.	Have detailed insights about how people view and interact with a particular Facebook Page, aggregated and broken down by demographic.

Who should create a Facebook Page?

Simply put, anyone who is in a position of promotional authority can build a Facebook Page. Small-business owners, event promoters, and advertising agencies can create a Page on Facebook to get attention and engagement from people. Facebook Pages are designed and optimized for the legitimate business seeking legitimate attention.

Popular categories for business Profiles include

- ✔ **Local businesses,** such as restaurants, bars, clubs, shops, and recreational spots.
- ✔ **Big name or national brands,** such as those that distribute products or provide a service. Starbucks, Verizon, and Coca-Cola are examples.
- ✔ **Nonprofit or government organizations,** such as schools and religious organizations.
- ✔ **Specific products,** such as certain car models, business mascots (such as Ronald McDonald), or high-end designer clothing lines.
- ✔ **News, media, and entertainment companies** can create Pages for their brands or their various offerings, such as movies, TV shows, and magazines.

The preceding list demonstrates that Pages are equally suited for businesses as well as for their products. The NBA, for example, has an NBA Facebook Page as well as a Facebook Page for each of its teams. CBS has a Facebook Page, as does each of its shows. The reason why many businesses promote themselves in this fractured way is because people may identify with particular parts of their business but not the business in its entirety. Creating different Pages for the different entities with which people may connect is important for maximizing engagement. Conversely, you want to avoid over-fragmenting your audience. For example, Six Flags amusement parks don't have to create a Page for every ride, Radiohead doesn't have to create a page for each album, and Starbucks doesn't have to create a page for every beverage.

Who shouldn't build a Facebook page?

A Page, just like a user's Profile on Facebook, represents a real identity and is managed by the real-life appointed authority of that entity. For example, if you're not Chuck Norris (or his PR person), you can't create a Facebook Page called Chuck Norris. And if you didn't write or publish *Fight Club* (or weren't hired by someone who did), you can't create a page for it. It doesn't matter how much you love *lite-mocha Frappaccinos, extra whip-cream;* unless you're the marketing rep for Starbucks, you can't create a Facebook Page for them. Well, you can, but your Page — and/or your account — may end up being disabled.

Good examples of names for hypothetical Facebook Pages are

- Amazon
- Anthony's Pizza
- Stephen Colbert
- Buffy the Vampire Slayer

Bad examples of Facebook Page names are

- **Amazon's Facebook Page:** Like a user's Profile, Facebook Pages are an online representation of your business. When users navigate to your Page and click Become a Fan, they're a fan of your business, not the page. When you send fans an update, you're sending it on behalf of the business, not the Page. The Page isn't a destination: It's a means. When people interact with your Page, they're actually interacting directly with your business, and it's important that the name reflects this.

- **Anthony's Pizza at 553 University Ave.:** Just like the thousands of Joe Smiths on Facebook, there may be hundreds of Anthony's Pizzas — but that's okay. People use the content on your Page, such as your photos or local address listed in your information fields, to identify the Anthony's Pizza they're after.

- **Stephen Colbert, Politician & Comedian Extraordinaire:** Stephen Colbert is welcome to specify his profession in his information fields. Additionally, in the body of his Page, he can declare himself *extraordinaire* over and over. However, his brand is his name, and that should be the name of his Page: *Stephen Colbert.*

- **Buffy the Vampire Slayer Is Awesome:** Buffy *is* awesome, and this would make a great name for a Facebook Group. However, there's no real-life entity with this name (that we know of); therefore, there shouldn't be a Facebook Page with this name.

Living in the Gray Netherworld between Pages and Profiles

You may have, by now, noticed a distinction between representing one person and representing a collection of people. So, while it's easy to choose between creating a Profile for the Dave Matthews Band, and creating a Page for the Dave Matthews Band, it may be harder to choose what to do if you want to create a something for just Dave Matthews.

Celebrities and public figures do have to make a choice about which service best fits their needs. In general, there are two relevant questions to ask if you find yourself in the public figure predicament:

✔ **Will I be the only one managing my online self?** In other words, do you have a staff assistant who is charged with keeping your Facebook presence up-to-date? Or will you be doing all of your own Facebooking?

✔ **Do I also want to share more privately with my real-life friends?** Some people want to have it all: they want to publish a photo album from the family reunion (even if that family has a last name like Norris), and keep that private, while still publishing interesting articles, thoughts, and less private photos to the world at large (especially the world that is pretty sure Chuck Norris can sneeze with his eyes open).

Yes, this is a "Choose your own Dummies adventure":

If the answer to both questions was yes . . . chances are you should still consider building a Profile. You will be the only one able to access it, and you can use the Publisher privacy controls we describe in Chapter 6 to choose who sees what.

If the answer to both questions was No, you should create a Page. It will give you the most flexibility in terms of who can manage it, and everything will publish to everyone — no special settings necessary.

If you answered no to the first question, and yes to the second question, you probably want to create a Facebook page for your staff to manage and a Facebook Profile just for yourself. The Page represents the public you, and a Profile can become the space where you share just with your friends and family.

If the answer is a combination of yes and no, a Page is again the more flexible, simple way to go, especially if it turns out managing your page is time-consuming and you change your mind on the answer to question one.

Creating and Managing a Facebook Page

A Facebook Page isn't equivalent to an account. Rather, it's an entity on Facebook that can be managed by many people with their own distinct accounts. This section will take you through all the steps of Page creation, administration, and maintenance.

Creating a page for your business

If you haven't already created an account on Facebook, we highly recommend that you do that first (although you don't have to). If you don't want to, you can start the process at Step 2 in the following steps; before completing Step 6, however, you're asked to create an account. The account you create here is a lesser version of a full Facebook user account, but it's still your account. You're asked to enter your e-mail address and birth date, and you should enter accurate information. That way, if you ever decide that you want a personal Profile, upgrading the account you create here is much easier than starting from scratch.

Pages can have multiple admins. If you plan to have other people managing the Page you're creating, they can do so from their accounts. There's no reason to share the e-mail address or password with anyone. In fact, doing so violates the Terms of Use. We hope we've gained your trust enough at this point of the book that you trust us here: ***Use your real e-mail address and birth date.*** This information won't be revealed to anyone else, and it makes your future interactions on Facebook much easier.

1. **Navigate to www.Facebook.com and log in with your username and password.**

2. **Scroll down until you can't scroll any further and then click Advertisers in the footer menu.**

   This is different than the Chat bar, which houses all of your applications and IM chats.

   The page you land on (www.Facebook.com/ads) gives you an overview of the Facebook integrated advertising system. Pages are free, but ads are not. That being said, when you are just starting out with your page, advertising can be worth the investment to help you build a base of connections and subscribers. Find out more about advertising in Chapter 15.

3. **Click the Pages tab, located just below the top menu.**

   You're welcome to read the copy on that page or click the Learn More link, but there's nothing there that's not in this book. (After all, we wrote both.)

4. **Click the Create a Page button.** It's the green button in the upper-right quadrant of the screen. This starts the Create Page workflow.

5. **Specify what kind of business you're trying to promote, as shown in Figure 12-2.**

   The reason for making an accurate selection here is twofold:

- Depending on the category you choose, your Facebook Page is created with a very specific set of fields and functionality. For example, specifying that your business is a restaurant allows you to specify your hours of operation, and specifying that you're a musician gives you instant access to a discography.

- You can help users find and identify you.

6. **Enter the name of your business and then click Create Page.**

   As we mention earlier, enter the exact name of your business, just like you'd sign up for Facebook with your real name.

   As soon as you click Create Page, you're the proud admin of a Facebook Page. You're not done, though. Now you have to configure and customize. Both of these processes are complicated enough that we're punting those explanations to a separate numbered list.

If all the excitement has gotten the best of you, continue on to customize your Page right away; the next section guides you through that process. If you plan to take a break, you need to know how to get back here.

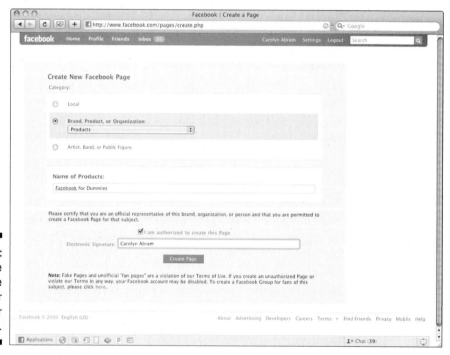

Figure 12-2:
Categorize
and create
a page for
your
business.

When you follow the preceding steps to create your first Facebook Page, you automatically have a new application added to your account called Page Manager (if you've ever run an ad, it may also be called Ads and Pages). Whenever you're logged in to Facebook, look for it in the Applications Menu (in the lower-left corner), and click this link to access, edit, and manage your Page. Page Manager is also where you go to see all the user-engagement statistics, which we talk about in the "Know-It-All" section, at the end of this chapter.

Making your page yours

Since its beginning, Facebook has operated under a different principle than most of its competitors. Many other sites encourage people to customize their online presence with backgrounds, colors, layouts, and songs to express their individuality. Facebook encourages people to express their individuality through the content they publish on their Profiles rather than through visual (or audio) display. The same is true for Facebook Pages. Most of the customization of your Page comes from what you say, link to, publish, and add as tabs for people to interact with. Businesses that are used to branding and customizing their Web sites may find this limiting, but think of the trade-off. Potential customers who arrive at your Facebook Page know exactly how to get the information they need and how to interact with your Page because they're already familiar with the format. The unified look and feel of Facebook Pages is designed for ease of navigation and to provide a seamless experience for Facebook users. Rather than view these limitations as a disadvantage, try distinguishing your Page by offering rich and engaging content and functionality.

We mention earlier that while creating your Page, you're asked to categorize your business. This category determines which information fields and default applications appear on your Page. Keep reading as we summarize the information fields as well as all the default applications that your Page may start with.

After completing the steps in the preceding section, you see your clean slate of a Facebook Page. An example is shown in Figure 12-3. At the top is your business, brand, or band's name, beneath which are two tabs waiting to be filled in with rich, informative, engaging information.

Much of your page can be edited from the page itself. Some behind-the-scenes settings, however, need to be edited from what we're calling the *Control Panel.* We call out whenever you need to go to the Control Panel, which you can do by clicking Edit Page right beneath your Profile picture.

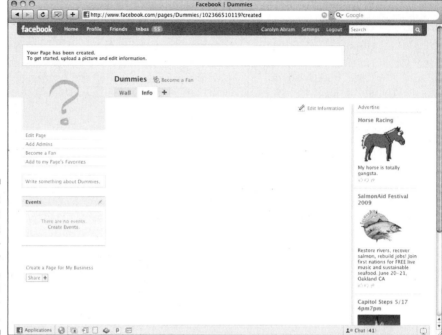

Figure 12-3:
A newborn
Facebook
Page—
after
creation,
before
configu-
ration.

People connect to your page the similarly to how they connect to other users, by clicking a big Connect button next to your name. For users, that usually says Connect as a Friend. For you, the button says Connect as a Fan. By default, when a user clicks that button, she starts receiving your posts on her home page in News Feed. We call this *subscribing.* We refer to your fans as connections, customers, and patrons a bit interchangeably, but when we talk about subscribers, we always mean people who see your posts in their News Feeds when they log in.

Getting your bearings

As you look around your newly minted page, all gangly limbs and blank spaces, you may notice something. It looks . . . just like a user Profile. It has an Info tab and a Wall tab and a Publisher. There's a space for a Profile picture, and a bio box running down the left column. Why, it's practically the same as a user Profile. If you don't feel like you're yet comfortable with the user Profile, we recommend skipping back a little bit to Chapter 6 because we're going to breeze through a bunch of the stuff we cover there in this section. But just as we do in that chapter, we're going to first talk about the main tabs, and then the other cool things you can do with your Page.

Information

The very first thing that we recommend doing is to set up a photo for your Page. This brings your Page to life, helping your fans identify you when they find you in Search or read about you in their friend's News Feeds. Set your picture by clicking Edit in the upper right of the Profile Picture box; then follow the instructions to upload a photo. The column in which the Photo is placed is 396 pixels wide and can be up to three times the width of your picture. Keep these dimensions in mind when trying to make or choose a high-quality photo for your Page.

Most Pages have three information sections within the info tab: Basic, Detailed, and Contact.

- ✓ **Basic information:** Here, enter information that is core to your business. For Basic information, bands list members, local businesses list their address, and big name brands usually list their Web sites, for example.

- ✓ **Detailed information:** This includes information fields unique to your type of business. This is where bands list their influencers, clubs state their dress policies, and movie studios list the awards they've won for certain films.

- ✓ **Contact information:** This one is pretty self-explanatory. Depending on the type of business you have, you can enter an e-mail address, phone number, and, in some cases, a mailing address.

Clicking Edit Information in the upper right of the info tab should expose all of these sections for editing. The more of these fields that you fill out, the more people know about you. Any field that you don't fill out simply won't appear when people visit your page.

The Wall

Whereas the Information tab lets people know about the basics, the Wall is where people get to know the real you. If you have a personal account with a Profile, the Wall will feel very intuitive to you. Check out the Wall for the satirical magazine *The Onion* in Figure 12-4 to get a feel for how a page can use its Wall to showcase what's new and exciting.

The Wall is where people who have connected to you will land when they visit your actual page. The content you publish in your Wall will also feed into their Home pages, assuming they've subscribed to your posts. In other words, it's a very important place to represent yourself honestly and engagingly through constant updates.

In Chapter 6, we describe in detail all the pieces of the Wall and how they fit together to tell the story of you. That story still needs to be told for you, even when you represent some sort of business. People are going to want to hear from you, they are going to want to learn about you, and the place they will go to do that is your Wall.

As a Page admin, the most important part of the Wall to understand is the *Publisher*. The Publisher, as shown in detail in Figure 12-5, is where you and fans create the posts that actually appear on the Wall.

Figure 12-4:
The Onion on Facebook.

Figure 12-5:
Use the Publisher to send posts out to fans.

The basic steps for using the Publisher are as follows:

1. **Click into the text field.**

   You'll see a few icons extend beneath you.

2. **(Optional) Select the icon that represents the type of media you wish to add.**

   If you want to add a link, click Link. If you want to add a photo, click Photo. You get the idea. If you don't want to add any sort of attachment, that's okay, too. In fact, it's quite common. Text-only posts are referred to as *Status Updates.*

3. **Type in your comment, either to explain your attachment or just to say whatever it is you're thinking about.**

4. **Click Share.**

Congratulations: Your Page is officially published. Posts you create here are sent as News Feeds for your subscribers to enjoy.

Wall Settings

Unlike user Profiles, Page admins have some control over how their Walls appear by default. From the Control Panel, you can open the Wall Settings section (shown in Figure 12-6) and access the following options:

✔ **Default View for Wall:** This setting controls what your subscribers and connections see when they land on your Wall. Some Page admins take great care to post regularly, and having a plethora of Wall posts from eager and enthusiastic fans — though wonderful — can push the newer content from the Page off the Wall very quickly. For this reason, most pages have a default setting that their connections will only see their original posts when they land on the Wall. Page admins who don't have a lot of time to update may consider making both original posts and posts from connections appear together because it keeps the Wall more current, even if they haven't updated themselves in a while.

✔ **Default Landing Tab for Everyone Else:** In Chapter 6, we talk about the feeling of landing on the Wall of a new friend and feeling like you just interrupted an incredibly interesting conversation. To prevent your potential fans from feeling that pain, you can opt for them to land on a tab of your choosing.

✔ **Auto-Expand Comments:** Comments on posts can be very interesting. If there are a lot of them, however, they can become unwieldy or irrelevant. This option allows you to keep these comments condensed. Users can still click to see them, but they won't show up until they click.

✔ **Fans can write on the Wall:** We strongly recommend keeping this one checked, but for some industries, it just isn't as possible for users to have the ability to comment at will. If you need to turn this one off, you can do so here.

✔ **Posting Ability:** Here is where you can control whether your fans are allowed to add photos, videos, and links as attachments to their posts.

Figure 12-6:
Wall
Settings.

Applications

We spend a lot of time in this book talking about how applications integrate with your personal Profile. Remember that when you first create your Profile, you have some default applications (which you can remove if you don't find them useful), as well as more applications that you can use to meet your specific needs. The same is true for your Facebook Page. Most Facebook Pages come prepackaged with a default set of applications, as shown in Figure 12-7. Depending on the category you choose, you may get a few choice extras. You're free to keep any of the preinstalled applications or remove them (with the exception of the Reviews application, which is required for all Pages in certain categories), and you're encouraged to browse and add more applications that you think your customers will find engaging.

Depending on which applications you use, you may want to consider adding a *tab* to feature its content. For example, if you add a lot of photos of your wares, a Photos tab gives people an easy way to see your full history of photo albums, not just the most recent one that may be at the top of your Wall. The same goes for any of the other applications you get by default. Additionally, if you add a lot of applications from third parties, you can create a Boxes tab that shows a small snippet of each application's content, each in its own box.

To add a tab, click on the little + (plus) sign next to the Info tab. This expands a menu and lets you choose which tab you want to add.

Photos

Use the Photos application to publish albums for your fans to enjoy. If you own a restaurant, you may want to take photos of your most popular dishes, creating one album for breakfast, one for lunch, and one for dinner. Bands may publish albums from their various concerts and events. Brands may use photos to show off people engaging with their products. For example, Nike might show women in Nike shoes, Starbucks might show a kid with whipped cream on his nose, and Blockbuster might show friends watching a movie. Add photos by clicking the Photos link in the Publisher (remember to make sure you're on your Page's Publisher, not on your Profile's).

If you choose, you can set the Photos application to allow people who've connected to you to add photos to your Page. These photos are shown in a separate section from the photos you add, which helps viewers distinguish the content you're adding to your Page from what your fans add. Publishing photos is often a great way to keep your Wall looking really diverse, and to generate interesting posts to go into your subscribers' News Feeds.

Events

If you ever host any kind of event for your business, you'll get a ton of value from the Events application. Stores create Events for their big sales, comedians create Events for their shows, and clubs create Events for their special-party nights. To create an Event, click the pencil icon in the upper right of the Events box on the Control Panel. Choose Edit from the menu that appears. This takes you to the Create Event page, where you can fill out the info and upload a photo (see Chapter 11 for more details on Event creation). Finally, send a message to all your subscribers informing them about your event. A bit later, we talk more about what sending messages to your fans entails.

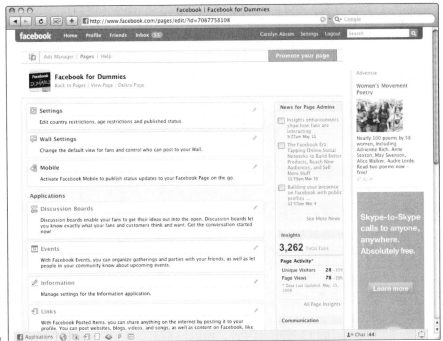

Figure 12-7: The Applications and Settings portion of the Pages Control Panel.

Discussion board

Every Page comes with a discussion board for your fans to congregate and discuss topics relating to your Page. A discussion board takes no setup on your side, which is why there's no box for it in the Control Panel. You can add it as a tab if you want to give people easier access to it. With the Discussion Board on your Page, users can instantly start topics and respond to others.

Video

The Video application for your Page works in a similar way than it does for your Profile (see Chapter 8). Just like with Photos, you can upload videos to your Page. For example, a coffee shop may show a video of a barista making a fancy drink, a singer may show clips from a recent concert, and a movie theater may show clips from an upcoming film. Zappos has added some pretty funny videos that include interviews and short skits done by its employees. It's a great way to put a human face on something very inhuman, like an online shoe store, in the case of Zappos. You can add videos from the Publisher.

Reviews

Besides being a way for you to represent your business or band, Facebook Pages are also a means by which real people get real information about the businesses around them. For this reason, users can count on the Reviews application on each and every Facebook Page in relevant categories. Unlike writing on the Wall (which can only be written on after people connect to you), anyone can write a review on any Facebook Page (although admins can't review their own businesses). Reviews are also different from the Wall in that each user can only ever write one review, although she can update that review if her impression of the business changes.

To do this, you need to first go to the Control Panel (Edit Page) and then click the Edit link (the pencil icon) in the upper right of the Reviews bar. Then click Edit in that drop-down list box.

More Applications

At the bottom of the Applications section of your Page's Control Panel is the More Applications box (refer to Figure 12-7). Depending on the category you initially selected for your Page, this box may already be populated with applications that Facebook thinks could be appropriate for your type of business. Restaurants, for example, may be encouraged to add the OpenTable application, which allows your customers to make reservations straight from your Facebook Page.

The Discography application comes recommended for movies and TV shows because many have sound tracks. To discover more about these applications, search for them in the Application Directory (which is covered in detail in Chapter 13) click the title to go to the application's About page. From there, if you like what you see, you can choose Add to my Page under the Application's Logo, with the other action links. To see more apps than those recommended, click the Browse More link in the upper right to go to the Product Directory. You'll already be in the For Facebook Pages section of the directory, and every application you see listed there can be added to your Facebook Page to increase your fans' engagement with your Page.

Most applications in the Application directory are built by companies other than Facebook. Although many of them make fantastic applications that can add a ton of value to your Page, some of them may be, um, inadequate. Facebook has rules to protect you from *malicious* applications, but not those that are simply low quality. After adding an application, we recommend that you check how it interacts with your Page and watch how your fans use it. Be sure that an application adds value before you decide to keep it.

Rather than browsing the Application Directory for good applications, some Page administrators check out their competitors' Pages to see what kinds of applications seem to be working well. If you do this and see one you like, look for links to the Application's main page in order to add it to your Page.

Settings

The very top of the Control Panel features a box for editing your Page's settings, of which, for now, there are only three, as shown in Figure 12-8:

- ✔ **Country Restrictions:** Because Facebook is an international site, it may be helpful to restrict your Page's visibility only to countries that speak the language your Page is in. Additionally, some Page type, like movies, may want to have a different focus or different admin in different countries. For those needs, each Page can be restricted by country.

- ✔ **Age Restrictions:** Put an age restriction on your Page in case you're promoting something that's illegal or irrelevant to those under a particular age, such as bars or matchmaking services.

- ✔ **Published Status:** This is basically a toggle for turning your Page on and off. You won't want to publish the page to everyone until you feel like it's ready, so after you get your basic information and a few posts up, you can change this to Published (publicly visible).

Some Page types, like bands, artists, or public figures may see an additional setting that allows them to change their Page's gender pronoun. If you're a band with more than one member, using *they* makes the most sense. An actress would select *she*. This pronoun is used in sentences, such as those that appear in your Page's Recent Activity. For example, "The Shins added a new album to their Discography," or "Blake Ross added edited his Photo Album."

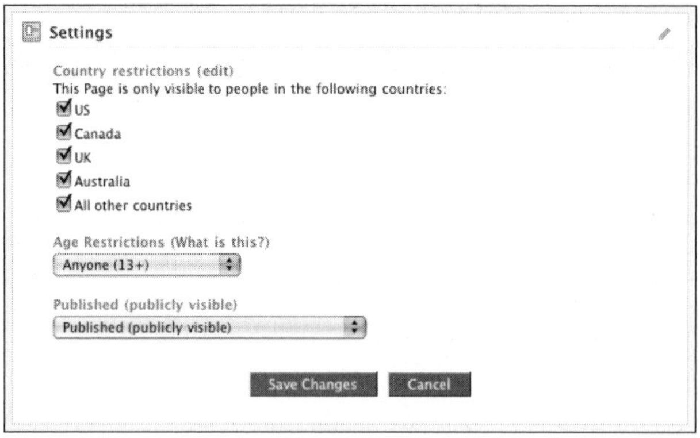

Settings

Country restrictions (edit)
This Page is only visible to people in the following countries:
☑ US
☑ Canada
☑ UK
☑ Australia
☑ All other countries

Age Restrictions (What is this?)
[Anyone (13+) ⇕]

Published (publicly visible)
[Published (publicly visible) ⇕]

[Save Changes] [Cancel]

Figure 12-8:
Fine-tuning
your
settings on
a Facebook
Page.

Mobile

If you want a little more flexibility in terms of *when* you create posts, you can use your phone as a direct link from the outside world to your Page. For example, you can update your status from your mobile phone, which updates your Facebook Page, as well as updates your subscribers' News Feeds with that information. This type of functionality isn't for everyone, but if you're representing people of any type, these types of quick updates make the Page feel much more authentic. This is the difference between sending a press release detailing a band's most recent concert and sending a short sentence saying, "Minor explosion during sound check. No one was hurt, and the show goes on." Which feels more real to you? Which do you want to pay more attention to?

Mobile for Pages has a few limitations, including the fact that there's only one phone per page, and only one page or Profile per phone. In other words, one phone needs to be imbued with the power to update the Page from afar. The phone you select needs to have basic text-messaging capabilities.

Your carrier's normal text messaging fees apply to texts you send or receive as a result of updating your Page via Facebook Mobile. Make sure you're okay with this cost before setting anything up.

After you've selected the phone you're going to use to update your Page, keep it close and follow these steps:

1. **Expand the Mobile section of the Control Panel by clicking Edit Mobile.**

   This is the same pencil icon that always indicates editable content on Facebook. It expands to reveal links.

2. **Click Register for Facebook Mobile Texts.**

   The Activate Facebook Texts dialog appears, as shown in Figure 12-9.

Figure 12-9:
The first
step toward
activating
mobile for
your Page.

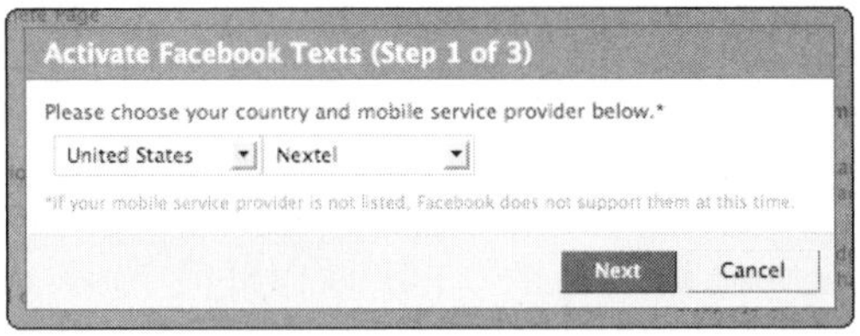

> **Activate Facebook Texts (Step 1 of 3)**
>
> Please choose your country and mobile service provider below.*
>
> United States ▼ | Nextel ▼
>
> *If your mobile service provider is not listed, Facebook does not support them at this time.
>
> [Next] [Cancel]

3. **Select your country and your mobile carrier, and then click Next.**

   The second screen appears, instructing you on a specific text message you should send to FBOOK (32665).

4. **Send the text message from your phone as instructed.**

   If everything worked, you should receive a text message back from Facebook almost immediately. It contains a confirmation code.

5. **Back on your computer, click Next.**

   The final step for activating mobile appears, as shown in Figure 12-10.

6. **Enter the confirmation code you received on your phone into the designated box within the dialog box. When you're done, click Confirm.**

   On your phone, you should get another text telling you that your phone has been confirmed. On your screen, the mobile texts Page appears with some instructions on how to use Facebook mobile as a Page owner.

Figure 12-10:
Enter your
mobile
confirmation
code.

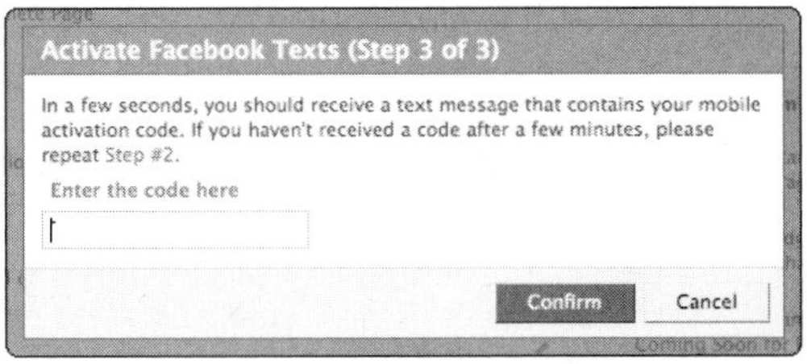

> **Activate Facebook Texts (Step 3 of 3)**
>
> In a few seconds, you should receive a text message that contains your mobile activation code. If you haven't received a code after a few minutes, please repeat Step #2.
>
> Enter the code here
>
> [   ]
>
> [Confirm] [Cancel]

Now, anytime you want to say something to your fans, you merely need to send a text message from the activated phone to FBOOK (32665) with the text of your post in the message. The post appears on your Wall, the only difference being that it will have a little mobile icon next to it, like in Figure 12-11.

Figure 12-11:
Status
updates
from your
phone are
denoted by
a mobile
icon.

Admins

Most businesses have more than one person sharing responsibility for promotion. Perhaps you're the co-owner of your restaurant, or you're part of a marketing team for several companies, or maybe you're the drummer of a band that's sick of the lead singer holding all the cards. Good news: Every Facebook Page can have up to 25 administrators, all of whom can admin the Page through their personal account. This means no password-sharing and no creating fake accounts. Whoever initially creates the Page simply needs to invite all the appropriate people to help administer the Page. Here's how:

1. **Navigate to the Control Panel of your Page.**

2. **In the Admins section in the right column (under which only you are listed), click Edit.**

3. **Invite people to be the administrators of your Page.**

   You can invite any person who already has a Facebook account and with whom you're friends on Facebook to be an admin by entering his name into the Friend Selector in the upper right of the Invite Admins page. You can enter the-mail address of any person who isn't on Facebook or with whom you're not friends in the box on the bottom right. In either case, the person you invite must accept the invitation in order to become an admin.

Promote your Page

To benefit from the viral nature of Facebook, you must seed your Page with people who want to become your fans.

Tell customers electronically

If you have an existing Web site or a mailing list, you may want to add a link or send a message to alert your existing fans or customers that they can now find you on Facebook. For those in your fan base who already have a Facebook account, they'll probably find that connecting with you there is way more convenient that remembering to go to your site regularly. And having them connect with your Facebook Page doesn't preclude them continuing to visit your Web site; rather, a Facebook Page gives you an extra opportunity to communicate with them about changes and updates on your site.

Tell customers physically

If you have a physical store, try sticking a sign on the window that tells customers to find you on Facebook. That way, they don't have to remember yet another URL. As long as they remember your business name and Facebook, they can look you up and connect with your business on an on-going basis.

Tell your friends

If you run a business, you probably already spend a lot of time marketing it to your friends. We'll go out on a limb here and hypothesize that you don't enjoy sending mass e-mails or constantly promoting your business to your friends and family. You never know who really wants to hear about it or who is just being polite by not complaining. Directing your friends to your Facebook Page solves two problems. They can choose to become a fan of your Page, and then they can choose whether to receive updates. This means the following:

✔ You update only those people who want to hear about it.

✔ You seed your Page with a slew of fans whose actions on your Page serve as passive referrals when their friends read about it in News Feeds or Highlights.

To share your Page with your friends:

1. **Navigate to your Facebook Page.**

2. **Scroll to the bottom and click Share.**

3. **Add up to 20 of your friends in the To line and welcome them to your Page.**

You can also stick the link in an e-mail. We don't recommend messaging your friends more than once in this way, though. If they want to hear from your business, they'll become a fan; if not, they're probably not great customers, anyway.

Advertise

In Chapter 15, we introduce you to the world of advertising on Facebook, with a special emphasis on how to advertise your Facebook Page. The beauty of advertising your Page on Facebook is that you're already targeting the audience most likely to understand what your Facebook Page is all about. Also, from the audience's point of view, it's a smoother experience to click an ad in Facebook, which navigates to another Facebook page. This is very different than how most Web advertising works, where clicking an ad opens a whole new window into a whole different Web site.

Engage your fans

If you've read this chapter to this point, you have your customized Facebook Page and are ready to drive traffic to your business. Now may be a good time to get up, take a little walk, a nap, or make a delicious turkey sandwich (extra cranberry, hold the mayo). You're done with the basic work required to allow people to find out about your business and connect with it.

To gain real attention and interaction, though, you can do a lot more. *Remember:* The richer your Page and the more you engage your fans, the more actions they take (and the more they have warm fuzzy feelings when they think of you), which generates News Feeds and Highlights stories for all their friends to see, thus giving you more visibility and attention.

Publish rich content

By *rich,* we mean informative and fresh. The more new and useful content you add to your Page, the more reason your fans have to come back and check it out. Here are some ideas to keep fans (that is, customers) lingering on your content:

- **Publish authentic status updates:** These short posts go into people's Live Feeds and News Feeds and remind them that you exist. However, if your posts get annoying, others are likely to hide you from their home page and other lists. Be as real as possible: User posts range from deep and thoughtful to silly to quirky; yours can also run the gamut. If it's raining and that changes something for your business, let your customers know. If you're in a band and you just landed in a new city, let your fans know. If you found an article that's relevant to your fans, let them know. If you're just starting on the second edition of a book on how to use Facebook, let your readers know. Don't end every post with a link to buy your particular good or service. Every once in a while, that's fine, especially if you're offering a discount or sale, but too much and it gets annoying.

- **Publish Photos, Video, Notes, and Links** to bring your Page to life, making it grow while your business does. If you sell stuff, you can continually add photos and videos of new products or of people using your existing ones. If you provide a service, you can add videos showing you or your employees at work — say, an expert barista pouring a latte, a sculptor whose fans would love to see him in action, or an auto technician offering tips on good car care. If your fans like what they see, they're very likely to use the Facebook communication tools to show your content to their friends, giving your business more attention.

✔ **Hold Events** to keep your patrons hooked. You use Facebook Events to invite fans to special parties, sales, or promotions. Some businesses hold events *just* for their fans on Facebook. When your fans RSVP your event, their friends may read about it on their Home pages. They can easily invite their friends along as well, or else their friends may just read about it, which is still probably good for your business.

✔ **Talk to your fans,** on behalf of your business. Your fans will be writing on your Wall and discussion board, and they'll be writing reviews. Wherever possible, feel free to contribute. If someone writes on your Wall about how they had a bad experience, don't delete it — respond! You can as easily comment on your own posts (or on posts from your fans) as your Page. In the case of the bad service experience, apologize and tell her you'll give her a free meal or discounted service if she comes back (and shows you her ID, which you'll know because her name is listed next to her Wall post). Other people who see the exchange will be impressed by your level of service.

If you're a shoe salesman and someone asks on your discussion board about finding the perfect shoe, fill him in. This public dialog has the benefit of informing other customers with the same questions. Any time you write on the Wall or a discussion board of a Page that you administer, your comments are listed on behalf of the business itself, rather than you. This helps viewers trust your voice of authority and doesn't expose your personal account to anyone.

Send Updates

There's a difference between the updates that you publish and the updates that you send. Updates that you publish are usually short, and relevant, and often time-sensitive. They are the types of information that can easily filter down a subscriber's Live Feed, and if it gets missed, it's probably okay. Updates that you send are more like newsletters or bulletins. They have some information that you don't want getting lost in the shuffle. Again, it's pretty important to send updates that are relevant; otherwise, your subscribers may opt out.

When looking at your Page, notice the action links beneath the profile picture. There may only be a few displayed, but clicking More reveals all the actions you can take, including a link to Send an Update to Fans. Updates on Facebook are different than other types of mailing lists. By clicking this link, you can compose a message that goes out to some or all of your fans.

Before writing an update for your fans, however, you should understand how Updates works from the user perspective:

✔ **People can opt out of Updates.** When users on Facebook find your Page, they choose to affiliate with it by clicking Become a Fan at the upper right of your Facebook page. Upon doing so, they're asked whether they would like to receive updates from your businesses in their News Feeds. You can comfortably assume that anyone who clicks OK wants to hear what you have to say. If a business ever sends updates that a particular person doesn't find valuable, he can opt out of Updates by clicking Opt Out directly from the update itself.

✔ **Updates are kept separate from Friend-to-Friend messages.** When your fans log in after you send an update, a notice on their Home page alerts them that they have a new update. Clicking that notice takes them to the special tab in their Inbox where updates from businesses reside. The reason for sorting business updates differently from Friend-to-Friend messages is simple: They're different. We're all familiar with the disappointment that comes from discovering that a new e-mail is promotional. E-mails from our favorite bands or businesses can be very exciting, if not for the fact that we're usually expecting a personal message.

✔ **Each business competes only with itself for its fans' attention.** The first time a fan receives an Update from a business, a new row for that business is created on that fan's Updates tab in her Inbox. Because every business gets exactly one row in its fans' Updates tabs, even if you send ten messages in a row, you're not adding any clutter to their lives. More Updates simply means that your row bumps to the surface, putting your most recent subject and snippet at the top.

Updates are organized within the Updates tab similar to how messages are arranged in the Inbox (which we describe in Chapter 9):

✔ Each row contains the picture of the business's page, the title, and a snippet of the most recent Update.

✔ A blue dot next to the subject line of an update indicates that unread Updates are in that row.

✔ The rows are ordered by the time at which the most recent Update from that business was sent.

✔ The narrow column on the right of the Updates tab acts like a table of contents, listing the businesses that have rows in the Updates tab. The number next to the businesses' names specifies how many new updates each business sent since the recipient last clicked through.

✔ As soon as a user clicks into a particular row, all updates from that business are immediately marked as read.

Okay, so fans experience updates from businesses very differently from how they experience promotional e-mails or paper mailings. What does this mean for you? It means that you should *update your fans*. They said they want to hear from you. The messages you send won't be misconstrued as spam because of the organization in the system, and users have full control to opt-out at any time.

In the next section, we show you how to track what effect your updates have on your fans' engagement. Use these metrics to help you monitor what types of updates and what frequency of updates optimizes your fans' attention.

Here are a few other things you need to know about updates:

- ✔ **You can include attachments in an update.** If you add a new photo, album, video, note, event, or other piece of content that you'd like your fans to know about, you can copy the URL for the page where that content lives and paste it into the message. In most cases, the content is automatically transformed into an attachment to your update, just like the Share feature we talk about in Chapter 9. Note that you can attach only one piece of content per update.

- ✔ **You can target your Updates.** When you're writing your update, you can select the Target Update option beneath Audience. This allows you to target by location, gender, and age. This is especially useful when promoting events, because people in Omaha may think it's a little mean-spirited to post about your 12 concert or performance dates in NYC.

- ✔ **You can access your sent updates from your Page's Control Panel.** In the right column, just under the Send an Update to Your Fans link, you can click See All Updates.

- ✔ **Fans who opt-in to receive your Updates have access to every Update you sent.** The first time someone receives an Update from your business, only that new update is marked as unread. If she clicks through on the row for your business, she sees all the updates that you sent before she became a fan. Cool, huh?

Know-It-All

In the beginning of this chapter, we mention various types of activities that business owners use to try to grow their customer base: running television and radio commercials; putting ads on buses, benches, and billboards; or hiring someone to dress like a chicken and dance outside your door. One of the hardest problems in advertising is figuring out what kind of effect your efforts have on your business. Facebook Insights are dedicated to unveiling this mystery. If you already set up your Page, follow along with this next section. If you haven't, this section may be the one that convinces you to.

Within 48 hours of publishing your Page, you start to see exactly how people are engaging with it. Click the Ads and Pages from the Applications menu to land on the manager application for all of your ads and Pages. Click on the Pages option at the top of that page, and then select View Insights for whichever Page you want on the subsequent list. This will take you to an *overview page* for that Page, which gives you 24-hour feedback about the current success of your Page. By default, you see two main graphs about your Page's metrics — interaction information and audience information.

The first graphs and stats you see deal with interaction. On Facebook, it's not just about page views or mass reach; the best indicator of your Page's effectiveness is if people are interacting with it. Facebook defines interactions as being a combination of comments, Wall posts, and likes (that is, when someone clicks the little thumbs up that means "I like this" in Facebook-land). In short, these interactions are going to be based on how people respond to the content you post.

The sample graph in Figure 12-12 shows the Interactions Graph Drop-down menu and the accompanying demographic break-down for interacting connections.

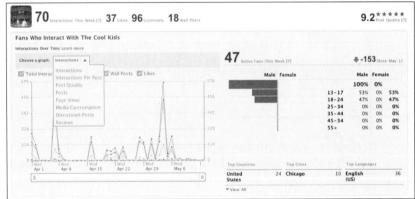

Figure 12-12:
Insights on interactions.

There are several graphs you can look at:

- ✔ **Interactions:** This one shows the total interactions on your page over 24 hours.

- ✔ **Interactions Per Post:** This graph tracks the average number of comments, likes, and Wall posts generated by each post you publish.

✔ **Post Quality:** Post quality is measured by calculating how much engagement results from each post coming from your page. A high Post Quality score means your posts are engaging and interesting to your connections. That's a good thing.

✔ **Stream CTR/ETR:** Stream click-through rate (CTR) shows how often people visit your page and come from a post you created that they saw on their Home pages. Stream engagement rate (ETR) shows how often people comment or like a post they see on their Home pages.

✔ **Posts:** This graph shows how many posts you've created.

✔ **Page Views:** A pretty standard Internet metric, this shows how many times your Page was viewed from day to day.

✔ **Media Consumption:** This graph shows how many times your photos, videos, notes, or other rich media get viewed by your fans.

✔ **Reviews:** Number of reviews created.

By default, all Insights graphs show you their information since the beginning of time . . . well, since your Page was created, anyway. You can change the time frame to more carefully inspect a particular month, week, or even day. Shrink the time window by dragging either corner of the bar below the graph toward the center. You can then scroll along the timeline.

The second set of graphs focuses more on fans and subscriptions and how they relate to each other. The sample shown in Figure 12-13 has the graph drop-down expanded. There is, once again, a demographic breakdown of people who have connected to you to the right of these graphs.

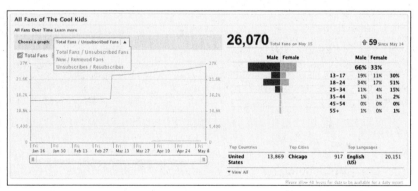

Figure 12-13:
Insights on
fans and
subscribers.

- ✔ **Total Fans/Unsubscribed Fans:** Total fans represents the total number of people who have connected to you. Unsubscribed fans represent all the people who connected you, but decided at some point that they didn't want to see your posts in their News Feeds. A sudden rise in unsubscribed fans may indicate that you are posting uninteresting content too often.

- ✔ **New/Removed Fans:** You definitely want to keep the new fans graph moving up and to the right, but keeping track of people who remove their connection to you may prove to be just as useful. If you're hemorrhaging fans, you should make sure you haven't done anything — on Facebook or off — to jeopardize your relationship with your customers.

- ✔ **Unsubscribes/Resubscribes:** This graph compares the number of times (not the number of people) people unsubscribe from your posts. In other words, the number of times people decide, "I don't want to hear from this guy anymore." A resubscribe occurs whenever someone says, "Actually, I didn't mean that at all." Again, paying attention to when these events happen helps you learn a lot about your fans and the type of content they like to see.

Part IV
Delving Further into Facebook

The 5th Wave   By Rich Tennant

"That's the problem-on Facebook, everyone knows you're a dog."

In this part . . .

We warn you upfront: By the time you've made it to this part, most people wouldn't refer to you as a dummy. In fact, your friends are possibly already calling you for help with Facebook. Now that you understand the basics of Facebook, you want to know how to make it even better, even more integrated into your life. And we can show you that.

This part covers bringing Facebook everywhere you go using Facebook Mobile, as well as making your experience richer through the use of third-party applications and ads. Hang on to your hats; this is going to be fun.

Chapter 13

Facebook and the Web

In This Chapter

▶ Understanding Facebook Platform and the social graph

▶ Seeing how applications can enhance your Internet experience on and off Facebook

▶ Discovering good, trustworthy applications

*F*acebook made headlines in May 2007 when it announced it was opening up its platform so that any developers anywhere in the world could develop applications on top of its social graph. About a year later, it announced that developers could now create applications outside of the Facebook frame. If this sounds like a lot of buzzwords, that's because it is. What this really meant was that applications — features like Photos and Events — that in the past had been built only by Facebook engineers could now be built by engineers who didn't work for Facebook. These applications built by people outside of Facebook could still integrate into the Facebook experience. Additionally, features that other Web sites wanted to add could now leverage Facebook info (with permission) to create a more seamless experience.

In this chapter, we give you the basic breakdown of what a platform is and how it works for you as a user. We then go into detail of the different types of applications and how they can benefit you. Finally, we talk about trust and Facebook Platform, and how to know if you're dealing with a good application. If you are a developer, check out the sidebar on good traits of applications, or look up *Building Facebook Applications For Dummies,* by Richard Wagner, published by Wiley.

Understanding What Facebook Platform Is

The most basic example of a platform is a soapbox. In ye olden times, people would take a crate that soap was shipped in, set it down in the middle of ye olde towne square, step on top of it, and shout out their ideas to ye olde crowde.

There are three players here: the soapbox, the person, and the crowde. While you keep reading, here are a couple things to keep in mind:

- ✔ **The soapbox didn't create the ideas.** The ideas belonged to the person shouting, the soapbox literally giving them a platform from which to enumerate them. A person could stand in the middle of the crowd, at the same level, yelling at everyone else, but they wouldn't be heard as well.

- ✔ **The soapbox means nothing without the crowd.** No matter how high the soapbox boosts you up and allows you to project your voice, if there's no one there to listen, your ideas can't spread.

If you've ever used a PC, you've probably used some version of Microsoft Windows (something like Windows 95, Windows XP, or Windows Vista). Windows is what's known as an *operating system.* It's the graphical interface used to access files and programs on your computer. You don't technically need an operating system. You could manually give your computer text commands to navigate the various files and systems, but that's much harder than using the interface that Microsoft provides. The operating system offers some core functionality that can then be used by various applications.

You've also probably used some version of Microsoft Word. This program was developed by Microsoft. However, you may have other programs on your computer that weren't built by Microsoft — maybe some sort of game, or something like Quicken, which you can use to track your spending. Because both Microsoft and Quicken can build applications, or programs, that work within Microsoft Windows, Windows is a platform for applications — whether built by Microsoft or a third party.

Facebook Platform, like a soapbox or an operating system, also offers core functionality that can be accessed to create applications. Facebook refers to its core functionality as the social graph. The *social graph* is the series of connections — Profiles linked to other Profiles via friendships — that makes up Facebook. Information spreads across the social graph in all the ways we've talked about in previous chapters — through messages, posts, and thousands of casual interactions that tell you the most recent information about all your friends based on your closeness and the relevance of the information.

For a long time, Facebook was the only company that could build on its own platform. And it did; it built Photos, Notes, Events, and Groups. All these applications use the connections that exist between individuals on the site to spread more information. These connections are what set Facebook applications apart from other sites, even ones specialized for various applications.

The classic example of this is Photos. Facebook has the number-one photo-sharing application on the Web. Facebook Photos doesn't have all the features of specific photo-sharing sites, like high-resolution storage or anything like that, but it's still more popular than the others. This is because of the connections — your ability to tag your friends in photos. When you do this, your friends are notified and they look at the pictures. This information is also spread through News Feed, where your friends can see your photos and comment on what they see. This, in turn, makes your friends more likely to use the Photos application the next time they want to share photos.

When Facebook opened up Facebook Platform, it enabled third-party developers anywhere to build applications that fit into Facebook as easily as Facebook Photos fits in. Like the soapbox, Facebook Platform lets application developers get their ideas and creations out to a crowd of people quickly and easily.

The soapbox — the platform — doesn't create the ideas or applications, and the platform means nothing without the crowd. You and your friends are the crowd, which is why Facebook applications can actually be useful to you.

Applications That Live on Facebook

In Chapter 8, we talk in detail about a few Facebook applications, built by Facebook, that live on Facebook. The biggest difference between these applications and the ones that you'll use and love from outside developers is that you had Photos, Notes, and Video waiting for you when you first signed up for Facebook. All of the pieces that made these work — tagging, notifications, posts to your Wall, and so on — were already at work behind the scenes.

When you use applications, you need to be a bit of the stage manager for how these applications work. You've been practicing for this moment as you set privacy and other controls on the various applications that Facebook built. Now that the curtain is about to open, you are ready to take command of all these aspects of each application:

- ✔ **Access to info:** Before an application can do anything interesting with the info about you and your friends, you need to authorize it to access your info.

- ✔ **Posts to your Wall and friends' News Feeds:** One of the key ways you (and your friends) learn about interesting things is through streams of dynamic information. For example, adding a photo album wouldn't be very useful if your friends didn't see that front and center on your Profile and possibly in their Home pages.

- ✔ **Bookmarks**: You probably see little icons for Photos, Events, and Notes in the Chat bar at the bottom of your page. As you use applications, you can add them there, or to the Applications menu. These bookmarks can also be used as filters on the Home page.

- ✔ **Invitations and requests you receive and send:** You can invite friends to Events; you can also invite friends to play games or support causes. These are actions you always have to do with some intent, regardless of whether the application was built by Facebook.

✔ **Notifications you receive and send:** Applications also spread information by notifying people involved when something happened that is relevant to them.

✔ **Boxes, Tabs, and Info Sections that display on your Profile:** Depending on what's important to you, you can decide what boxes people see in the left column of your Profile, what tabs you add to your Profile, and what sections you add to your Info tab.

✔ **Privacy settings:** Just like with applications built by Facebook, you control who sees boxes and tabs that live on Facebook.

✔ **Special Permissions:** There are a number of unique permissions that you can grant to applications that are usually only required by certain types of applications or certain reasons. For example, a desktop application will usually need a Special Permission to access your info even when you're not browsing the Web.

This is a bit general, so in the next section, we go through the process of actually using an application. We highlight where all of these parts appear.

Checking out Causes

Causes is a Facebook application that lets people gather around — you guessed it — causes they want to promote or support. Causes is built for Facebook, and in fact has no Web presence outside of Facebook. That makes it a great candidate to show how a Facebook application fits into the Facebook experience and all the ways that you get to choose how you want it to fit in.

If you want to follow along on your own screen, you can find Causes by searching for it in the upper-right corner. For the purposes of our example, we start from the Causes application page, as shown in Figure 13-1.

To actually get started using Causes, click on Go to Application, which takes you to the Allow Access screen shown in Figure 13-2.

Does this sound familiar? It's the first bullet in the list of ways you control how applications integrate with Facebook. The Allow Access? screen is a reminder that the application you're about to use wasn't built by Facebook, and therefore Facebook can't make any official promises about how your information will be used after you agree to give an application access. Facebook policy prohibits some things, like storing your data for extended periods of time, or circumventing Facebook's privacy rules. For most applications, like for Facebook, it's in everyone's best interests for the application to be honest and to respect your trust. However, part of trust is that everyone takes part. It is your responsibility to make sure you trust an application before you agree to allow it access to your info.

Figure 13-1:
The
Application
Page for
Causes.

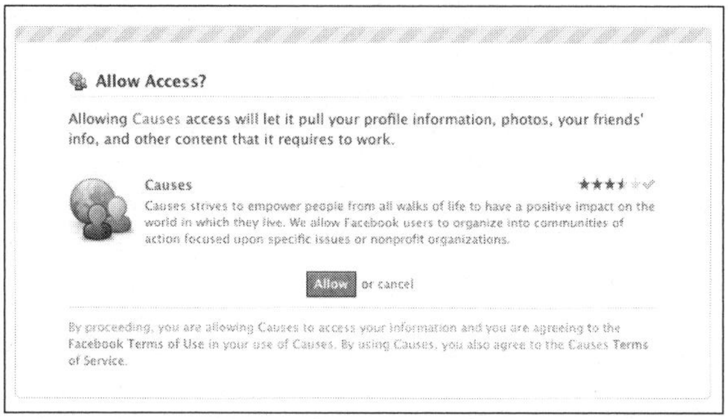

Figure 13-2:
Do you want
to allow
Causes to
have access
to your info?

We talk more about how to recognize trustworthy and untrustworthy applications later on in this chapter, in the section, "Signs of a trustworthy application." Assume for now that you've have done your homework in this case, and know that Causes can be trusted. Click that big Allow Access button.

After you've clicked Allow Access, you see a screen similar to Figure 13-3.

The Causes Home page, much like the Facebook Home page, or the landing pages for applications for Photos or Groups, is a gateway into the various actions you can take (like creating or joining a cause). When we say that applications "live" inside Facebook, this is what we mean — Causes Home is surrounded by the Facebook navigation menus, as if it's any other page.

One of the actions you can take from the Causes Home page is to create a new cause. To do this, click on the Find Causes menu at the top of the page and select Start a Cause. The screens you see when you create something from an application vary depending on the application, just as creating a photo album is different from creating a note. We've started creating a cause in Figure 13-4.

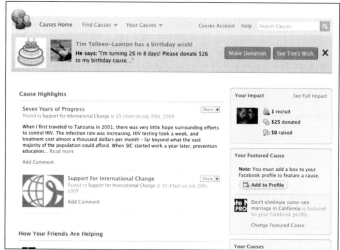

Figure 13-3:
The Causes
Home page.

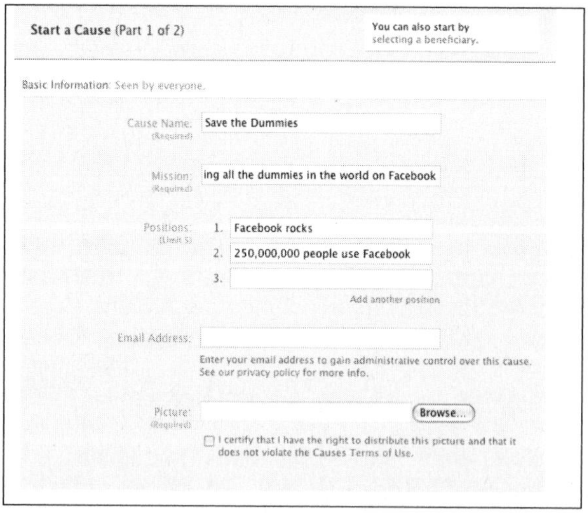

Figure 13-4:
Creating a
new cause.

After you create a Cause, you see a small prompt that explains that you need the ability to receive e-mail if you want to have an original cause. This is important because Facebook usually limits applications' access to e-mails because it doesn't want applications to spam users without permission. That's why opting into e-mails requires a Special Permission, in this case, permission to e-mail the user. All Special Permissions should have headers similar to that shown in Figure 13-5, although the nature of each permission will vary.

Figure 13-5: Special Permissions for e-mails.

After you create your cause, a Publisher prompt appears, as shown in Figure 13-6. This allows both you and the application you are using to gain distribution by pushing information out to your friends through their Home pages. In this example, any of Carolyn's friends may see this cause, decide to join, donate, or decide to use Causes to collect money for an organization they want to support.

Figure 13-6: A prompt to publish to your Wall and your friends' Home pages.

The final step of the creation flow for Causes allows you to invite friends to support your cause, and also gains distribution for Causes, because your use of it may imply to your friends that you like the application, making them more likely to check it out as well. Figure 13-7, in a display of both information and meta-ness, shows the confirmation dialog box that you would need to approve to send invitations. That dialog box shows what the actual invitation will look like.

Figure 13-7: Sending invites.

If someone chooses to join the Cause we just created, a notification, like that shown in Figure 13-8, lets us know so we can continue to interact with other people through Causes. Lots of applications send notifications for any number of reasons; if any of them are bothering you, mouse over the application you don't like and click on the little X. This gives you a prompt to stop all notifications from that application, and you can even mark notifications as spam if you believe it is spamming you.

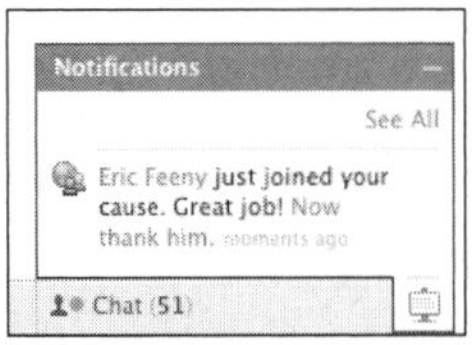

Figure 13-8: Receiving notifications.

On the Causes Home page, at the Chat bar at the bottom of the page, is a prompt to Bookmark Causes. Bookmarking applications means that you always have easy access to it from the bottom Chat bar, either via an icon, like those you see in Figure 13-9, or via the Applications menu.

Also from the Causes Home page, a small prompt explains that if you want to feature a cause on your Profile, you first need to add a box to your Profile. In Chapter 6, we talked about how Profile boxes can help you feature stuff you really care about or really want your friends to see when they visit your Profile. So if you really want to feature a cause like "Save the Dummies," you may elect to add a Profile box. The Add Causes to Your Profile Box dialog box is shown in Figure 13-10. The top row lets you choose where exactly you want this Profile box to live — in the left-hand column of your Wall and Info tab or in the Boxes tab. The Boxes tab, which we also talk about in Chapter 6, is a tab on your Profile that is just a home for application boxes.

Some applications prompt you to add an Info section instead of a box. Info sections are designed to live on your Info tab and fit in with static information like your favorite books and work history. Usually they are much more text-heavy and don't change as often as the content in boxes.

Figure 13-9: Book-marking causes.

Figure 13-10: Add a box to your Profile.

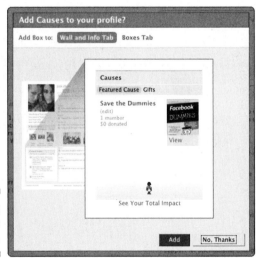

From your Profile, you can also choose to add a Causes tab. Because tabs are big and very prominent on your Profile, this is something you would normally do for the applications you care about most and want people to see the most. To add a tab, like in Figure 13-11, click on the plus sign (+) to the right of your rightmost tab and select the application you want to add.

Figure 13-11:
Adding an
application
tab.

| Carolyn Abram self-improvement is hard. 32 minutes ago clear |

Wall Info Photos Boxes ➕ Add a new tab

What's on your mind?

🌐 Causes

📅 Events

Attach 📷 📹 🔗 🌐 ▼

📝 Notes

Share

Imagine the Causes you support and feature on your Profile are a bit controversial. You may not want co-workers, or certain friends, or people who are
visiting your Profile for the first time to see your Causes. Facebook allows
you to use privacy to control who sees the Profile boxes and tabs, but keep in
mind that these settings don't apply to posts you create. Anyone who can get
to your Wall can see posts that you create related to Causes. To set privacy
on this application, follow these steps:

1. **Click Applications in the lower left-hand corner of the screen, in the
   Chat bar.**

2. **Click Edit Applications.**

   This takes you to the Edit Applications page, which we talk about later
   in the "Managing Your Applications" section of this chapter.

3. **Find Causes and click Edit Settings.**

   This brings up a dialog box similar to what's shown in Figure 13-12.

4. **In the Privacy drop-down list, choose the visibility level or create a
   custom setting for that application.**

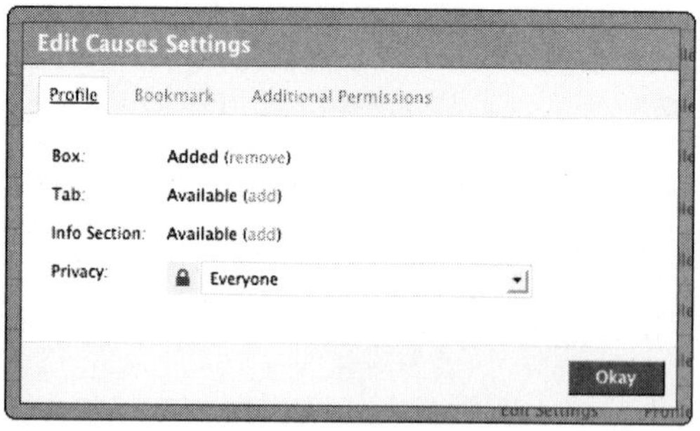

Edit Causes Settings

Profile   Bookmark   Additional Permissions

Box: Added (remove)
Tab: Available (add)
Info Section: Available (add)
Privacy: 🔒 Everyone   ▼

Okay

Figure 13-12:
Edit settings
here.

The privacy setting you create here only applies to the boxes and tabs you
add to your profile. It does not apply to posts you create that go to your
friends' News Feeds and Live Feeds.

Keep in mind that Causes is just one example of how an application might fit into your Facebook experience. Different applications may want to post content more frequently, or may strongly encourage you to invite friends. The important thing to keep in mind is that _you_ control what applications get to do. You don't have to add boxes or publish posts if you don't want to. Don't be afraid to show your applications who's boss.

Figuring out why to use applications inside Facebook

Well, you certainly don't need to use applications to have a completely wonderful, rich Facebook experience. If you aren't comfortable with applications, or haven't found one that you'd find useful or relevant, they aren't required, and they don't provide you with any Facebook expertise. Plenty of Facebook experts use very few, if any, applications. That being said, there are a few good reasons to use applications:

- ✔ **They offer functionality Facebook doesn't.** Facebook has rules about creating Profiles only for real people, and many a pet-lover, over the years, has had the misfortune of seeing Fluffy's fake Profile taken down. Dogbook, an application that lets you create a Profile for your dog within your own Profile, means people have the ability to represent this important part of their lives on Facebook, without violating Facebook's terms. Similarly, music-related applications, or course-related applications for students, have filled the gaps that exist for specific groups of people on Facebook.

- ✔ **They can be really fun.** Do you like word scrambles? Do you like to type? Do you like to pretend you own a restaurant? Do you like Texas Hold 'Em? Really, any game you can imagine is offered as a Facebook application, and it pairs the delight of a game you love with the cutthroat competition that can only happen among friends. For example, a simple typing game like Typing Maniac becomes much more entertaining when you are vying for first place with one of your good friends.

- ✔ **They connect you in new ways to the people you care about.** All of the applications on Facebook help you learn more about people and stay in touch with them in different ways. Whether that's knowing what concerts a friend all the way across the country is going to, or finding out that Carolyn is, in fact, Eliza Bennet via the "Which literary heroine are you?" quiz application, all of this information enriches your relationships in small, subtle ways.

Exploring Applications That Live Outside of Facebook

Imagine all the things you do on the Web. Maybe you buy gifts for friends at Amazon.com. Or perhaps you blog, or like to comment on blogs that others write. Maybe you look up movie reviews. Maybe you rent movies through sites like Blockbuster or Netflix. You do any number of things, all of which, we would wager a small sum, would be better if your friends were there.

Wish you had a better sense of whose Yelp reviews you could trust? Looking for a movie recommendation? Don't actually like dealing with strangers on the Web? Welcome to *Facebook Connect*.

Facebook Connect is the blanket term we use to talk about applications that live on other Web sites. These applications may or may not be similar to the applications you use within Facebook. It may be more accurate to say that these applications use a Facebook link that you establish to make your experience on their sites more social.

There's no one single application that can explain all of the integration points for Facebook Connect because most applications only need one or two of these points to make use of Connect. So we go through some of the implementations you see as you browse the Web and what you should expect.

What to look for

Figures 13-13 and 13-14 show two examples of types of prompts you may see to connect another site with your Facebook account. Figure 13-13 shows a prompt that lives on a Home page; clicking the connect button here basically enables you to skip the process of creating a new account for that site.

Figure 13-13:
Create your Digg account through Facebook Connect.

Figure 13-14 shows an example of a Connect prompt that may occur after you've already created an account. Often this type of prompt can be found in the Account section of other Web sites.

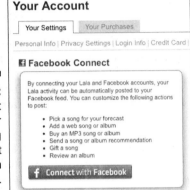

Figure 13-14: Connect your existing account with Facebook.

If a Web site is promoting its Facebook Connect implementation, you usually see some version of that little Facebook "f" (we call that the Facebook *favicon*) along with text like "Log in with Facebook," or "Connect with Facebook." If you're not sure if a Web site has Connect integration, try checking out that Web site's help pages and searching for "Facebook Connect."

Login

The first way Connect can improve your Web experience is to eliminate the need to create a brand new account for every. Single. Web. Site. Ever. The Web forms that ask for your name, your e-mail, subsequent prompts to upload a Profile picture and find friends — these are things of the past. As an example, we're going to log in to post a comment on a blog.

Normally commenting on a blog post at a Gawker news site like Jezebel (www.jezebel.com) doesn't require a lot. You need to at least enter your e-mail address, and if you want to be able to comment more in the future, you create a username and password as well. If you don't want Gawker to have your e-mail, or if you're worried about forgetting your password, maybe you just won't comment. However, when you go to log in at this Web site, you also have the option to log in via Facebook. Now, all you need to do is verify that you want to connect Jezebel to Facebook.

Figure 13-15 shows the Connect login dialog. There are a few important things you should notice about this. The first is that Carolyn's name is already displaying in the bottom of this dialog. This is because she was already logged in to Facebook when she clicked the Connect prompt. If you aren't logged in to Facebook, you see a Facebook login screen in this space, where you have to enter your Facebook login e-mail and password. Also, if you share a computer with other Facebook users, make sure that the name displaying in the bottom of the dialog box is, in fact, yours.

Figure 13-15:
Connect
Jezebel with
Facebook.

The second thing to remember is that this dialog box is basically asking you for the same thing that the Allow Access screen did for Causes — in order to work, this site needs access to your Facebook info. For the most part, sites that use Connect need this info for legitimate purposes, but you should still make sure you trust the site that you're using before you click Connect here. WellknownMcgoodreputation.com? Probably okay. SleazyMcSpamerson.com? Maybe do a little more research first.

Figure 13-16 shows how easy it now is to comment on this particular blog post. There's the space for a comment to be entered, as well as the option to publish the comment back to Facebook (more on that in the next section). Notice how it pulled Carolyn's Profile picture to display next to her comment? Instead of a long registration process, including finding an appropriate photo to upload, Carolyn was able to comment in seconds by just plugging in her Facebook info.

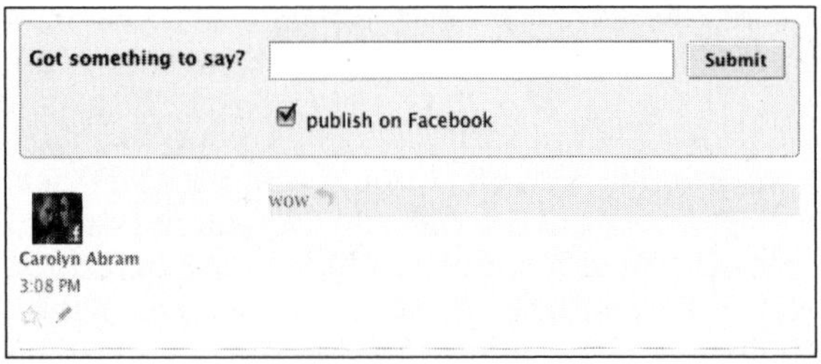

Figure 13-16:
Commenting
is as
easy as
connecting.

> **Got something to say?** [   ] [Submit]
>
> ☑ publish on Facebook
>
> WOW
>
> Carolyn Abram
> 3:08 PM

Sharing with Facebook friends

When you use other Web sites, you take any number of actions that your friends may find interesting. Ratings of restaurants and movies may help a friend the next time he's looking to plan a date night. Scores from a game or comments on a news article may give a friend the urge to compete or just read. Before Facebook connect, unfortunately, all of these actions lived in isolation on their respective Web sites. You could share them with whatever friends you had made on that Web site, but building out that list required a lot of time, time you had already spent doing the same thing on . . . Facebook.

With Facebook Connect, you can easily share posts about content you create on other sites on your Profile and in your friends' News Feeds. Figure 13-17 shows an example of a post about an action taken elsewhere: in this case, the making of a reservation through OpenTable.com.

Figure 13-17:
More
friends,
more info,
more better.

> Andrew 'Boz' Bosworth made a last minute reservation so April and I can grab a nice meal before she takes off. Worried about my neck but trying not to let it stop me from fun stuff.
>
> Andrew made a reservation for **Manresa – Los Gatos** using **OpenTable.com**
>
> See reviews for Manresa – Los Gatos
>
> Thu at 7:04pm · Comment · Like
>
> Yun-Fang Juan It's a great restaurant! The chef beat Bobby Flay in Iron Chef
> Thu at 8:13pm

The great thing about this is that your friends are more likely to see info that you want them to see because it's showing up someplace where they already are. Additionally, Facebook features like commenting and liking make the slightly dull experience of making a reservation more interesting because people can offer their own opinions and ask how the evening went. Connect makes even the most mundane parts of the Internet more social.

Help from Facebook friends

Much as you can share with your Facebook friends, your Facebook friends can share lots of great information with you through various Connect implementations. Figure 13-18 shows a part of the Web site Citysearch (www.citysearch.com). By connecting her account, Carolyn is able to see exactly what her friends from Facebook have already reviewed, in case she missed the original post they created when they first wrote the review.

Figure 13-18: Get the right info from the right people.

Entertainment through Facebook info

This category is a little bit weirder. It tends to apply to marketing or advertising campaigns that use Facebook Connect, which is a much less obvious "benefit" of Facebook Connect (oh great, now I'm connecting my account to the advertisers). But done right, this sort of use can lead to a great advertising experience for marketers and consumers alike. One example (a bit hard to fully capture in one screenshot) shown in Figure 13-19 was a campaign by the Discovery Channel to get people to watch the "Frenzied Waters" program about sharks. An animation prompts you to see "your story." After connecting the site with your Facebook account, you get to witness the aftermath of your death by shark, including a photo-montage of your life flashing before your eyes, quotes from your friends, and the obituary constructed from your work and education info. In short, it's hilarious, and you'll probably want to learn more about sharks afterwards.

Figure 13-19:
Oh, the
tragedy.

Discovering Other Applications

The most common applications you encounter on Facebook are the ones that live inside Facebook and the Connect Web sites that provide functionality elsewhere. However, there are many other categories of applications that you may find use for over time.

Applications for your business

If you are a Page owner, many applications are designed to live on your Page and provide additional functionality for your business. For example, musicians may want to add the Discography application to show off their different albums or the YouTube application so fans can easily share the YouTube videos they've posted from live concerts.

Applications for your desktop

Desktop applications require you to download something to your computer (as opposed to just making information available to the application). These applications often provide functionality like allowing you to read your News Feed and comment on the posts there without having a Web browser open.

Or, they may take your Facebook events and import them into whatever calendar program you use. In a nutshell, they let you use Facebook outside your browser window.

Applications for your phone

The most basic mobile application is actually just Facebook, itself, which you can learn more about in Chapter 14. However, as Facebook Connect continues to grow, many new mobile applications are being created that allow you to, for example, play mobile games against your Facebook friends on your iPhone. Mobile Platform applications can often feel like a mash-up of Facebook Mobile and an application that often lives within Facebook. The same features, like posting, commenting, or notifications, make these types of applications effective and relevant as you wander around the world, phone in hand.

Finding Your New Favorite Application

With so many applications, it's hard to predict which ones you'll want to use, and which ones will be fun, relevant, and useful to you. We've gone over a few examples here (and for even more of Leah and Carolyn's picks, check out Chapter 16), but the reality is that you have your own tastes, so you may have to do some exploring on your own to find the right applications for your life.

You'll probably discover many applications through your friends — posts they create and invitations they send will tip you off on what you may enjoy. But if you want to go out and find an application *right now,* you need look no further than the Application Directory.

The Application Directory

The Application Directory is pretty much just what it sounds like; a directory of all the applications you can use. To get to the Application Directory, follow these steps:

1. **Click Applications in the bottom-left corner of Facebook.**

2. **Select Browse More Applications.**

   It should be the option closest to the bottom of the list. This brings up the Application Directory, as shown in Figure 13-20.

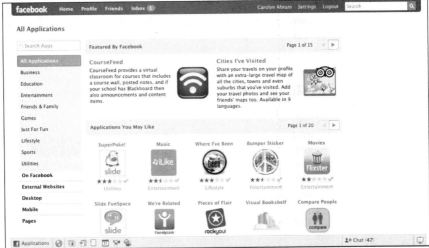

Figure 13-20:
The
Application
Directory.

The Application Directory has several distinct pieces:

- ✔ **Search Apps:** The little search box in the upper-left corner of the screen allows you to search for certain applications by name.

- ✔ **Application Filters:** The filter that opens by default when you land in the Application Directory is All Applications and offers sub-filters by categories, which let you start to browse more specifically. Look more closely at the other filters in bold: On Facebook, External Websites, Desktop, Mobile, Pages. Sound familiar? If not, reread the last few sections.

- ✔ **Featured By Facebook:** At the top of the page are applications that Facebook has chosen to highlight. These applications are often some of the best that the platform has to offer, so this is a good place to start looking for a new application.

- ✔ **Applications You May Like:** These applications are recommended algorithmically, based on what your friends use and also based on the average rating of the applications. Look for the green check mark to signify whether an application has been "verified." We talk more about verification in the next section.

- ✔ **Recent Activity from Friends:** This may look a bit like your Home page, and it *is* a bit like your Home page. It's a constantly updating list of posts by your friends, but it's filtered to show all posts from applications. This is just another way to bring applications that you are likely to enjoy (because your friends enjoy them) to the front of the page.

As you navigate the Application Directory, you can click on any application to learn more. This will take you to the application's Page. You can see an example of an application's Page in Figure 13-1. The most important part of this page is the Go to Application link right below its logo. Before you click this link, however, you need to decide whether you want to trust that application with your information. We talk about how to tell whether an application is trustworthy in the next section.

Signs of a trustworthy application

Any application's Page is a rich source of information that helps you know whether the application will behave in a way that is respectful of your information and of your friends. You don't want an application that uses your photos in ways you don't like, nor do you want an application that's going to spam your friends every time you sneeze. Here are some things to look for:

✔ **It's Verified:** Facebook Verified applications are applications that go through a review by Facebook employees to make sure the application adheres to Facebook's standards of behavior. This check makes sure the application is being respectful of your information and data, and isn't doing anything creepy or evil. Look for the green check mark or the "Verified" badge on application Pages to signify that an application is trustworthy.

✔ **Your friends are using it:** Verification can make you breathe more easily that an application won't abuse your trust, but your friends using an application proves that beyond that, it may also be a useful, fun application that you will enjoy.

✔ **Its reviews are generally positive:** Click on the Reviews tab on any application Page. There you can see ratings as well as explanations of those ratings. Lots of comments like "Spammed my friends" or "Too slow" should tip you off that this may not be a good experience.

✔ **It provides some level of support:** Whether through FAQs or responding to Wall posts, good applications respect their users and try to at least help you out a bit if you get stuck. Now, some applications may be developed by one guy in a garage, so their level of support may not be as high as one developed by a big corporation, but the gesture is what signifies a good application.

Managing Your Applications

If you've been authorizing every application we've name-dropped so far, you may have found that your application menu has grown faster than a magic beanstalk toward the top of the page. This is fine for now, but depending on how you wind up using applications, and how you feel about the ones you've added, there may come a time when you want to change some things up. After you reach that point, there's one place you need to be: the Application Settings page.

The Application Settings page

The Application Settings page lets you control many of the aspects of your applications that's we've already discussed in this chapter. You can see what the Application Settings page looks like in Figure 13-21.

You can get to this page in two ways: either from the Settings drop-down menu in the top navigation bar, where you can click Application Settings, or from the Applications menu in the bottom Chat bar, where you can click Edit Applications. (We know, that's kind of confusing. Sorry.)

By default, when you arrive, you see the applications that you've used most recently. Next to each application's name, there are three links: Edit Settings, Profile, and a little X. The X can be used to remove an application entirely. Clicking it not only removes any boxes or tabs you have on your Profile, but will also remove your authorization of it, meaning that application won't have any access to your info. If you want to use it again, you need to go through the authorization screen again.

The Profile link takes you to that application's Profile (we also call it an Application Page in this book), so if you want to quickly leave a review or check out any information about that application, you can do so from here pretty easily.

Figure 13-21:
The
Application
Settings
page.

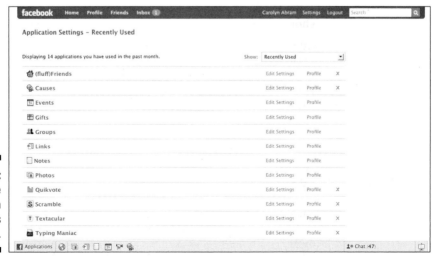

The whole purpose of this page, however, is the little Edit Settings link, which pops up the Edit Causes Settings dialog box, as shown in Figure 13-22. (The name of the dialog box varies depending on the name of the application you're working on.)

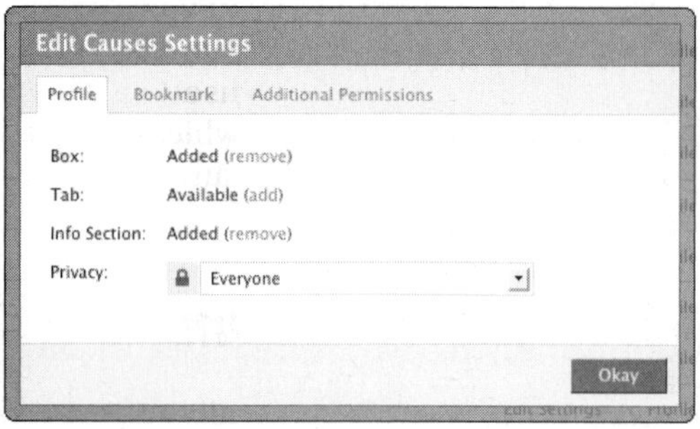

Figure 13-22: The Edit Causes Settings dialog box.

Most of these settings are aspects of applications we've already talked about, so here's a quick run-down of all of the options and exactly how they change your relationship with that application:

- ✔ **Profile>Box:** If you've previously added a Profile box for this application, this space reflects that. You can remove that box from here, or add one if you haven't already.

- ✔ **Profile>Tab:** If you've previously added a Profile tab for this application, this space reflects that. You can remove that tab from here, or add one if you haven't already.

- ✔ **Profile>Info Section:** If you've previously added a Profile Info section for this application, this space reflects that. You can remove that section from here, or add one if you haven't already.

- ✔ **Profile>Privacy:** This control lets you set privacy on who can see any Profile boxes, tabs, or sections you've added. This doesn't control who can see content that you post to your Wall and friends' News Feeds.

- ✔ **Bookmark:** The bookmark tab has only one setting — if you want to add or remove a bookmark for that application to your Applications menu.

- ✔ **Additional Permissions:** As we talked about earlier, Additional Permissions cover a broad range of things. The thing to keep in mind here is that any permission you've granted in the past can be revoked from here. Additional Permissions are at the discretion of the developers, if they are needed at all, so you usually won't see options here that you haven't been prompted for before.

When you add a Profile box, tab, or info section, that setting only controls the existence of the box, tab, or section. To edit the content (or what people are seeing there), you need to go to your Profile or to the application.

You'll notice at the top of the Application Settings page that you can choose different ways to display your applications. You can see, for example, all the applications you've bookmarked, or all the ones you've added to your Profile in one way or another. Most of these categories are covered in the preceding list. If you want to see all applications you've ever used, select the Authorized item in the drop-down menu. Any applications for which you want to revoke *all* permissions simply need to be deselected from any of these views.

Controlling what you see from friends

You know that aunt you have who shows up for family events wearing crazy hats and talking a little too loudly about her opinion of everyone? More than one family member may have listened to her lecture on the virtues of macro-tastic vitamin supplements and responded simply with, "To each, her own." Similarly, you may have some friends on Facebook who just don't have the same taste as you when it comes to applications. Maybe they take a ton of quizzes, which flood your Home page with information you don't find particularly enlightening. Or maybe they are always challenging you to games of Scrabble, and you've been boycotting that game since that one time you got two triples in one word and knew you would never top yourself. There are a few pro tips you should keep in mind that will keep your Facebook just the way you like it.

- ✔ **Block an application:** If you find an application offensive, or if it keeps sending you some sort of invites, you can block it from its Page. Simply look below its logo for a link to Block Application. This prevents the application from being able to contact you at all, even if your friends are using it.

- ✔ **Ignore a Friend's Invites:** Remember that crazy aunt? She may be sending you invites or requests from multiple hat-related applications. Look beneath that request to find a link that lets you ignore all invites from that friend. You can still be friends, but you won't receive all the annoying invites anymore.

- ✔ **Hide from News Feed:** If you're looking at your Home page and it's inundated with one type of post that you just don't like to look at, use the Hide links (which you can find in the upper-right corner of that post when you mouse over it) to hide all posts for that application. Alternatively, if all the annoying posts are coming from one person using many different applications, you can hide that person.

Best practices for developers

If you are a developer thinking about creating any sort of Facebook application, the best advice we can give you is this: Be excellent to your users. If you need something more specific than that, here are some tips:

✔ **Don't spam.** Users hate spam. If they associate spam with your application, they will probably hate your application.

✔ **Be useful.** People use Facebook as a way to keep in touch with friends and get the information they need about people. If your application is useful, it's more likely to spread virally.

✔ **Be social.** Folks use Facebook to keep in touch and interact with friends and family in a new way. Your application spreads quickly if it has an inherently social aspect to it. People want to connect with their friends. Give them new ways to do so.

✔ **Be clear about what you do.** It's very important that people understand what they're doing when they add your application or interact with it. No one likes deception.

✔ **Be competitive.** Numerous people are developing on Platform, so distinguish your application from others that may be similar. Make sure it has the absolute best feature set you can build.

✔ **Listen to your users.** Facebook users are passionate and vocal. Use that to your advantage. Read the reviews and discussions on your application's page, take suggestions seriously, and respond to negative posts when you can.

✔ **Be reliable. And fast.** No matter how good your application is, if a user is always hit with a "Down for Maintenance" message, or has to wait 30 seconds per page load, she stops using your application. Spend time and resources planning on how to scale quickly for a large user base.

Chapter 14

Facebook on the Go

In This Chapter

▶ Capturing and sharing the moment with Facebook Mobile Uploads

▶ Keeping yourself connected with Facebook Mobile notifications and texts

▶ Staying up to date with Facebook Mobile Web

▶ Discovering special versions of Facebook designed to work on your phone

Throughout this book, we show you how Facebook enriches relationships and facilitates human interaction. Nevertheless, what can Facebook do to enrich your relationships while you're *not* sitting in front of a computer? Life is full of beach weekends, road trips, city evenings, movie nights, dinner parties, and so on. During these times, as long as you have a mobile phone, Facebook still provides you a ton of value.

We don't propose that you ignore a group of people you're actively spending time with to play with Facebook on the phone (unless of course you *want* to ignore them). Moreover, we don't think you should tune out in class or in a meeting to Poke your friends. We do suggest that knowing the ins and outs of Facebook Mobile actually enriches each particular experience you have — while you're having it. With Facebook Mobile, you can show off your kids' new photos to your friends, or broadcast where you're having drinks, in case any of your friends are in the neighborhood and want to drop by.

Facebook Mobile serves another function — making your life easier. Sometimes you need *something,* say, a phone number, an address, or the start time of an Event. Maybe you're heading out to have dinner with your friend and her boyfriend whose name you can't, for the life of you, remember. Perhaps you hit it off with someone new and would like to find out whether she's romantically available before committing yourself to an awkward conversation about exchanging phone numbers. (Just a heads-up: This conversation can be awkward even *if* you find that person is single. Facebook can do a lot for you, but not everything.)

In this chapter, we assume that you have a mobile phone and know how to use its features. If you don't have a phone, you may consider buying one after reading this chapter; this stuff is way cool. Mobile texts simply require that you own a phone and an accompanying plan that enables you to send text messages. Facebook Mobile Web requires a mobile data plan (that is, access to the Internet on your phone). Facebook Applications require that you own any one of the several types of phones that Facebook can currently support.

Is That Facebook Mobile Web in Your Pocket . . . ?

In many ways, using a mobile phone can augment your experience using Facebook on the computer. In this first section, we talk about how you can easily add information to and get information from Facebook when you're not physically in front of the computer. These features are primarily for people who do most of their Facebooking on the computer, but sometimes interact through their phone. In later sections, we talk about how you can experience most of Facebook without ever logging on to a desktop or laptop computer.

Getting started

This chapter teaches you almost everything you need to know about using Facebook with a mobile device. However, if you ever find yourself asking questions about it while near a computer but NOT near this book, you can go to www.facebook.com/mobile for much of the same information. You can always get to this page by scrolling down to the bottom of any Facebook page and clicking the Mobile link.

To get started with Facebook Mobile, you first need to enter and confirm your phone number into the settings page:

1. **Scroll down to the bottom of any page and click the Mobile link.**
2. **On the right side of the page, under Get started, click the Edit Mobile Account.**
3. **Underneath Activate a Phone, click register for Facebook Texts and follow the instructions to activate your phone.**

If your carrier isn't listed under the drop-down list, some features of Facebook Mobile are not available to you.

After you've activated your phone, and put your phone in your hand, much of the Facebook Mobile experience is at your fingertips.

Mobile uploads

In this section, we show you how to spend only one magical moment to capture, save, and publish the real magical moments in life.

Three types of people can be found at social events. The scrapbookers who always remember to bring their fancy-schmancy camera to every gathering. (You know who they are because they tell you to "Smile!" a lot or sometimes say "Act natural.") The person who never intends to take photos, but who, when the birthday girl blows out her candles, the host spills wine on himself, or someone arrives wearing a hilarious, slogan tee shirt, is ready with the low-quality mobile phone camera. (Hey, it captures the moment, right?) And the person who doesn't take photos even though his phone has a camera because, "What good is a picture on a phone?" (Where do you go from there?)

For the scrapbookers of the world, we recommend Facebook Photos. After the social gathering, plug your camera into a regular computer, weed out the embarrassing photos, and upload the rest to a photo album. However, if you're the second or third type of person, we recommend you check out Facebook Mobile Photos. With mobile photos, you have no time for weeding, editing, or second thoughts. Mobile photos pave the way to instantaneous documentation.

Here's how to upload a mobile photo:

1. **Make sure you have a phone with a camera and you know how to use it to take a picture and/or take a video.**

   If you're unsure, check your phone's instruction manual, or ask just about any teenager. Leah has a few nephews you can borrow.

2. **Go to www.facebook.com/mobile and look underneath Upload Photos via E-mail for a personalized e-mail address.**

   This e-mail address, of the form aaa111parsec@m.facebook.com, makes it possible for you to upload photos to your Profile from your phone. Optionally, you can click Send My Upload E-mail to Me Now. From there, you can ask Facebook to either e-mail you the address or text it to your phone. Either way, you want to add that personal e-mail address to your phone's contacts so you can easily message it in the future.

3. **Wait for something hilarious to happen and then take a picture or video of it.**

4. **Send an e-mail to the address you found above, with the picture or video attached.**

   The subject line will be the caption, so choose wisely. *Note:* If your phone doesn't support e-mail, but does support MMS (multimedia messaging service, which enables the sending of audio, video, photos, and rich text), you can send your mobile photos or videos to mobile@facebook.com.

5. **(Optional) To make any edits or changes to your mobile photos, go to your photo albums and click the Mobile Uploads album. To make changes to your video, go to the video application and edit there.**

Note that the default visibility of your mobile uploads is "everyone." You can change this by going to the mobile album from the photos tab of your Profile, or the video application from the application bar on the bottom, and adjusting the privacy level.

Mobile texts

You're out and about and realize you need the phone number of someone who isn't stored in your phone. What do you do? Call a mutual friend? What if she doesn't answer? 1-411? What if 15 Robert Johnsons live in your city? For this scenario and several others, you send an *SMS,* or text message, to 32665 (FBOOK) containing a code word that tells Facebook what kind of information you're trying to access. For example, the word *cell* informs Facebook that you're trying to access a cellphone number. The results of your inquiry are sent to your phone via SMS.

To follow along with this section, head to the Mobile Tester:

1. **Click Mobile in the bottom right of any Facebook page.**

2. **From the Mobile page, underneath Facebook Mobile Texts, click Learn more about Mobile Texts.**

3. **On the bottom right of the Mobile Texts page, you can enter text into the field just below the image of a mobile phone to simulate mobile texting.**

The texter tester (say that three times fast) shown in Figure 14-1, is a nice way to learn about how Mobile Texts work without having to pay texting fees, and without using your friends as test subjects.

The tester allows you to try various commands and see the result as if it were from a real phone. Typing **Poke Carolyn Abram** into the tester tells you that doing so from a mobile phone would actually Poke Carolyn, but doing so from the tester won't actually do this. The Mobile Text tester is free — Facebook Mobile never charges you for using any feature, although your mobile plan may charge you per text message. Here's the lowdown on what you see in Figure 14-1:

 ✔ **Update your status** by typing @ in the body of the SMS followed by whatever you want your status to be. For example, **@ on a ski lift** changes your status to *<Your Name> is on a ski lift.* You receive a text message from Facebook stating that your status has been updated.

✔ **Get Profile information** for a particular friend by sending the name of the person you're looking for. If Facebook finds an exact first and last name match, you receive the Profile information that person has given you permission to see. For example, if Leah sends an SMS to 32665 containing **Carolyn Abram**, within seconds, she receives a text from Facebook containing Carolyn's mobile phone number, e-mail address, status (she's at a party right now), relationship status, and networks.

✔ **Get someone's cellphone number** by sending a text containing **Cell** followed by the name of the person whose number you're after. For example, **Cell Carolyn Abram** returns Carolyn's cellphone number (as long as you have access to it via her Profile). This time, though, if multiple matches appear for the name you entered, Facebook sends you the first four matches and their numbers (if they're listed and visible to you). Again, if the name you're looking for isn't in the list, simply reply with *n* for more results.

✔ **Message someone's** Facebook Inbox by typing **Msg** followed by the first and last name of the person you'd like to message and the body of the message. For example, Carolyn could send a text to 32665 that reads, **Msg Leah Pearlman Stop writing and come to this party.** Leah immediately receives the message in her Inbox.

If you enter a name for which Facebook finds more than one match, such as **Carolyn**, you receive a text message asking, *Which Carolyn?* with a list of the four most-likely matches among your Friends and then your networks. Each result is accompanied by a number. (For Leah, Carolyn Abram is first.) When you see the result you're looking for in the list, reply to that text message with the number associated with the matching result. Facebook then sends you the Profile information. If you don't see a match, reply with *n* to see the next set of results.

Figure 14-1: The Facebook Mobile Tester lets you try the Texts service.

- ✔ **Poke someone** by texting **Poke** followed by the person you'd like to Poke. If Carolyn sends a text message containing **Poke Leah Pearlman**, Leah is immediately poked. Just as with Profile information, if Facebook finds multiple matches for people you might be trying to Poke, you receive a text message containing a list and a request that you clarify whom you're trying to Poke. Reply with the number associated with the right name.

- ✔ **Post on a friend's Wall** by writing **Wall** followed by your friend's first and last name and the contents of the post. Leah could text **Wall Carolyn Abram I'll come to the party after writing about Facebook Mobile** to let Carolyn and everyone who looks at Carolyn's Wall know why she is late to the party.

- ✔ **Add a new Facebook friend** by sending **Add** and the person's name. While Carolyn waits for Leah to come to the party, she might make a new friend, named Blake Ross, say. Carolyn can text **Add Blake Ross**. She might have to choose from multiple Blake Ross's, but then the request is automatically sent. Blake can confirm when he's back at his computer. Using your phone to immediately *friend* a person you meet is less formal than exchanging business cards, less awkward (and more reliable) than exchanging phone numbers, and gives you more flexibility later for how you want to get in touch. However, remember that by *friending* someone, you give away access to your Profile, so think twice before you Add.

- ✔ **Write a note** by texting **Note** followed by the contents of a note to 32665. The best Mobile Notes are often written when someone finds himself trapped in some interesting situation with nothing but a mobile phone. We've seen several Mobile Notes written when someone is locked out of her house, for example. Another popular Mobile Note comes from someone in a long line, such as one for a new Harry Potter book, the latest Xbox release, or the next hot iToy from Apple. Mobile Notes also come from airports, runways, and sporting events — even dentist, doctor, and hospital waiting rooms.

Mobile Texts is currently available only in the United States and Canada. Mobile Texts works on any mobile device as long as it can send and receive text messages and is one of Facebook's supported carriers. You'll know whether the last part is true if you start to sign up and don't see your carrier listed in the drop-down list. Facebook never charges you for any text messages you send, but your carrier might — check your plan to know what to expect on your bill.

What's all the buzz about?

An old wives' tale claims that when you feel your ears burn, someone is thinking about you. (Maybe it just means to back away from the campfire.) Here's a slight modification: Someone, somewhere, is thinking about you when your phone starts vibrating. Turning on Facebook Mobile texts means that you'll be notified via SMS when someone Pokes you, sends you a Facebook message, comments on your photos and notes, writes on your Wall, or requests to be your friend.

To activate Facebook Mobile texts, click Mobile from the bottom of the page, click Edit Mobile account settings, and then select Texts Are On (shown in Figure 14-2).

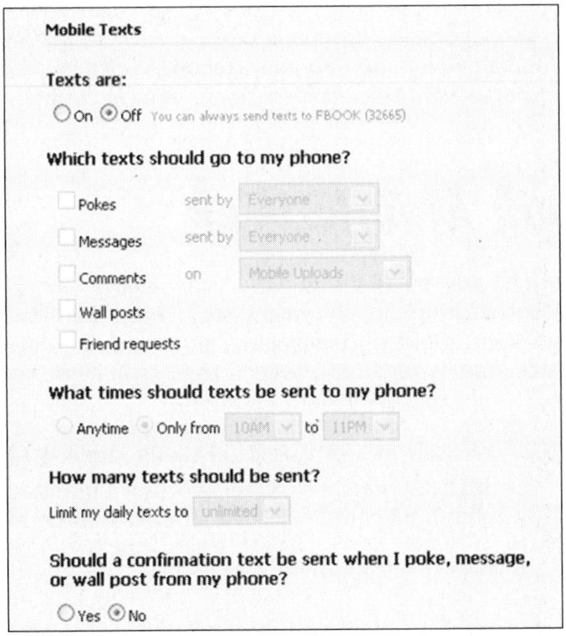

Figure 14-2: Set up your preferences for receiving notifications on your mobile phone.

The Mobile Texts page offers a number of granular settings:

- ✔ You opt-in to most of the Mobile text notifications, including when you receive Message, Wall posts, Comments, Friend requests, Photo Tags, or Posts. For Pokes and Messages, you specify whether to receive notifications about all of them or just those from your friends.

- ✔ You can specify what time you prefer to receive text notifications, so that if someone Pokes you at 2 a.m., you don't have to wake up for it. (Maybe you *only* want to know who's trying to Poke you at 2 a.m. No judgment here.)

- ✔ If you have a mobile plan for which you're charged per text message (and you're exceedingly popular), use the settings that limit the number of messages Facebook sends you per day.

✔ You can select whether to receive confirmations about the success of the Pokes, messages, or Wall posts that you send from your mobile phone.

✔ Finally, as covered in Chapter 9, this is another entry point for specifying which of your friends' statuses you want sent right to your phone.

If you subscribe to the status of someone who doesn't spell very well but is conscientious about it, you may receive several texts as he tries to get his status just right.

From this page, you can also jump into your Account settings, change your mobile phone number, or add another number to your account.

Using Facebook Mobile Web

Have you ever noticed how some things are smaller than other things? Bunnies are smaller than elephants; toy cars are smaller than real cars. How about the fact that your mobile phone is much smaller than your computer? If you haven't noticed *that,* you clearly haven't tried to access the Web on your phone.

Viewing a Web page from your phone can be extremely difficult because the information that is normally spread across the width of a monitor must be packed into one tiny column on your phone. Facebook is no exception to this, which is why the very first tip in this section is this: Never go to www. facebook.com on your mobile phone. You'll regret it.

But fear not, you still have a way to carry almost all the joys of Facebook right in your purse or pocket. On your mobile phone, open your browser application and navigate to m.facebook.com — a completely new window in Facebook designed specifically to work on a teeny-tiny screen.

If you use an iPhone, or a few select phone types, entering www.facebook. com redirects you to iphone.facebook.com, which we talk about in more detail a little later on.

The first time you arrive at m.facebook.com, you're asked to log in. After that, you never (or rarely) have to re-enter your login information unless you explicitly select Logout from your session, so make sure you trust anyone who you lend your phone to.

If you plan to use the Facebook Mobile Web site frequently, we recommend that you have an unlimited data plan that allows you to spend as much time on the mobile Web as you like for a fixed rate. The Facebook Mobile Web site is nearly as comprehensive and rich as the computer version. You can spend hours there and, if you're paying per minute, spend your life savings, too.

Currently, Facebook Mobile Web is supported in the United States for people using Boost, Cingular, Nextel, Sprint, and Virgin USA. Bell Mobility, Aliant, Fido, Solo, Rodgers, TELUS, SaskTel, and MTS support Facebook Mobile Web in Canada. Facebook Mobile Web works with many other carriers besides these, but Facebook makes no guarantee about the quality of your experience if you use a different carrier.

Mobile Home

After you log in, you see the mobile version of the Facebook Home page. Although the design of the mobile site is somewhat based on the design of the regular Web site, it has some significant differences. Some of the differences exist simply because of less space; the mobile site must cut to the chase while allowing you to get more information on a particular topic. For example, the mobile Home page shows only five News Feed stories rather than 25. You can get more stories if you want them, but you'll damage your thumb if you have to scroll through 25 News Feed stories to get to any of the links at the bottom.

The other differences arise because people using Facebook on a mobile phone often have different needs than those at a computer. For example, one of the first pieces of information you find on a friend's Profile is her phone number (if she has it listed), because if you're looking up someone on a mobile phone, you may be trying to contact her by phone.

To follow along with this section, click Mobile in the bottom right of any Facebook Page, and then click Learn More About m.facebook.com on the right.

Either way, the Mobile Web page appears, as shown in Figure 14-3. By default, the preview for the mobile Home page appears in the mobile phone graphic on the right. Click any of the other links (Profile, Friends, Inbox, and Photos) to see a preview of those pages. In this section, we detail what you see on the mobile Home page; we cover the other pages in the following sections.

Scan this list for a tour of the mobile Home page:

- ✔ **Home, Profile, Friends, Inbox:** these are the main navigational links you'll see at the top of any Page on the mobile Web. Home brings you back to the page you see when you sign in, Profile takes you to your own Profile, Friends takes you to a list of your friends, and Inbox takes you to your written messages.

- ✔ **New Messages or Notifications:** When you reach the mobile site, you find whether you have any unread messages, Events, or notifications right at the top of the page. These links only appear if you have something waiting for you. If you have a new message, remember the name of the sender always links to the sender's Profile, so be careful to select the word *Read* if you want to jump straight to the message.

✔ **Status Updates:** When you use Facebook from your mobile phone, you're probably not sitting at your home office, workplace, or school. You may be trapped in jury duty, a bachelorette party, or waiting in line for a roller coaster (wheee!). Facebook makes it super easy to spread the news the moment you're doing something that you want people to know or when you want people to meet you:

- *Your Status:* Shows you what you're status is set to. If your status isn't set, you'll be encouraged to set it.

- *Update Your Status:* Lets you enter your status using the letter keys on your phone. When you're happy with what you've entered, select Update. If you don't want a status, select Clear.

- *Friends' Statuses:* The five most recent statuses set by your friends. To see more than this, select See All. To see a particular friend's status, we recommend going straight to his Profile, which we show you how to do in a minute.

✔ **Birthdays:** If you have any friends with birthdays in the next three days (who have those birthdays listed on their Profiles), the big days show up below statuses on the mobile Home page. If you see none listed, you can probably put away the wrapping paper . . . for now.

Figure 14-3:
Explore
Facebook
Mobile Web
from the
comfort of
your
computer.

✔ **Upcoming Events:** If you've received (and have not declined) invitations to Events that are in the next three days, you see the primary information here. If you have no Events in the next three days, this section won't appear on the mobile site. To see your Events, you have to get to them in another way, which we talk about later.

- *Name of the Event:* Takes you to more information about the Event.

- *Location:* An extremely handy feature when you can't remember the address of where you're going.

- *RSVP Status:* This makes it easy for you to change your mind at the last minute.

- *Time:* The start time helps you avoid arriving too early or too late, which is good, because that's embarrassing. The end time helps you plan your after-party or arrange for a ride home.

- *See All:* Shows your upcoming and past Events.

✔ **Mobile News Feed:** Shows you the most recent stories that you would see on your computer. To save space, the stories have a little less information than the stories you're used to. Click through to a story to get more information about it. Select See All at the bottom of the Mobile News Feed section to see all the stories your heart desires. At the top of the Mobile News Feed, you'll see a set of filters. Filters pare your News Feed down to the particular types of stories that interest you most:

- *Top Stories:* The same as the stories listed in the right column of your home page. These are the posts that have been created in the last couple weeks that have generated the most hubbub from your friends. Maybe they have a lot of Likes or Comments, for example. These are the stories that are likely to crop up in social situations, so if you only read a subset of your news feed stories, it should be these.

- *Status:* Lets you filter down to only the status updates from your friends. This allows you skip over photos and links to get to get a more likely set of updates about what people are actually doing at any moment.

- *Photos:* By contrast, lets you see all the current photo stories in your News Feed. This can be a great way to pass time while waiting in line at the grocery story, for the bus, or in the corner of a boring cocktail party where you want to look important by spending time on your phone.

- *Live:* Shows you all stories your friends are posting in chronological order.

- *Bookmarks:* Links to let you filter News Feed down to Photos, Note, Group, and Event stories specifically. Clicking through to any of these filters also offers you other ways to interact with those applications. Filtering to Notes, for example, and then scrolling to the bottom gives you an easy way to navigate to your own notes, or write a new one.

✔ **Inbox:** Where you see all the messages people have sent you. You can read entire threads and take action on a particular thread, including Reply, Mark as Read/Unread, and Delete. Navigate to Sent messages by scrolling to the bottom of the page.

✔ **Navigations Links:** The primary navigation links are at the bottom of every mobile page. The first four links are the same as the links on the blue bar at the top of the regular site, and the top of the mobile site. In addition, you also have a link to recent notifications as well as the Facebook phonebook: a list of all your friends and their phone numbers, provided they have phone numbers on their Profiles.

✔ **Search:** The search box on the mobile site is designed to help you find people. When you enter text, the search results show your friends, the people in your network, and everyone else — in that order. There's no full-blown search or browse functionality from your mobile phone, just the search box, which is usually good enough.

✔ **Bottom Links:** Much like the bottom links on the regular site; a catchall of other stuff.

  • *Settings:* Allows you to opt-in to applications that you'd like to use on your mobile phone. This list contains every application you've added to your Profile. Not all of these applications have a mobile component, but if you check the box next to an application, you get access to that application on your phone if that application adds mobile support.

  • *Logout:* The only way to end your mobile session. We recommend that you log out regularly if anyone else has access to your phone.

  • *Help:* A misnomer on the mobile site — it's actually more like an About page that explains the value of the Facebook Mobile Web. We recommend that Facebook update this page to make it actually *help*ful.

Mobile Profile preview

Profiles on the Facebook Mobile Web are designed differently than Profiles on the regular site. As we mention in the previous section, a lot of information from specific applications may be absent from your Profile. Moreover, the structure is ordered such that the information you're after is closest to the top. When you arrive at any mobile Profile, you see the most usable and actionable subset of the available information. A See Full Profile link at the bottom gives you access to the rest.

Access to information on mobile Profiles is the same as on the regular site — when you look at your Profile on the mobile site, you see your information, but that doesn't mean everyone has access to it. They have access only to what you specify via the privacy settings on the regular site:

✔ **Message, Poke, and Call:** These are at the top of the Profile for quick *thinking of you* (or whatever your Poke means) communications. Your friend is guaranteed to get your message if he has Facebook Mobile Notifications set up, which we talk about earlier in this chapter. A call only appears if he's listed a phone number for himself, and a message and Poke depend on his privacy settings.

✔ **Status:** At the top of a person's Profile after her name, you see her status and the last time it was updated. When you see that your friend is *at Starbucks, come join,* the time stamp is helpful for knowing whether she updated it one minute ago or four days ago. You can also see how many people Liked or Commented on their status, and add to those counts yourself by doing the same.

✔ **Profile Picture:** Next, you see the current Profile picture. Selecting it shows you other photos used as Profile pictures in the past.

✔ **Wall tab:** This is the same as the Wall tab the Profile on the Web site. If you're looking at your own or your friend's Profile, it's selected by default. If you're looking at a non-friend's Profile, you have to click the Wall tab link beneath the Profile picture to see it. The Wall tab shows you the last several stories that person (or you, if you're looking at your own Profile) added to her Profile.

✔ **Info Tab:** To see the Info tab, you likely have to click the link to it beneath the Profile picture. This shows the same information you can see on that person's Info tab on the normal site, but reordered to be mobile friendly. Contact info is right at the top of the Info tab because when you look someone up on a mobile phone, you're often after a number or address. If the person has his phone number listed here, you can select it to start the call. After that you see all the other information he may have added to his Profile, including his networks and basic info, his favorites, and where he went to school or worked.

✔ **Friends List and Other Tabs:** Beneath the main contents of the Profile, you can see that person's friends, as well as jump into any other tab that user may have on her Profile, including her photos.

Mobile Friends List

The Friends link takes you to a list of your friends with the most recently updated statuses. The reason for this default is that when you're out (and on your mobile phone), it's nice to see where everyone else is out and about. At the top and bottom of the page, you have access to a few more filters for viewing your friends:

✔ **Phonebook** filters your Friend List down to only those friends who have a phone number listed on their Profiles.

✔ **Everyone** shows you an alphabetical list of your friends' names, which you can use to navigate to their Profiles. Just like in normal Facebook search, you can message your friends without having to go to their Profiles.

✔ **Recently Added** friends are all your friends in the order in which you became Facebook friends, starting with the most recent first. This is handy when you've recently friended someone, at a dinner party, say, and want to sneak off while she's not looking to learn more about her.

✔ **People You May Know** are not your Facebook friends, but they can be! This is the same set of people who are featured on the right side of your Home page on the computer. These are people with whom you have mutual friends or other things in common who you're quite likely to know, and may want to become friends with. It's not really the kind of thing you'll probably spend much time on while using your phone, but who knows how boring your family reunion might be? You might welcome any distraction.

Mobile Inbox

The Mobile Inbox functions the same as the Inbox on the regular site, but you access it in a compacted view. In the Mobile Inbox, your messages are sorted by the time the last message on a thread was sent. Each thread includes the subject, the sender's name, the time the last message was sent, a snippet of the message, and quick links to Reply, Mark as Read/Unread, or Delete. The Mark as Unread link is particularly handy because often you read a message on your mobile phone, but don't have time or energy to type out a response right then. Marking it as Unread reminds you to respond when you return to your computer.

Here's one major design difference between the Inbox on your phone and the Inbox on your computer: When you enter into the mobile thread, the newest message is at the top with the Reply box beneath it. You can scroll down to read the previous messages in the thread. In the regular Inbox, the order is flipped because it generally makes sense to read a conversation from the top of the page to the bottom. When you open a thread on the regular Inbox, the oldest message is at the top of the page, but the page automatically scrolls down to the newest message. This scrolling behavior isn't possible on a mobile phone, so the order of the messages is reversed.

Your Sent messages appear as a separate tab in the regular Inbox. In the mobile Inbox, you access your Sent messages by scrolling to the bottom of the Inbox and selecting the Sent link.

Facebook Mobile for the touch screen

As we mention earlier, if you navigate to Facebook on your iPhone, you actually end up at a completely different version of the site designed specifically for touch screen phones. Because only a fraction of people who use Facebook use it in conjunction with a mobile phone, and only a fraction of those people use it with a touch screen, we're only going to touch on the topic. (Get it? Touch on it? Ha!) If you have an iPhone or similar device, you are a) cooler than Leah, who had to borrow her 16-year-old nephew's phone to research this section, and b) you can follow along on your phone. If not, you can skip past this section entirely, or go to x.facebook.com on your computer to see what you're missing.

Touch screen layout

The touch screen site is organized really similarly to the computer version of the Website except you get about a tenth the functionality. The beauty is, it's the tenth that most people use, most of the time, so you'll rarely miss the rest.

✔ **Status:** In the upper-left corner of the touch screen site is a link to update your status. As mentioned before, this is because when people are out doing crazy things, they often have crazy things to say. In your authors' experiences, mobile status updates are among the most amusing and useful. Right now in Leah's News Feed, a mobile status is letting her know that a couple friends are having an impromptu picnic near her house. If she wasn't writing a book right now, she'd join them.

✔ **Search:** In the upper-right corner, you have a link to search for people on the site. As you type, your phone will start digging up matches for you.

✔ **Home:** The Home page is broken into two sections, News Feed and Events. The reason News Feed is the primary view is because it's often nice to know what your friends are up to right now so you have the possibility of meeting up or having a real-time exchange. The reason Events are also front and center is that often when people are out and about using Facebook on their phones, it's because they're at or on their way to an Event. Having the time, address, and attendee list of an Event right in your pocket can be key to making sure you show up at the right place and time.

✔ **Profile:** Profiles are organized into the same Wall, Info, and Photo tabs as Profiles on the site; however, each is abbreviated, and any additional tabs that might exist on the real Profile aren't on this version of the Web site. The Info tab only has basic and contact information. The Wall tab lists only the items other people have posted on that person's Profile. To add something to your Wall, you can touch at the empty space in the top and start typing. The Photos tab features the photos of, and by, the Profile owner. Again, the brevity here is for readability on a small device.

✔ **Friends:** The touch screen Friends page is organized into three views. The default lists all your friends who've recently updated their statuses. You can switch that to view all friends who are currently online and available to chat. Or you can see all the most recent photos uploaded by your friends.

✔ **Inbox:** This is where you access all your messages. From here, you can either compose a new message, delete a message, or reply to one.

The lowdown on mobile downloads

Facebook Mobile Web sites can be highly useful when you have Facebook needs and are far from your computer. However, they can also be highly . . . slow. The speed of Facebook Mobile depends on the speed of your phone, and when it comes to speed, phones aren't exactly Superman just yet. If you have an iPhone, Blackberry, Nokia, Android, Palm, or phone that uses Windows Mobile, Motorola, or Sony Ericsson, you can probably improve your Facebook Mobile experience by downloading a special Facebook application built specifically for your phone. More details about each are listed beneath the Facebook for Your Phone heading at www.facebook.com/mobile.

Chapter 15

Facebook: A New Kind of Advertising

- -

In This Chapter

▶ Understanding the key difference between good and bad advertising

▶ Touring Facebook's advertising solution

▶ Improving your return on advertising investment by managing your ads

- -

There are two kinds of people in America: those who watch the Super Bowl and those who watch the Super Bowl commercials. It's odd that, for a few hours every year, most of us actually seek out advertising, while the rest of the year we resent it. We fast-forward commercials, we change radio stations, we chuckle at the occasional billboard (but mostly we complain about how they ruin the skyline). What's the cause for prejudice? Is advertising inherently evil?

If you're someone who runs a business or is responsible for driving customers to a business, you know the answer is *No.* Advertisers have no malicious intent (usually), and they're not out to annoy, distract, or interrupt us. They simply have a product or service that they believe could improve our lives, if we only knew about it. So they tell us. They tell us three minutes before the end of our favorite TV shows; they tell us with their tee-shirt logos, hood ornaments, and catchy jingles; they stand on the corner with signs that read *Lemonade 5 cents.* And if one person among us responds well to an advertiser's particular message, that advertiser has no problem yelling across an entire crowded room to make sure that person hears it.

Realizing How Advertising Has Improved

Yelling across a crowded room has been the model of advertising for years. Advertisers operate under the somewhat accurate principle that the wider the distribution, the better the chances of reaching someone who cares — that's why Super Bowl slots are the most expensive of the year. It's not because football fans are more likely to buy stuff; it's because more people simultaneously watch the Super Bowl than anything else on TV. More people equals more customers.

However, there is a cost. People have only so much attention to lend to advertising. Therefore, if 2, 3, 4, or 5 million advertisers start yelling across the room, people hear none of it. When too many messages fly, people tune out, leaving advertisers with no recourse other than being the *loudest, brightest,* or *catchiest.* Anyone who has stood in the middle of Times Square in New York City understands exactly what we're talking about. And that has certainly been the model of advertising on the Internet. The flashier an ad, the more in your face, the more distracting — the more likely you are to click it.

Advertising has a bad rap because of this. Every now and then, you see an ad for something you were craving, something that intrigues you, or features something that just entertains you. In those times, you probably don't mind the advertising at all; in fact, you might appreciate it. Nevertheless, 99 times out of 100, an ad is a nuisance, which is how *ad* has practically become a dirty word. Understanding these flaws with the modern advertising landscape led to the formulation of principles for the Facebook Ad system:

- ✔ Consumers are happiest if they see fewer total advertisements and the ones they do see are most relevant to them.

- ✔ Advertisers are happiest if they *don't* throw away cash and *don't* dilute consumer attention. In other words, advertisers want to deliver their messages primarily to those people who actually care about them.

- ✔ When consumers are exposed to relevant, high-quality advertisements, they're more likely to pay attention to advertising on the whole, making each ad that much more valuable.

- ✔ To get people's attention, advertising is usually weaved into some product or service that already has consumer attention, such as TV shows or Web sites. People enjoy a TV show or Web site more if its ads are relevant, high quality, and not harmful to the user experience. As a result, they spend more time watching that channel or using that Web site, thereby seeing more total ads. Therefore, responsible TV stations or Web sites are rewarded for good advertising behavior. Customers are happier, advertisers are happier, and the product or service provider is happier.

Advertisers have to yell across the room because they don't know who, in a crowd, may be listening. Now, because each Facebook user enters so much personal information, Facebook can enable its advertisers to deliver their messages only to the people most interested (while completely protecting its users' privacy).

No more yelling.

Imagine Times Square in this model. Rather than everyone looking at thousands of flashy signs, each person would see five or six messages about things that actually interest them, making more room for flowers, and sky, and, we'll go ahead and say it, *non-commercialism.*

Defining Social Ads

On Facebook, users see three types of advertising. One is *syndicated advertising.* On a certain percentage of Facebook Pages, Microsoft has a special location carved out where it can run ads from its ad network. Microsoft pays Facebook for the use of this location, and other businesses pay Microsoft for getting their ads exposure. For a while, this was Facebook's primary source of revenue. The second type of advertising is fancy expensive *engagement units* such as videos and sponsored event invites, which appear on the right side of the Home page. Although these are super-cool and high-performing, they require a direct personal relationship with the Facebook Sales team and cost a pretty penny. This chapter focuses on self-service social advertising, which are the third type of ads on Facebook. These are the ads from which anyone who has something to sell can benefit. A *social ad* is an ad that businesses create and upload to Facebook directly to circulate on Facebook. No middleman. Social ads have a number of interesting characteristics:

- ✔ Social ads appear in the right column on most Facebook pages.

- ✔ Social ads are composed of the same set of optional components: a title, a photo, an ad body, and the option for inclusion of social actions (which we explain in the next section). Therefore, social ads are uniform in their appearance, so advertisers must get your attention with content, not form.

- ✔ Social ads are demographically targeted to users based on information they list in their Profiles, including geography, age, sex, interests, school, workplace or profession, political views, or relationship status.

- ✔ Using social actions, social ads are targeted to people whose friends have shown an interest in the product or service.

Social actions

Previously in this chapter, we refer to *social actions.* If you haven't heard this term in advertising before, don't be surprised. It's currently exclusive to Facebook. Social actions are best described via examples:

- ✔ Wiley Publishing makes a Facebook Page (described in Chapter 12) to advertise *Facebook For Dummies.*

- ✔ At some point, Carolyn publicly becomes a fan of the *Facebook For Dummies* Page.

✔ Wiley Publishing creates an ad on Facebook. Characteristics of the ad include

- A subject that reads something like, "Facebook For Dummies. Do you know someone who needs help understanding Facebook? More help than you can give?"

- A picture of the book's cover.

- A targeted audience of 30–40 year-olds.

In addition, Wiley Publishing *opts-in* to appending social actions to the ad.

✔ Because Carolyn has already pledged allegiance to Dummies, the social ad system tries to show the *Facebook For Dummies* ad to Carolyn's friends who fit the 30–40-year-old demographic.

The system automatically appends to the ad the social action, composed of Carolyn's Profile picture and the News Feed story, "Carolyn Abram is become a fan of *Facebook For Dummies.*"

Social ads plus social actions rules

Carolyn's friends are way more likely to be interested in *Facebook For Dummies* if they already know that Carolyn liked it. At the very least, if they're intrigued, they might ask her for more information. When authorized by an advertiser, the Facebook system looks at all the people within the targeted demographic for an ad, and then tries to show the ad to people whose friends have already had a positive interaction with that company. Here are a few important points about social advertising:

✔ **No one's actions are ever shown to people who couldn't also have seen that action as a story in their streams.** In other words, the only people who can see the ad with the social action are those to whom Carolyn has made her action visible. By default, becoming a fan of a Page is a publically visible action, so, most likely, anyone connected to Carolyn will be able to see her story appended to the ad.

✔ **You cannot append a social action to your ad unless you also have a Facebook Page or application.** Users must have a place to interact to generate the social actions in the ad.

✔ **Even if you opt-in to social actions, this doesn't guarantee that a social action is always appended to your ad.** If there's not enough engagement with your Page, there may not be enough social actions to append to your ad. To increase the likelihood that this happens, you must ensure that your Facebook Page or application is seeing a lot of activity.

Who uses social ads?

Anyone who has access to a computer, a credit card, and something to promote is a great candidate for using Facebook social ads. People use social ads for all kinds of different things:

- Drawing attention to your Web site or business
- Telling people about a new deal or offering
- Campaigning for an election
- Promoting a college event
- Driving traffic to a Facebook Event, Group, Page, or application
- Raising awareness of a cause
- Wishing friends a happy birthday
- Promoting a concert or a new CD
- Directing traffic to a listing on Marketplace
- Recruiting for a job opening

Social ads target your ad to an audience as small as a single school or as wide as a whole country, and they're applicable to just about every promotional effort. The only audience Facebook can't currently target is people who don't use Facebook. But you can spread your message to them some other way — dress up like a chicken and hand out flyers in front of your store, perhaps.

Creating a Social Ad

Creating an ad on Facebook is extremely easy; creating a good ad may require some extra effort. In this section, we walk you through the basic how-to of creating an ad on Facebook, while providing lots of tips and tricks to ensure your ad is as effective as possible. We call out what steps are required, and what steps are recommended.

Getting started

Log in to Facebook and navigate to www.Facebook.com/adversting. You can access this Page at any time by scrolling to the bottom of any Facebook Page and clicking Advertising. You can also click Create an Ad on the right side of any page above the ads that are displayed in the right column. Click Create an Ad to get started.

If you don't have a Facebook account, you can skip the login part, but you are asked to create a personal account (use your e-mail address, password, and birthday) before completing your ad purchase.

Designing your ad

Figure 15-1 shows where you add some basic information about your ad, as described here:

- **Destination URL:** The destination is the landing page for people who click on your ad. If you already have a Web site for your business, enter your business's URL (or the URL of the page you want people to land on when they click your ad). If you're trying to advertise something you have on Facebook, such as a Facebook Page or an Application, select the link below the URL box that says I want to advertise something I Have on Facebook and choose the relevant Page, Application, Group, or Event from the drop-down list. If you want to link your ad to a Facebook page you haven't yet created, hop back to Chapter 12 to set up your page first.

- **Title/Body:** When you enter the ad title in the Title field and body in the Body field, use the preview on the right to see what your ad will look like. You have 25 characters for the title and 135 for the body, so remember to invite your inner editor to the ad creation process.

- **Image (Optional):** You can upload a photo — the way your photo shows up in the Preview is how people see it in your ad.

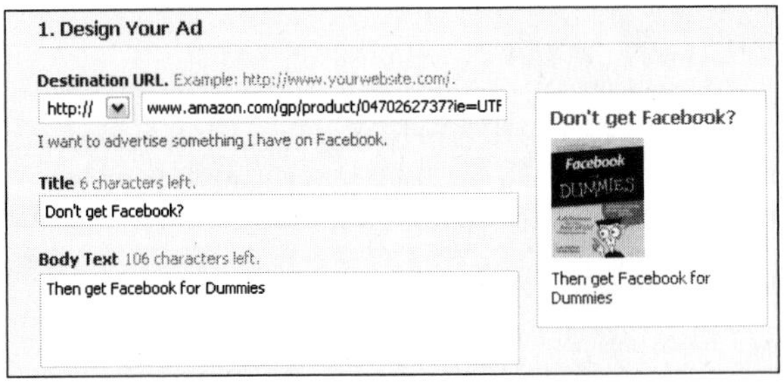

Figure 15-1:
Creating a
Facebook
ad.

1. Design Your Ad

Destination URL. Example: http://www.yourwebsite.com/.
http:// ☑ www.amazon.com/gp/product/0470262737?ie=UTF
I want to advertise something I have on Facebook.

Title 6 characters left.
Don't get Facebook?

Body Text 106 characters left.
Then get Facebook for Dummies

Don't get Facebook?

Then get Facebook for Dummies

After you make your choice, continue on to the next section.

Targeting your ad

On Facebook, an engaged man or woman is likely to see ads for wedding photographers, whereas sports lovers may see an ad for coverage of the big game. An older married man may see an ad about anniversary presents, and if you're a 23-year-old female who likes poetry and traveling, don't be surprised if you see an ad for a women's writing workshop in Europe. (Recently, this happened to Carolyn, who was so thrilled by the ad, she went on to get more info about the workshop.)

As we mention in the beginning of this chapter, targeting your ad may be the key to good advertising. If you narrow your message to the specific people most likely to respond, you pay much less for the same amount of attention.

The goal of targeted advertising is to try to be as specific as possible, without alienating anyone who may be interested. To that end, Figure 15-2 shows the options for the Facebook targeting system, and this list helps demystify them:

✔ **Location:** If your product or service is relevant to consumers only in a particular location, be sure your ad is shown only to those people. A traveling circus, for example, might make a whole series of ads targeted at different locations to let people know when to break out their clown noses and floppy shoes. Currently, Facebook doesn't allow an ad to be targeted at more than one country at a time, so if you have an international company, you need to make separate ads for each country.

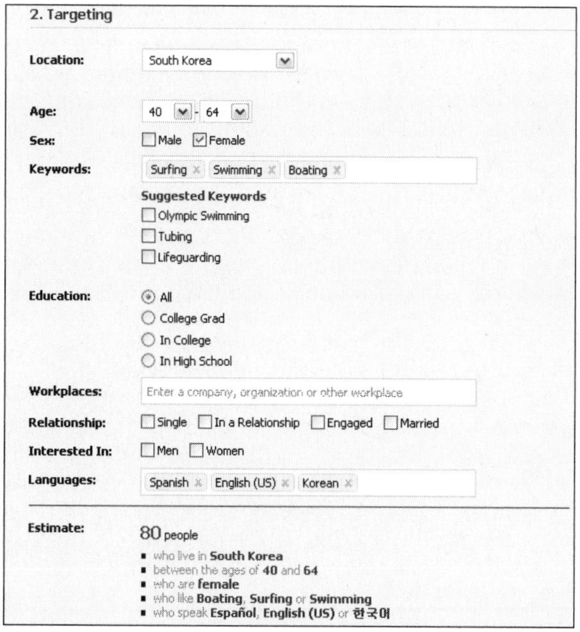

Figure 15-2: Your ad's targeting options.

✔ **Age:** Specify the minimum and maximum age for your ad. The default is 18 years old because any ads targeted at people under the age of 18 are reviewed before being shown.

✔ **Sex:** Selecting either male or female ensures your ad goes to only men or only women. If you check both of these boxes, or if you leave them both unchecked, your ad is delivered to both males and females.

✔ **Keywords:** When Facebook users create their personal Profiles, they enter various terms that describe their activities and interests. When enough people enter the same term, that term is used for keyword targeting. You know a term is valid for targeting if you start to enter it and a drop-down list appears to automatically complete the word. If the word you're thinking of doesn't appear, come up with a synonym. If the word you're looking for *does* appear, you probably still want to come up with a few synonyms and target those as well. For example, if you sell books, you may want to target to *Reading, Read, Books, Reading Books,* and *Literature.* Play around with this step and see how the audience size estimator fluctuates with various combinations. The audience size estimator takes the criteria you've entered, and quickly figures out approximately how many people on Facebook match that criteria so you know a rough idea of the audience you're targeting. It's not exactly accurate because calculating the audience fast is quite difficult technically. Also, more than a million people sign up on Facebook daily, so your audience size is shifting constantly.

✔ **Education:** This field allows you to reach the people in a particular life stage, such as high school, college, or college graduate. You can also target people at (or from) a particular school. If you're targeting kids in college, you can reach out to a particular graduation year if that's relevant. You can target particular majors. For example, a computer company could create an ad and target it to all the computer scientists and engineering seniors from the top schools. If you're planning an alumni event for Amherst College, you can target everyone who is listed as alumnae of Amherst. If you want to wish your collegiate child a public happy birthday, you can buy an ad and target it only to her school.

To specify a specific school or major, select the education level and then start typing the name of the school in the field. The name of the school most likely autocompletes for you; if not, it's not in the system and can't be targeted.

✔ **Workplaces:** You can target everyone who works at a particular company by filling out the Workplaces field. This is most relevant for those who want to target an ad at their own company (or another company) for recruiting purposes. If the company you're looking for isn't listed, click Help Center in the bar at the bottom of every Facebook page and suggest it to the User Operations team.

✔ **Relationship:** People with different relationship statuses are likely to respond differently to different products and different messaging. There are many good examples of advertisers who effectively change the tune of their messaging depending on the relationship status. Selecting all or none of the check boxes leads to identical targeting.

✔ **Interested In:** This field allows you to target to people who have expressed a particular sexual orientation. Why would you want to run ads targeted toward a particular sexual orientation? Here's an example: In a recent California election, there was a proposition to make gay marriage illegal. Adversaries of the measure used this targeting option to run ads aimed at getting people to the polls to vote the proposition down.

✔ **Languages:** Targeting people based on the language they speak is a very practical way of targeting your ad. Many of the people who use Facebook in the United States do so in Spanish. You may get wider appeal if you target an English ad at English speakers and a Spanish ad at Spanish speakers.

✔ **Estimate:** As you adjust the parameters of your audience, the Estimate section automatically updates to tell you the number of people you're targeting. As you add more specifications, the number drops. This is good because it means you're focusing your message to a specific audience. If you're too specific with your parameters, however, you may lose your audience entirely. There just may not be many 64-year-old, Spanish-speaking, South Korean women who like to surf, no matter how much you'd like to advertise to them. If the number dips too low, you should consider relaxing your requirements. In this example, you could expand the age and language requirements, or add other hobbies such as swimming or boating. In the Estimate section, you'll see your target audience reflected back to you in plain English. After checking a bunch of boxes and choosing from drop-down lists, it maybe be tricky to be sure you've targeted correctly. Checking the Estimate section allowed can help reassure you that you've chosen your settings correctly.

We spend a lot of time emphasizing how valuable targeting can be if you have a message that's relevant to only certain kinds of people. However, what if you have a product everyone can enjoy? You still target your ad — with tailored messaging for different people. Say, for example, you are the promotion's manager for a jewelry store. You can create one ad targeted at women with a message about treating one's self, and another ad targeted at men that emphasizes gift-giving. You can be more specific by targeting married men with an ad about buying gifts for their wives, or targeting young men with an ad about gifts for their mothers, for example.

Figuring out campaigns and pricing

Figuring out the price of an ad isn't quite as straightforward as listening to a vendor yell, "Hot dogs, 99 cents, get your hot dogs!" The amount you pay for your ad depends on all kinds of factors, including how you target it, whether you care that people click your ad or just see it, and how you've set your campaign and your budget (see Figure 15-3).

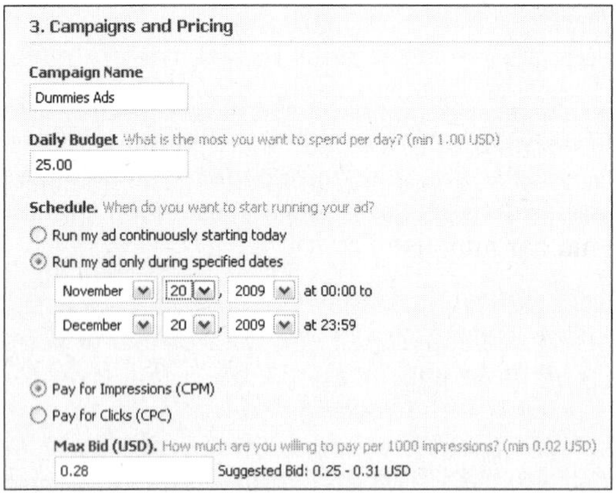

Figure 15-3: Pricing your ad.

- **Campaign Name:** A campaign refers to one or more ads for which you want to run and pay for as a group. You may have created several differently targeted ads to bring an audience to your band's concert ten days from now. Grouping all these ads into the same campaign allows you to set a single budget and schedule for the entire group of ads so you don't have to spend time and effort optimizing for the ads that are performing better or worse. The first ad you create on Facebook is automatically put in a campaign. When you create more ads, you're able to add them to various campaigns or create now campaigns.

- **Daily Budget:** You're charged based on how many people click or view your ad (up to your maximum daily budget, which you set by entering it into the Budget field). If you set a maximum daily budget of $10, and offer to pay up to 10 cents per click, you hope that approximately 100 people click on your ad. The Facebook Ad system does some fancy behind-the-scenes math to figure out how many people must see your ad to get you your 100 clicks. If the system shows your ad to too few people, you won't end up paying the full $10, Facebook makes less money, and you may not get the response you were hoping for. If the system shows your ad to too many people, you may end up getting some free attention you don't have to pay for. Good for you; not so good for Facebook. The system is constantly being improved to deliver your ad to exactly as many people as it takes to get the response you're willing to pay for.

✔ **Schedule:** You can choose to either start running your ad right away or specify the start and end dates for your ad. When you select Run My Ad Continuously Starting Today, you stop your ad when your goals are met; otherwise, you're charged per day continuously.

✔ **Pay for Impressions(CPM)/Pay for Clicks (CPC):** When you set your budget, you see two tabs: Pay for Clicks and Pay for Views. Select Pay for Clicks if the goal of your ad is that the audience ends up on your actual Web site or Page. Amazon (www.amazon.com) is an example of a company that would likely choose Pay for Clicks because customers buy products on its Web site.

Other examples of Pay for Clicks advertisers would be application developers who want people to use their applications, bands who want people to try their music, or non-profits who want people to contribute to their causes. Coca-Cola may be the kind of company that would use Pay for Views to simply get its brand and slogan in front of people. Someone selling his car may use Pay for Views after putting a photo and all his contact info in the ad.

✔ **Max Bid:** Besides filling out your daily budget, you also specify how much you want to bid for a click or a set of 1,000 views. Say that five advertisers want to target men who have the text *tattoos* in their Profiles. All five advertisers bid differently for clicks. Each time men with *tattoos* in their Profiles log in, the ad system shows them the ad from the highest bidder, until that advertiser's budget is exhausted. Then the system shows the ad of the next highest bidder. For each click or view, advertisers are charged the price of the next highest bid beneath their own (except that the second-to-lowest bidder pays 1 cent higher than the lowest bid). If an advertiser bids 10 cents per click and another bids 5 cents, and all the others bid 3 cents, the first advertiser ends up paying 5 cents, the second advertiser 4 cents, and all the others 3 cents as well.

Facebook has a lot of users, but it doesn't show each user very many ads. The value in bidding high is that it's the safest way to get the response you're after. The value in bidding conservatively is that you may pay less for the same number of clicks or views. The bid system helps advertisers pay exactly what a click or impression is worth to them. Moreover, the companies that take the time to make highly targeted and quality ads often end up bidding higher than those companies that produce low-quality ads; therefore, users are more likely to see high-quality and relevant ads.

Reviewing your ad

After you create your ad, target your audience, and set your own budget, it's time to admire all your handiwork on the Review Ad page. Rather than just applauding yourself for a job well done, review all the information carefully to make sure you're getting exactly what you're about to pay for. Speaking of paying for things, when you're done reviewing all the information, fill out the standard credit card information on the bottom half of the page and place your order. But first, we highly recommend you read the advertising guidelines and advertising policy linked on the right side of this page before you begin your Facebook advertising adventures. When you're confident all the information is accurate, click Finish.

After you created a few ads, you may want to create similar ones to those you've already created. Say you're the manager of a small chain of restaurants in California. You may want to run two nearly identical ads: one targeted toward Los Angeles residents, pointing them to your L.A. location, and the other targeted at San Francisco residents, directing them to your S.F. location. Besides these slight differences in targeting, the body, copy, image, social actions and everything else about the ads are identical. Rather than duplicate your effort, you can make one of the ads first, and then when you come back to create an ad again, click the drop-down menu at the very top of the page that says Copy an Existing Ad. From there, select the first ad you created, and watch how every form is automatically prefilled with the information from the previous ad. Then you can simply make the necessary edits and quickly proceed.

Managing Your Social Ads

After you start running an ad on Facebook, you're more than welcome to just cross your fingers and hope for the response you're after. However, with the Ads Manager, if you want to know exactly what kind of responses your ads are getting, and if you want to improve the performance of your ads, you can always pause ads while you make changes to optimize your efforts:

✔ To manage your ads, go back to www.Facebook.com/ads and click the link that says Manage Your Existing Ads beneath the Create an Ad button. You can also sign in to Facebook and click Ad Manager (also called Ads and Pages if you're the admin of a Page in addition to running ads) in the Applications menu in the bottom-left corner of any Facebook page.

✔ Ad Campaigns (at the top, not pictured) shows you much more detailed information about each of your ads in an ad summary table (grouped by campaigns). This is the tab you land on by default when you click Advertisers, after having created ads, as shown in Figure 15-4. Information here includes the following:

  • The status of the ad (not started, running, or completed)

  • Your max bid (which you can change inline at any time)

  • Type of ad (Cost per Click versus Cost per View)

- The number of total *impressions* (the number of times someone sees your ad)

- The number of clicks so far

- The click-through rate (CTR), which is the average number of times your ad is clicked on each time it is viewed

- The average cost you're paying per click (if your ad is a Cost per Click or CPC ad)

- The average cost per million (CPM) to you each time 1 million people view your ads

- Your total spent so far

In addition, you can specify whether you want to see all these metrics for the last 24 hours, 7 days, or to date, using the drop-down menu above the ad summary tables.

✔ On the front page of the Ad Manager, you see a graph of the performance of your most active ad campaigns. The overview graph shows clicks, impressions, and the click-through rate over time. You can use the Choose a Graph drop-down menu at the top of the graph to isolate any one of these pieces of information. If you're interested in how many people saw your ad, for example, you can select impressions. If you only care about who clicked on it, select Clicks. CTR, or Click-Through Rate, tells you how many people clicked on it divided by how many people saw it. A CTR of 0.5 means that one out of every two people who saw it clicked it. The bottom of the Overview page shows the performance of your ad today compared to yesterday.

✔ Clicking the name of an individual ad shows you all the detailed information at the campaign level, but this time about the performance of that particular ad in a campaign. This page also shows the preview of the ad and reminds you of your targeting information. From this detailed view of an ad's performance, you can choose to pause or stop your ad at any time.

Between graphs and detailed statistics, the ad management interface gives you all the information you need to help customize your ads to get the absolute best return on your investment. This isn't as selfless as it sounds. If you're having the most success possible, it's likely you're making extremely high-quality ads with accurate targeting; therefore, it's a better experience for Facebook users and a better experience for Facebook. To this end, Facebook plans to continue building these tools to create one of the most robust, valuable advertising networks on the Web.

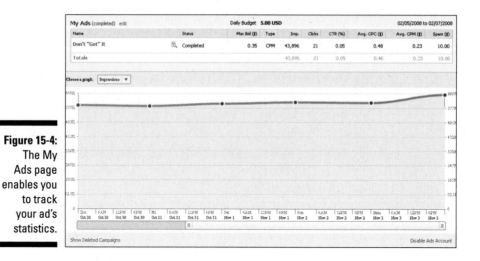

Figure 15-4:
The My
Ads page
enables you
to track
your ad's
statistics.

Spam Is Not Delicious

Good user experience is key to the success of Facebook and, therefore, key to the advertisers who advertise on Facebook. In order to preserve good user experience, Facebook puts most ads through a review process before they're allowed on the site. Your ad must be generally relevant to the people you target. The text and image of your ad must not be misleading in any way. The content of your ad, and the site that it links to, must be appropriate for any audience. Ads may be rejected for other quality metrics, such as misspellings, too much capitalization or punctuation, and so on. Generally, if your ad is clear and tasteful, you won't have any problems.

Part V
The Part of Tens

The 5th Wave

By Rich Tennant

"Jim and I do a lot of business together on Facebook. By the way, Jim, did you get the sales spreadsheet and little blue pony I sent you?"

In this part . . .

In the earlier parts of this book, we focus heavily on options and hypothetical situations. So, to ensure that you have some concrete examples of what's really happening on Facebook, we present to you the Part of Tens.

In this part, we don't make claims about what's the *best* of anything on Facebook because every experience is unique. However, you can see how much your taste matches ours by checking out our favorite applications. Additionally, you can see how Facebook has made an impact on people's lives — and how it might just have an impact on yours. In case you forgot some of what you read earlier (we know, it's a lot of info), we include some of the most common questions we get from our family and friends. And finally, we recount some of our favorite anecdotes about people reconnecting via Facebook.

Chapter 16

Ten Great Third-Party Applications

Traditionally, Facebook has focused on offering the most general types of functionality that just about anyone would find useful. But, in life, different people have different needs and desires. Students like to know what courses their friends are taking. Athletes sometimes trade exercise tips; some record their workouts. Foodies often swap recipes. Music lovers share new music discoveries; movie buffs rate and review films. In an attempt to be all things to all people, Facebook has empowered the masses to add all the specialized functionality that can transform Facebook from a general social network into a specific, tailored tool for managing one's lifestyle — no matter what that lifestyle consists of. This specialized functionality includes all of the previous examples, tools for students, business people, hobbyists, families, and more. Here's a variety of applications that we think are good examples of what Facebook has to offer.

Typing Maniac

On the surface, measuring the speed of one's typing sounds like something only professional stenographers would want to know. However, Typing Maniac, a game played on Facebook, tests that theory. As words float down the screen, you must type them before they hit the bottom. As you move up the levels, the words get longer and move down the screen faster.

Of course, the part of the game that is most entertaining is that you can track your progress among your friends. As Typing Maniac posts to your Profile about your progress from caveman to alien, your friends are alerted and can start to compete against you. We strongly suggest that you not use this game as a "break" from work, as you will never want to stop playing.

Austin City Limits

Austin City Limits is a music festival that takes place in Austin, Texas, every year. If you go to its Web site (www.aclfestival.com), you can connect with your Facebook account to see which of your friends will be attending the performances by various artists. Additionally, you can leave comments on certain performances that can get published back to Facebook. You can also see comments your friends have left.

Even if you have no intention of attending Austin City Limits, keep in mind that lots of concerts, festivals, and tours are making more and more use of Facebook Connect. It's great for promoters because it gets people talking about the event, and it's great for users because you can better organize with your friends.

Lala

Music listening and discovery are two of the most common activities people do online. Functionality related to music (with the exception of Pages for musicians) is notably absent from Facebook, and is certainly a hole for most people, who feel that their music is a big part of their identity.

Lala is a music site (www.lala.com) whose Facebook Connect implementation allows you to see what your friends are listening to. It also allows your actions on Lala (things like reviewing albums or sending recommendations) to show up as posts on your Wall. From Lala, you can follow certain friends to see what they are listening to, and if you're the friend with the good taste in music, well, your friends can follow you and find out about your favorites from their Facebook home pages, as well as from their time on Lala itself.

Groupcard

Groupcard is an application that lives on Facebook that replicates the real-world experience of passing a card around to be signed at a party. Groupcard allows you to choose a card type and the basic look and feel of the card and then invite others to sign it. Each person who signs it can select a variety of fonts, as well as pulling from his photos to find an appropriate one to send with the card. After everyone has signed, the card then gets "sent" to its intended recipient.

We like Groupcard because although it's not required for wishing someone a happy birthday or congratulations, it makes the experience of doing so a little more personal and special.

Digg

Self-described geeks out there are probably avid users of Digg (www.digg.com), a news site that allows its users to *Digg* or promote certain news stories that they think are the most interesting or relevant. By connecting Digg with your Facebook account, you can publish your Diggs back to Facebook. This ability means that you can tell your friends, as well as the larger Digg community, what you think is interesting or newsworthy.

Also, if you're not finding anything interesting on the Digg home page, you can see what your friends (who have also connected their Facebook accounts with Digg) have Dugg in the last few days. Another example of how Facebook connect works to make Facebook as well as its companion site more interesting and social.

Graffiti

Graffiti is a simple and beautiful application that allows users to add the ability for their friends to draw pictures for them on their Walls. A friend can leave a little visual gift for another friend, and mutual friends can discover the art in their Home pages.

We like Graffiti because it's a mix of the *thinking-of-you* Poke and the more labor- and time-intensive task of writing a card and mailing it. Receiving a Graffiti drawing is rewarding because someone devotes time to you in a public way, which shows the world that person cares about you and that you are worth their time. Goosebumps.

Carpool by Zimride

The Carpool application allows people to offer and request rides to wherever they need to go. It can be used to organize regular carpools to and from work (especially useful when people at your company have actually joined your workplace network), or to find company for longer, one-time road trips.

There are plenty of other services online that people use to find rides, but what's great about the Zimride Carpool application is that it adds the layer of identity that is easy to find on Facebook, and difficult to find elsewhere. Carpooling with a stranger can be worrisome, but carpooling with someone who has friends in common with you might be more comfortable. Even if that's not the case, the mere ability to check out potential carpoolers and see if they seem like someone you could tolerate being in a car with for a few hours can make a world of difference.

Visual Bookshelf

Visual Bookshelf, an application by Living Social that lives on Facebook, pretty much proves the assertion that a recommendation from a friend is worth more than a recommendation from a stranger. You and your friends can leave reviews and share favorites with each other straight from Facebook. You can feature Visual Bookshelf on your Profile as a box that allows your friends to see what you're reading now. (For example, *Facebook For Dummies*, and it is *amazing!*)

Visual Bookshelf actually has a pretty smart connection with Amazon (www.amazon.com), so that as you see books you want to read, you can easily go buy them and get down to reading and reviewing them.

My Diet

Let us be clear: You look great. You definitely don't need to go on a diet, but we do want to point out the My Diet application, and others like it, can help people get themselves organized around something happening in their lives. Some applications are for brides planning their weddings; others are for students studying for classes. All of them help you keep track of metrics (in the case of My Diet, calories in and calories burned) and share what's going on in your life with your friends. This can be especially helpful if you and your friends are all starting a workout regime together. It lets you support each other even when you're not with each other.

And for the record, if you cut a cookie into pieces, it's zero calories.

Restaurant City

If you like games that you play over time and that allow you to make lots of decisions — Monopoly players, we're talking about you — you will most likely love Restaurant City. This game allows you to start a restaurant and hire your friends to work there. As your restaurant makes money, you can hire more of your friends, redecorate, and start to compete with your friends' restaurants. Simple fun, right on Facebook.

Chapter 17

Ten Ways Facebook Uniquely Impacts Lives

Sometimes people are dismissive of Facebook, saying, "I keep up with my friends by calling them and visiting them. I don't need a Web site to do that for me." This is true. However, we try to make the point throughout this book that Facebook doesn't replace real friendships — it supplements them. You can still communicate and share information with your friends without Facebook; however, it's easier and faster to do with Facebook. Some things are always a part of life; Facebook just makes them better, faster, and stronger.

Keeping in Touch with Summer Friends

Carolyn once spent a summer leading a troupe of seventh graders into the wild. After two weeks of backpacking, kayaking, climbing, and bonding, the kids were given a big list of e-mail addresses and phone numbers, said their goodbyes, and were packed off to their respective homes. Carolyn (about to return to Facebook headquarters) lamented the fact that the kids were too young to be on Facebook because they almost assuredly would lose that sheet of paper. Carolyn quickly "friended" her co-counselors (who were all old enough to be on Facebook) and keeps up with them through photo albums, notes, and the occasional Poke war. As an added bonus, years later, when her co-counselor needed a reference, he knew exactly where to find her.

Not just for Carolyn, but for thousands of high school students, the best-friends-for-the-summer — who had a tendency to fade away as school and life took over — are now a thing of the past. Camp friends immediately become Facebook friends, and on Facebook, no one gets lost. Plus, it's easy to share the memories of a fun summer via Facebook Photos. If you're interested in finding out what's new with your camp friends, they're only a click away. Additionally, it's easy to plan camp reunions without needing to find everyone's new info.

Preparing to Head Off to School

Everyone has a story about leaving for college. Whether they're dropping off a child or an older sister or heading off themselves, people remember some form of anxiety, nervousness, or blinding fear of the unknown. Who were these people in the hallway or sharing the bathroom? Who was this so-called roommate?

Now, college students go off to school having been introduced to their future dorm mates, roommates, and residence assistants via Facebook. Students can list their residences and easily pick out the people they'll most likely meet on the first day, thus dulling the fear that they won't know anyone.

In the time between acceptance letters and orientation, college freshmen spend their time Wall posting, friending, and getting to know their future classmates. Therefore, they join groups and support one another through a big transition. Suddenly, school is less scary.

Going on Not-So-Blind Dates

Ever been a matchmaker? Ever had a particularly difficult "client" — a friend who has a million requirements for "the one"? Ever been embarrassed because you didn't realize just how picky your friend was until after the date? Enter Facebook. Now, "He's smart, funny, has a great job, lots of cool hobbies, a nice family, and nice friends" can be condensed into a Facebook message with a shared Profile. From there, both parties can decide based on the Profiles — looks, interests, or the combination of all the information — whether they want to go on a date.

Some of our friends have gone so far as to say, "No Profile, no date." Given the circumstances, this is reasonable. Not only do you get a little window into a person's world, but you also prepare for talking about the various interests and activities that you see there. This way, "So I saw you like snorkeling. Where does one do that when you live in Idaho?" can be a much better conversation starter than, "So, what do you do?"

Think of it as *far-sighted* dating rather than blind dating.

Meeting People in Your New City or Town

When Leah moved to California from Seattle, the first thing she did was look up all the people she knew who were in both the Brown University network and listed their current city as San Francisco. She figured it was as good a place as any to get a handle on what her new social life was going to be.

Many people are making themselves comfortable this way in new cities around the world. Carolyn got the following message from her friend, Shelby, who was living in Abuja, Nigeria, at the time.

> *So I was friends with this Marine in Liberia. We lost touch when I left Liberia. He joined Facebook two weeks ago, and requested me as a friend. We started talking again. He put me in touch with a friend who works for the U.S. Consulate in Lagos, Nigeria. I Facebooked her. She found my blog address on my Facebook Profile, and forwarded it to her friend who works for the U.S. Embassy in Abuja.*
>
> *Tonight, I went out with this girl from the Embassy and a bunch of other Embassy people. And I have plans (finally!!) for a couple of days next week with these people.*
>
> *And all of this is because of Facebook.*

Shelby's story is just one example of how Facebook makes moving less of an ordeal — a neighborhood is waiting for you when you arrive.

Reconnecting with Old Friends

Long-lost friends. The one who got away. I wonder whatever happened to her. Have you heard about him? These are just some of the ways people talk about the people they somehow lost track of along the way. Whatever the reason for the loss, this sort of regret can be undone on Facebook. Finding people is easy, and getting in touch is, too.

Many recent graduates exclaim that going to a reunion is unnecessary — you already know what everyone is doing five years later; you found out from Facebook. But even for the not-so-young alums, the Find Classmates and Find Coworkers features provide a direct line to search anyone who's on Facebook that you remember from way back (or not so way back) when.

Facebook gets e-mails every so often about people who find birth parents or biological siblings on Facebook. However, the majority of the time, people are looking for and finding their old classmates and reminiscing about the good old days. Better yet, they are reigniting a spark in a friendship that can last far into the future.

Keeping Up with the 'rents

Face it: Keeping your parents in touch with everything that's going on is difficult. However often you speak, it sometimes feels as though you're forgetting something. And visits often feel rushed, as though you don't have enough time to truly catch up.

Facebook Photos and Video applications are two of the best ways to easily and quickly share your life with your parents. Because you can upload photos so quickly, they can feel as though they were present at the *<insert activity here>*. Whether a dance, party, or concert, it's as though you came home and immediately called to tell them about it.

Additionally, Facebook creates the casual interactions that are so often missing from a long-distance parentship. The *How was your day?* is reinstated by daily status updates. *Good morning* replaced with Poke. If you still don't feel as though you're actually home for a visit, you could add a game like Lexulous, an application that lets you play Scrabble with anyone (at any time) from anywhere in the world. It's perhaps the best way to keep in touch with your parents.

Keeping Up with the Kids

If you've read much of this book, you know (from your authors' gentle reassurances) that everyone is welcome on Facebook and that Facebook is for everyone. If you happen to be the parent of a teenager, you may hear a distinctly different story, something more along the lines of, "Stay out of my life!", followed by the sound of a slamming door.

Well, Facebook *is* for everyone, and it can be a great way to keep up with your children when they go away to college and beyond. Our parents love the ability to look at our photos, Poke us when we haven't called, and say things like, "Your status said that you're stressed. Is everything okay?" If you're looking to be friends with your child on Facebook, here are some tips:

- ✔ **Respect their boundaries.** At some ages, kids just don't want their parents to have access to their social life. Don't be hurt if your child doesn't accept your friend request or doesn't let you see all of her info. Like all relationships on Facebook, share what you're comfortable with, and your kids can share what they're comfortable with.

- ✔ **Don't friend all of their friends unless given permission.** As funny as it can be to say, "See? Johnny thinks it's cool that I'm on Facebook," this can also be really irritating and breaks Rule 1: Respect boundaries.

- ✔ **Have your own social life.** Yes, Facebook can be a great way to feel connected with your child at any distance, but use Facebook to connect with your own friends and share content with everyone — friend and family alike.

- ✔ **Don't worry too much.** Yes, you might see some parts of your child that you didn't know about. Just as you're a wonderful, multi-faceted human (as represented by your Profile), so too is your child. Get excited that you're getting to know the person you helped shape.

Assuming that your child accepts your friend request, start keeping up. It's easy to check her Wall if you haven't heard from her in a few days, weeks, or months. A simple status like *Carolyn is writing Facebook For Dummies all the time* can explain a lot of lost phone time. (Sorry, mom and dad!)

Facebooking for Food (or Jobs)

If you've ever found yourself job hunting, you probably are acquainted with the real-world version of *networking*. You ask friends for their friends' numbers and job titles; you take people out to coffee; you go on interviews; you decide whether the company is right for you; you repeat the whole process.

Although finding the right job hasn't gotten any easier with Facebook, a lot of the intermediate steps have. Asking your friends for their friends' info is as easy as writing a note. Better yet, scan through your friends' networks to see whether any of them are working at companies that interest you. After you receive some names, send them a Facebook message (or e-mail, whichever is most appropriate) to set up the requisite "informational coffee date."

After interviewing, a great way to get information about a company is to talk to people who work there. Use Find Coworkers to search people who've listed that company in their Profiles.

The only caveat to this approach is that you're now using Facebook to represent a professional portion of your life. If you contact people via Facebook and they feel a little uncomfortable with the content in your Profile, whether that's your Profile picture, a recent status that can be easily misinterpreted, or a Wall post from a friend that reveals just a little too much information, it could make a bad first impression — just as if you'd shown up to the interview in torn jeans and the shirt you slept in. As a well-educated user of Facebook (because you *have* read all previous 16 chapters without just skipping directly to this one, right?), you're well aware of the myriad privacy settings that enable you to tailor what different parties see and don't see. However, if anything on your Profile might be particularly misunderstood, simply hide it until you sign your offer letter.

Goin' to the Chapel

A small bit of Facebook trivia: There has, in many circles, arisen the idea of *Facebook Official (FBO)* — the act of moving from *single* to *in a relationship* and listing the person that you're in a relationship with on your Profile. For any fledgling couple, this is a big deal for their personal lives; however, becoming Facebook Official also serves notice to friends and anyone who happens upon one's Profile: I'm taken.

Because of this relationship function, Facebook has become the fastest way to spread a wedding announcement to extended friend groups. Of course, people still call their parents and their closest friends, but *everyone* can find out and share in the happiness via News Feed. Congratulatory Wall posts ensue, as do copious numbers of photos with *the ring* tagged front and center.

Hey, Facebook Me!

Before Facebook, in both romantic and platonic contexts, it was hard to get from "Nice to meet you" to "Will you be my friend?" Now, the simple phrase, "Facebook Me!" expresses this sentiment and so much more. "Facebook Me!" can mean, *get in touch, look me up,* or *I want you to know more about me* but in a pressure-free way. It doesn't mean *take me to dinner,* or *let's be best friends forever and ever.* It's simply a way to acknowledge a budding friendship.

"Facebook Me!" can also be how good friends say, "Keep up with my life, I want you to know about it," which acknowledges that people are busy and that it's difficult to find time to see each other or talk on the phone. However, even when people are incredibly busy, a quick check on Facebook can make you feel connected again and secure that your friend is doing well.

Chapter 18

Ten Questions That Leah and Carolyn Get a Lot

As Facebook employees, Leah and Carolyn often get an insider's look at the specific complications, confusions, and pain points people come across while using Facebook. At dinner parties, group functions, family events, or even walking across the street wearing a Facebook hoodie, someone always has a suggestion or a question about how to use the site. It's understandable. Facebook is a complex and powerful tool with a ton of social nuance, much of which has yet to be standardized. Questions like "When should I send a Facebook message instead of an e-mail?" "When is it OK to request someone be my friend?" and "How do I turn down requests?" are popular questions for which there are no concrete answers because the social norms are still being formed. However, because your authors have heard a lot from friends, our families, and strangers about the experiences they've had on the site, we have been able to form some opinions about and recommendations for some of the fuzzier Facebook questions.

What follows is the set of questions Leah and Carolyn hear most often from friends and family, often with strain in their voices or pain in their eyes. The goal of highlighting the more complicated questions is to save you the stress of encountering these issues yourself and wondering if you're the only one of the 250 million who just doesn't get it.

Is My Computer Infected with a Virus?

That is such a total bummer, and if your computer is infected with a virus, you have our deepest, most sincere sympathies. But first, make sure you really have one. One of the main ways people discover they got a virus through Facebook is if a friend received a message from you that looked like spam. If this situation happens to you, your first step should be to change your password by clicking the Forgot Your Password link from the login page, or going to Account settings. Often, viruses hack an account and change the associated e-mail address or password to take control. If you can't change your password, that's probably what happened. If that's the case, contact Facebook customer support immediately by clicking the Help link and searching for "hacked" for related questions and answers. Finally, you should run a virus scan of your computer to help remove any malware that might have ended up on your computer as a result.

Much more information about Facebook-related viruses can be found at www. facebook.com/security. You'll find recommended virus scanners, steps for fixing problems, and information about any new viruses as they crop up. By becoming a fan of the Facebook security page, you can get information in your News Feed from the Facebook security team, which can help keep you on the lookout for any suspicious-looking links. That, in turn, brings us to the most important reminder about viruses.

The best way to deal with a virus is not to get it in the first place. The best way to *not* get a virus on Facebook is to not click on any links you don't trust. When a friend sends you a link though a message or a Wall post, make sure that the friend's message is significantly personal to your relationship, such as "Hey, mom, remember how we were talking about the singularity the other day? Check out this video." If it's impersonal, such as, "Hi! Check out this link, you'll like it." That's a vague message that could easily be a virus in disguise. The second to thing to check is that you recognize the domain name of the link. URLs for well-known sites such as www.youtube.com, www.facebook. com, or www.flikr.com, and so on are likely legitimate. If you don't recognize the URL, don't click. Instead, write back to your friend and ask him if he meant to send you the message. If he did, no harm, no foul. If he didn't, you've just alerted him that he has a virus, and you should tell him about the Facebook security page and recommend a good virus scanner.

Do People Know When I Look at Their Profiles?

No. No. And oh, yeah, no. When people see stories about their friends pop up on their home page, they sometimes get a little anxious that this means Facebook is tracking everything everyone does and publishing it to everyone else. That's not true. Consider two types of actions on Facebook: Creating content and viewing it. Creating content means you've intentionally added something to Facebook for others to look at or read, such as uploading a photo, a video, writing a note, or posting a status. These types of actions are all publishable posts — that is, stories about them may end up on your

Profile or in your friends' News Feeds — although you have direct control over who exactly gets to see these posts. The other type of action on Facebook is viewing content such as flipping through photos, watching a video, following a link, or viewing someone's Profile. Unless someone is looking over your shoulder as you browse, these types of actions are strictly private. No one is ever directly notified about them, and no trace of the fact that you took that action is left on your Profile or in your friends' News Feeds. So now you can check people out to your heart's content.

I Have a Problem with My Account — Can You Help Me?

Carolyn and Leah, along with every other Facebook employee, frequently get asked to help fix the accounts of friends and friends of friends and friends of friends of friends of . . . well, you get the idea. Sometimes the problems are Facebook's fault, and sometimes they are user error, but either way, you'll be surprised to learn that, quite often, your average Joe Facebook employee *can't* help fix most account problems. There are two reasons for this. The first is that the site is very large and changing constantly, and many employees don't know the details of site functionality outside their specific area. The second reason is that many account problems can only be resolved by employees with special access to the specific tool required to fix an account. Here are a few of the account questions we've received recently, and the answers given:

- **I can't remember my password. Can you reset it for me?** Answer: No can do. Resetting a password requires a special tool — it also requires that an employee verifies you are who you say you are by verifying your answer to your security question. This prevents someone from pretending an account is hers and duping an employee into handing over access.

- **My account got deactivated because it said I was sending too many messages. Why? and Can you fix it?** Answer: Leah recently had this happen to two friends, one who was using his account to promote his music career, and one who was distributing his poetry to many, many friends through messages. This is Facebook spam detection at work. When an account starts sending a lot of messages in quick succession, especially when those messages contain links, this looks a lot to the system like spam. In most cases, the person is warned first, but if the behavior continues, his account is disabled. The only way to have this action reversed is to write in through the Help pages and request reactivation. To write in, click on Help Center in the lower left of any Facebook Page. Look for an FAQ titled My Account is disabled from the Site, and follow the instructions for requesting reactivation. This can sometimes take several days.

✔ **I changed my name to a fake one as a joke, and now I can't change it back, can you do it for me?** Again, a special tool is required. Click the Help Center link at the bottom of any Facebook Page, and search for Name Change. The first FAQ gives you directions and a link to write in and request a name change. These requests may take up to a week to fulfill. This example also serves as a heads-up to everyone else. Facebook only allows one name change without having to write in and get permission. This is to preserve the authenticity of the accounts. During the 2008 U.S. presidential election, many Facebook users added the middle name "Hussein" to show their support of Barack Hussein Obama. The fact that you still see so many at the site with this name reflects the fact that people used up their name changes and can't change them back without writing in.

What Do I Do with Friend Requests I Don't Want to Accept?

This is a tough question. As far as we know, there isn't exactly a social convention for this yet, so the answer to this question is pretty personal. Just know that there are a number of actions you can take:

✔ **Many people just leave the request sitting there forever.** Carolyn and Leah don't recommend this action because it just clutters up your account — it's better to make a decision.

✔ **Click Ignore.** This is Leah's favorite option. Although people are never directly notified that you've rejected their request, they may notice later that you're not friends and make the correct inference you did not accept. If you do ignore a request, you also need to prepare your follow-up if she asks you about why you ignored her request. Because there is no social convention for this situation just yet, most responses work well here, such as "I'm sorry, I like to keep my friend list down to only my closest friends," or "It's OK, I don't use Facebook often anyway." You can try "Weird, Facebook must have messed up, I don't think I got it," but then you'll have to accept her request when she likely tries again.

✔ **If you don't want to accept because you don't want that person having access to your Profile, we recommend adding him to a special restricted Friend List (see Chapter 5).** You can go into your Privacy settings and exclude that friend list from seeing any parts of your profile. Then anyone you add to that list will be restricted. In this way, you can accept the friend request without giving up access to your Profile.

✔ **If you don't want to accept because you don't want to read about that person in your News Feed, no problem!** Simply hit Accept. The first time she shows up in News Feed, hit the Hide button in the upper right of the story. This action removes her from your News Feed for good until you choose to add her back.

What's the Difference between Facebook, MySpace, Twitter, and LinkedIn?

It's likely there are graduate students across the globe writing theses on this particular topic. Needless to say, it's a tough question to answer in a paragraph or casual conversation, so anything you read here is a gross generalization and subject to opinion:

✔ **MySpace has its origins as a tool for local bands to promote their music.** Because many people love music, many people flocked to MySpace (www.myspace.com) in order to connect with their favorite musical artists. A key rule of advertising is to go where the people are, and because so people were going to MySpace, other businesses and celebrities got involved to garner public attention as well. To this day, MySpace is still oriented toward the relationships between people and media and people and celebrities. The site is designed in a way to make it maximally easy for popular figures to achieve wide distribution and large audiences, or even everyday Janes and Joes to become popular figures.

✔ **LinkedIn is a tool geared to help people connect primarily for business purposes.** LinkedIn (www.linkedin.com) users try to connect with as many people as they can so that if and when they need a new job, or they're looking to hire someone to come work with them, they can flip through a vast network of friends and friends of friends to find a reliable lead. People can write and request letters of recommendation for one another, and often recruiters reach out to LinkedIn users whether they're actively looking for a job or not.

✔ **Twitter allows people to engage in real-time sharing.** Whenever a Twitter member has something interesting to share, he blasts out some text, 140 characters or less, that everyone who is "following" him has the option to see. What differentiates Twitter (www.twitter.com) from Facebook is its extreme simplicity and single focus on real-time exchange of ideas. Facebook is a place where you build longstanding relationships with people; you have access to their static content like their phone numbers and photos; you can message them privately or interact with them through groups and events. Twitter is a place where your friends (and anyone else) find out the information you're sharing at any given time, and vice versa. Popular uses of Twitter are link sharing for interesting Web sites and news, short opinions about current events, or enabling people to meet up when two people are both out and about at the same time.

I Keep Getting Invites for Those App Thingies — Should I Accept Them?

Different Facebook employees might give you different advice on this question. Here's how your authors would handle this situation personally. Accept the invitation if the app invite is from a company or Web site you already use and like, *or* if you've heard personal accounts from friends that that particular application is worth trying out. Ignore the rest: Your friends won't be offended, or if they are and ask you about it later, you can just tell them you weren't sure what it was. (It's easy to play dumb when you have a copy of *Facebook For Dummies* sitting on your shelf.) Leah personally only uses two or three applications, and has probably ignored 30 or 40 requests. The whole notion of applications on Facebook is still a bit of a work in progress — one day, we expect that we'll find more worthwhile applications we can accept, but for now, feel free not to accept anything that confuses you.

How Do I Convince My Friends to Join Facebook?

One sneak attack we don't recommend is creating a fake account for your friend and interacting with his friends on his behalf. This is against the Terms of Use, but we've seen it be highly effective in convincing a hapless victim to come take the reins on an account that's out there acting on his behalf. Careful with that strategy if you want to retain your friendship.

Other methods involve showing (rather than telling) your friend the value by sending him links to the photos you post on Facebook, putting his e-mail address on the invite of event and group invitations, or even sending him links and messages (again, by putting his e-mail address on the To line) from the Facebook Inbox.

You can tell her anecdotally the ways in which Facebook has enriched your life: Maybe you're interacting with your kids more, you're keeping in touch with friends you thought lost, or you have a place to put your thoughts and photos where your friends might actually see them. You can let him look over your shoulder as you use the site, so he can see the experience himself — ask him questions about whether there's anyone in particular he'd like to look up. The more information he sees about the people he cares about, the more likely he is to make the next step.

One common complaint from people who haven't joined the site is that they "don't have time for yet another computer thing." To this concern, one common response is that Facebook is an efficiency tool that often saves a person time compared to using old-school methods. Messaging can often replace e-mail, and events are easier to coordinate over Facebook. Sharing phone numbers is easier. Sending and receiving links are easier. Finding rides to the airport, restaurant recommendations, and who is heading to the park on Saturday are all faster and easier than trying to use e-mail, phone, or other.

Finally, for some people, it' s just not their time. No matter what you say, they'll stick their fingers in their ears and sing la-la-la until you start talking about sports or the weather or the circus coming to town next week. You can't force them to Facebook; you have to let Facebook come to them. Over the years, Carolyn and Leah have watched many a non-believer eventually cross over and discover the value. Patience may be your only weapon for these die-hards.

What if 1 Don't Want Everyone Knowing My Business?

To those who ask that question and don't have time to read Chapter 5 of this book, which goes into great detail about how to be a private person on Facebook, we simply try to impart the following message: You can be an extremely private person and still derive nearly all the same value out of Facebook as anyone else. All you have to do is learn how to use the Privacy control, and lock down all your information and access to your Profile to those you trust. From there, you can interact in all the same ways as anyone else without feeling like your privacy is being compromised. Oh, besides learning the Privacy settings and taking the initial time to adjust yours until they feel just right, you're going to have to do a little extra work to be private on Facebook and still derive comparable value. You'll likely have to put in extra effort connecting with friends. The reason for this is that the more locked-down your information is, the harder you make it for not-yet-Facebook-friends to find your Profile, and the harder it is for your friends to find you, identify you, and connect with you. As long as you're willing to do the work of seeking out your friends and connecting with them, however, your experience should be nearly identical with everyone else's.

1 Heard Facebook Owns Everything 1 Put on There — True?

In a legal sense, yes. You also own everything you put on Facebook, and whenever you delete any of your content, it will be deleted by Facebook. What Facebook doesn't own (but you do) is the rights to transfer ownership of any of your content to anyone else. So it's completely illegal for anyone else to take your content from Facebook and use it for their own or any commercial use. In early 2009, many Facebook users banded together to express concern about this legal stipulation (which exists for any site you upload content to, by the way). In response, Facebook published a statement of rights and responsibilities that makes a commitment about what Facebook will and won't do with your information. These commitments were voted on by every Facebook user who chose to participate and govern the companies use of any material you add to the site. Read about these rights and responsibilities in greater detail at www.facebook.com/terms.

Does Facebook Have a Feature That Lets Me Lock Myself Out for a Few Hours?

Short answer: not really.

Long answer: Many people do deactivate their accounts, their reason being "I spend too much time using Facebook." The benefit of such an action is that you're guaranteed not to get notifications about messages, picture tags, Wall posts, or anything else. The downside is that it will cause a lot of confusion among your friends who suddenly can't message you, tag you, or write on your Wall. If they have your e-mail address, they're likely to bug you anyway to ask why you disappeared from Facebook.

The reason it's not a real solution is because all you have to do to reactivate at any time is to enter your password (just like signing in), and you're completely back to normal. So if you're remotely curious how your social group has evolved without you, you might have trouble truly staying away. Which brings us to our next suggestion: Have some self control. Just like many good things in life, the key to keeping them good is moderation. French fries are delicious, but too many give you a tummy ache. Dancing is a blast 'til your feet are full of blisters. Television is educational and entertaining until it's 3 a.m., you're watching your fifth infomercial, you forgot to feed that cat, put out the trash, and you find yourself wondering what life is all about. Facebook is no different. It's a brilliant utility when used to make your life easier and your social interactions richer. When you find yourself flipping through two-year-old vacation photos of a friend of a friend of a friend of a friend, it's time to blink a few times, step away from the mouse, and go out for ice cream, or dancing, or whatever else it is that gives you joy.

Chapter 19

Ten True Facebook Tales

*W*e've hopefully impressed upon you all of the awesome ways Facebook can impact your life and how you communicate and share with your friends, but you may still think we're pretty far from the truth. However, truth is indeed stranger than fiction, and trust us, there are endless possibilities for what Facebook might wind up meaning to you. If you're still skeptical, take the following true tales as our proof, though by all means imagine us with flashlights below our chins as we tell them.

If you're looking for more stories like these, pay attention to your local news or even national news. More and more, Facebook gets referenced as a source, a cause, or the news itself. Also, poll your friends: chances are many of them have their own true tales about finding a long-lost friend, reconnecting with an estranged family member, or improving a strained relationship through Facebook.

I'm Kelly — I'm Kelly, Too

According to ABC News (www.abcnews.com), Florida resident Kelly Hilderbrandt (woman) was curious who else in the world shared her exact same name. She went on to Facebook and searched for it. She found exactly one match: Kelly Hilderbrandt (man), living in Texas at the time.

According to she-Kelly, he-Kelly's profile picture was rather attractive, so she sent him a message, and they began a long-distance friendship. Eventually, they decided to meet in person, and their long-distance friendship blossomed into a romance, and eventually, an accepted marriage proposal.

If you're single, running out of options, and have a first name that could be shared by someone of the gender you prefer to date . . . just know, it might work for you, too.

One Million Voices

If you ever doubted the ability of one person to make a difference, we encourage you to read more about Oscar Morales, the creator of a Facebook group called "Un Millon de voces contra las FARC." FARC is a terrorist organization in Colombia that is said to have taken more than 700 hostages. Oscar Morales at first intended just to start a Facebook group, but as it quickly grew (according to the BBC, 250,000 users quickly signed up), it soon became a full-fledged, worldwide demonstration.

As reported in the BBC, in more than 100 cities worldwide, between 500,000 and 2 million people showed up to march in a demonstration. They wore the group's slogan, which roughly translates to: "No more kidnapping, no more lies, no more deaths, no more FARC."

Although it's unclear what the lasting effect of such a demonstration will have on its targets, what is clear is that one person can reach thousands upon thousands of other people. The little diagrams of a completely interconnected world aren't just the stuff of airline magazines; it can happen.

Fighting for Darfur

In 2008, two students in Massachusetts were appalled by the genocide happening in Darfur. They decided to hold a dance to raise money to donate as much as they could raise to the Genocide Intervention Network.

In order to get maximum attendance, they did all of their dance promotion using Facebook Events. The two teens expected one or two hundred attendees, and were almost saddened to have to turn away hundreds of guests when more than 1,100 people showed up to their small venue. The dance, after costs were paid for, raised $13,000 for their cause. After discovering how successful fundraisers run through Facebook could be, the two began making plans for their next event.

Elsewhere in Massachusetts, college student Brandon Sabbag was equally appalled by the Sudanese tragedies. He began channeling his discontent by organizing conversations with fellow students. According to Catherine

Holahan, Sabbag began using Facebook to organize benefit concerts and huge protests. Sabbag describes his method of promotion as posting information about his events to groups who share his sentiment.

Facing Autism

Barbara Fischkin wrote her story for Facebook as part of Autism Awareness Month. The story was published on the Facebook blog in April 2009. Her son, Dan Fischkin, 21, suffers from a severe form of adult autism. Due to his condition, he had formed very few social connections throughout his life.

His mother once blogged about her son's condition, and a woman with a high-functioning form of the same type of autism reached out to Ms. Fischkin and asked to connect with Dan on Facebook. Due to the specific nature of Dan's autism, Facebook turned out to be a much more comfortable way for him to interact with people. It offers lots of pictures, brief text exchanges, and most importantly, the ability to meet people from all over who understand, from personal experience, what Dan is going through. Through this first friendship, and a group of Facebook members with a similar form of autism, Dan's social group grew.

After a number of months on the site, Dan developed a rich social life, consisting of more than 150 online friends. His mother expresses how watching him interact with friends has taught her much about his social interactions.

A Social "Sorry"

In Australia, National Sorry Day commemorates the mistreatment of the aboriginal population by the government. It is meant to acknowledge the grievances of the past, as well as provide a moment from which the entire nation can move forward. In 2008, as reported by News.com in Australia, thousands marked the occasion by joining Facebook groups related to National Sorry Day, as well as by changing their statuses to "So-and-so is sorry."

Within the group discussion boards, meanwhile, talk brewed about what it meant to be sorry about something many of the members had not been alive to witness. People spoke about what the government ought to do to make reparations, and about whether apology even was the proper first step. Even without complete agreement, the entire incident reflected how easy it was for average citizens to say how they felt about their country's past, as well as make their priorities clear in a semi-public forum.

Twenty-Year Reunion

As reported on Canada.com, a mother who had given her son up for adoption when she was only 17 later found him through Facebook. She described how she'd wanted to find him her whole adult life, but the nature of the adoption records left her clueless because all she had was a name.

Eventually, a friend recommended that she try to find him on Facebook, where she could look him up by name, and also see a picture that might give her some clue. According to mom, a number of results matched her son's name, but one picture gave him away. She sent him a message tentatively asking about his identity. He, knowing right away that this was the birth mother he'd also been wanting to meet, wrote right back. His adoptive family was supportive of their reunion, and the two have grown very close since their first meeting.

Activism Like an Egyptian

As Facebook spreads across the world, people within every country can be more connected and more organized. This was the case in Egypt, where Facebook was widely used to coordinate political dissent and activism like marches, protests, and boycotts. In particular, a group of Facebook activists called for one nationwide strike in May 2008 to protest the rising prices of food and other basic commodities. As reported by the *Wall Street Journal*, Facebook activists were detained by the government. Their imprisonment, including that of Esraa Abdel Fattah, was protested on Facebook as well.

The story of activists being arrested by their own government is never a happy one to tell. But the fact is that in this case, such an act was not quietly hushed up; her arrest was not a secret act. Rather, it drew more notice to the cause, and *they could not be silenced.* The fact that so many young people (indeed, people of all ages) had a forum with which to connect — that they could do more than pass out fliers or mark money to let people know about protests and events — speaks volumes about the future of all nations.

Kids with Compassion

As a freshman in high school, Brett Bassock wanted to do something for his grandmother, Elaine Fox, who suffered from Parkinson's. He started a group on Facebook, pledging to donate 17 cents to Parkinson's research for each member who joined. Elsewhere in the world, Michael J. Fox, the actor who has been living with Parkinson's for much of his adult life and has a Parkinson's Research foundation named after him, caught wind of the group. Actor Fox offered to sponsor the 17 cents himself in Grandma Fox's name.

At the time of reporting, the group had more than 6,000 members. At that time, Brett brainstormed other ways he could raise funds in honor of his grandmother. He started a Web site to organize walks for Parkinson's as well as brainstorming how to organize other events. Today, nearly 900 groups on Facebook that organize people interested in Parkinson's Research. The Michael J. Fox Foundation has nearly 15,000 members.

Robyn Doolittle of the *Toronto Star* interviewed 13-year-old David Robertson about his use of Facebook for fundraising. At his fifth-grade birthday party, he asked his friends to donate money to the Santa Claus Fund, a drive put on by the *Toronto Star* that collects money to buy needy children gifts at Christmas. David raised $500 dollars from people he knew, so he decided to expand his efforts to include those he didn't. He started a group, pledging to give $1 to the fund for every person who joined his group. In a short time, his group had 120 members. It's a modest number, but given that he had to earn the pledge money through doing household chores, it's probably appropriate the group not grow too large.

Virtual Support Network

In 2007, monk-led protests in Myanmar led to a massive crackdown on such demonstrations by the ruling junta. The junta tried to restrict images of their actions from leaking to the outside world, but with the Internet and Facebook chugging along, that effort proved to be impossible.

As reported by the Associated Press, the Facebook group, "Support the Monks' Protest in Burma," grew to more than 100,000 members in about ten days. Although it was started by someone in Britain, the group became a storage area for reports of what was happening from within Myanmar. Citizens posted photos, videos, and observations — the showdown couldn't be hidden from the outside world. Although the international connections couldn't physically support the monks and people of Myanmar, they could provide the global attention required to bring such showdowns to slightly better conclusions.

From a Skinny Kid to President

Now, we know the 2008 presidential election got almost no press coverage. The whole thing was a foregone conclusion, with almost no heat in the primaries, and certainly no voter interest in the general election. (Did we lay it on thick enough? We're just joshing you . . .) Well, if you can handle one more interesting look into how the presidency was won, regardless of your own personal vote, you need look no further than Facebook. As reported in the *Washington Post* about a month after Barack Obama's win, it turned out the president-elect had had a massive following on Facebook (see Figure 19-1).

With more than 3.2 million listed supporters, Barack Obama was able to use the page he had created to drive traffic, organize rallies, and collect donations. He distributed content from the campaign trail on his page, and his supporters were able to interact with his team (and a little bit with him) directly. No one's saying that he couldn't have won the presidency without Facebook, but Facebook is one of many technologies that changed the way politicians campaign. Across the world, politicians can be found on Facebook, connecting with their constituents and trying to keep their jobs.

Figure 19-1:
President
Barack
Obama's
Facebook
page.

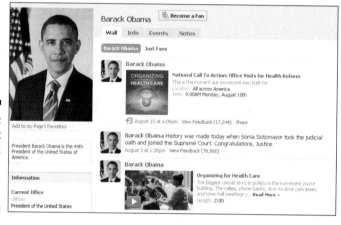

Index

• *D* •

Business/Accounting & Bookkeeping

Bookkeeping For Dummies
978-0-7645-9848-7

eBay Business
All-in-One For Dummies,
2nd Edition
978-0-470-38536-4

Job Interviews
For Dummies,
3rd Edition
978-0-470-17748-8

Resumes For Dummies,
5th Edition
978-0-470-08037-5

Stock Investing
For Dummies,
3rd Edition
978-0-470-40114-9

Successful Time
Management
For Dummies
978-0-470-29034-7

Computer Hardware

BlackBerry For Dummies,
3rd Edition
978-0-470-45762-7

Computers For Seniors
For Dummies
978-0-470-24055-7

iPhone For Dummies,
2nd Edition
978-0-470-42342-4

Laptops For Dummies,
3rd Edition
978-0-470-27759-1

Macs For Dummies,
10th Edition
978-0-470-27817-8

Cooking & Entertaining

Cooking Basics
For Dummies,
3rd Edition
978-0-7645-7206-7

Wine For Dummies,
4th Edition
978-0-470-04579-4

Diet & Nutrition

Dieting For Dummies,
2nd Edition
978-0-7645-4149-0

Nutrition For Dummies,
4th Edition
978-0-471-79868-2

Weight Training
For Dummies,
3rd Edition
978-0-471-76845-6

Digital Photography

Digital Photography
For Dummies,
6th Edition
978-0-470-25074-7

Photoshop Elements 7
For Dummies
978-0-470-39700-8

Gardening

Gardening Basics
For Dummies
978-0-470-03749-2

Organic Gardening
For Dummies,
2nd Edition
978-0-470-43067-5

Green/Sustainable

Green Building
& Remodeling
For Dummies
978-0-470-17559-0

Green Cleaning
For Dummies
978-0-470-39106-8

Green IT For Dummies
978-0-470-38688-0

Health

Diabetes For Dummies,
3rd Edition
978-0-470-27086-8

Food Allergies
For Dummies
978-0-470-09584-3

Living Gluten-Free
For Dummies
978-0-471-77383-2

Hobbies/General

Chess For Dummies,
2nd Edition
978-0-7645-8404-6

Drawing For Dummies
978-0-7645-5476-6

Knitting For Dummies,
2nd Edition
978-0-470-28747-7

Organizing For Dummies
978-0-7645-5300-4

SuDoku For Dummies
978-0-470-01892-7

Home Improvement

Energy Efficient Homes
For Dummies
978-0-470-37602-7

Home Theater
For Dummies,
3rd Edition
978-0-470-41189-6

Living the Country Lifestyle
All-in-One For Dummies
978-0-470-43061-3

Solar Power Your Home
For Dummies
978-0-470-17569-9

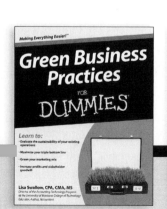

Internet

Blogging For Dummies,
2nd Edition
978-0-470-23017-6

eBay For Dummies,
6th Edition
978-0-470-49741-8

Facebook For Dummies
978-0-470-26273-3

Google Blogger
For Dummies
978-0-470-40742-4

Web Marketing
For Dummies,
2nd Edition
978-0-470-37181-7

WordPress For Dummies,
2nd Edition
978-0-470-40296-2

Language & Foreign Language

French For Dummies
978-0-7645-5193-2

Italian Phrases
For Dummies
978-0-7645-7203-6

Spanish For Dummies
978-0-7645-5194-9

Spanish For Dummies,
Audio Set
978-0-470-09585-0

Macintosh

Mac OS X Snow Leopard
For Dummies
978-0-470-43543-4

Math & Science

Algebra I For Dummies
978-0-7645-5325-7

Biology For Dummies
978-0-7645-5326-4

Calculus For Dummies
978-0-7645-2498-1

Chemistry For Dummies
978-0-7645-5430-8

Microsoft Office

Excel 2007 For Dummies
978-0-470-03737-9

Office 2007 All-in-One
Desk Reference
For Dummies
978-0-471-78279-7

Music

Guitar For Dummies,
2nd Edition
978-0-7645-9904-0

iPod & iTunes
For Dummies,
6th Edition
978-0-470-39062-7

Piano Exercises
For Dummies
978-0-470-38765-8

Parenting & Education

Parenting For Dummies,
2nd Edition
978-0-7645-5418-6

Type 1 Diabetes
For Dummies
978-0-470-17811-9

Pets

Cats For Dummies,
2nd Edition
978-0-7645-5275-5

Dog Training For Dummies,
2nd Edition
978-0-7645-8418-3

Puppies For Dummies,
2nd Edition
978-0-470-03717-1

Religion & Inspiration

The Bible For Dummies
978-0-7645-5296-0

Catholicism For Dummies
978-0-7645-5391-2

Women in the Bible
For Dummies
978-0-7645-8475-6

Self-Help & Relationship

Anger Management
For Dummies
978-0-470-03715-7

Overcoming Anxiety
For Dummies
978-0-7645-5447-6

Sports

Baseball For Dummies,
3rd Edition
978-0-7645-7537-2

Basketball For Dummies,
2nd Edition
978-0-7645-5248-9

Golf For Dummies,
3rd Edition
978-0-471-76871-5

Web Development

Web Design All-in-One
For Dummies
978-0-470-41796-6

Windows Vista

Windows Vista
For Dummies
978-0-471-75421-3

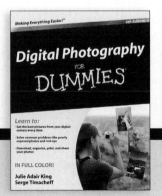

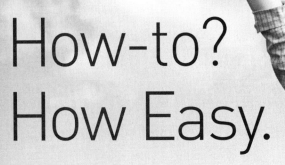

How-to?
How Easy.

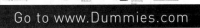
From hooking up a modem to cooking up a casserole, knitting a scarf to navigating an iPod, you can trust Dummies.com to show you how to get things done the easy way.

Visit us at Dummies.com

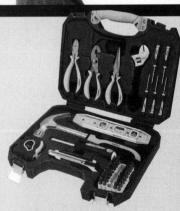